D1602585

Refuge of a Scoundrel

The Patriot Act in Libraries

Herbert N. Foerstel

A Member of the Greenwood Publishing Group

Westport, Connecticut • London

Library of Congress Cataloging-in-Publication Data

Foerstel, Herbert N.
    Refuge of a scoundrel : the Patriot Act in libraries / by Herbert N. Foerstel.
      p. cm.
    Includes bibliographical references (p.) and index.
    ISBN 1–59158–139–7
    1. Library records—Law and legislation—United States. 2. Library surveillance—United States. 3. Bookstores—Records and correspondence—Law and legislation—United States. 4. Libraries and state—United States. 5. United States. Uniting and Strengthening American by Providing Appropriate Tools Required to Intercept and Obstruct Terrorism (USA PATRIOT ACT) Act of 2001. I. Title.
    KF4315.F64 2004
    344.73'092—dc22   2003065950

British Library Cataloguing in Publication Data is available.

Library of Congress Catalog Card Number: 2003065950
ISBN: 1–59158–139–7

First published in 2004

Libraries Unlimited, 88 Post Road West, Westport, CT 06881
A Member of the Greenwood Publishing Group, Inc.
www.lu.com

Printed in the United States of America

The paper used in this book complies with the Permanent Paper Standard issued by the National Information Standards Organization (Z39.48–1984).

10 9 8 7 6 5 4 3 2 1

Contents

Introduction

The "war on terrorism" is this nation's most loosely defined war, yet it has already been accompanied by more fundamental reductions in our constitutional rights than any other American conflict. Our political leadership has warned us that it is a war without end, and that the devastating changes it has wrought in our social and political fabric may therefore be permanent. Even the meaning of "terrorism," the alleged enemy in this permanent war, is unclear, as the tortured attempts to define it in the USA PATRIOT Act have shown.

Some years ago I heard a now-forgotten conservative commentator declare, "There is good terrorism and there is bad terrorism. There is terrorism for a good cause, and there is terrorism for a bad cause." Indeed, a quick look at America's varied responses to terrorism in places like Chechnya, Kosovo, Nicaragua, Afghanistan, Turkey, and Iraq suggest that identifying terrorists is a process that changes with the political winds.

The American Civil Liberties Union warns us that the term "terrorism" is "enormously elastic." The ACLU points out that the State Department labels as terrorism such unlikely crimes as erratic behavior by the mentally ill, drunkenness by passengers on airplanes, and convicts rioting for better food.[1]

Under the Patriot Act and successive legislative and administrative actions, peaceful political or religious groups can be investigated and prosecuted without probable cause. Libraries, bookstores, and places of worship are now routine targets of surveillance. The disturbing excesses of government power granted by Congress after the 9/11 attacks and the broad public support for these new federal powers were motivated by fear. Fear can often be our best teacher. When we learn that certain circumstances are dangerous, our fear leads us to avoid them. When we learn that certain aspects of our own behavior are dangerous, our fear leads us to modify them. Thus, fear can instruct us to act in our own interest and in the broader community and national interest. But when fear is generalized or directed at scapegoats, it creates an atmosphere of confusion in which hidden monsters threaten us at every turn, and repression, isolation, and ignorance are our only shelters.

In his award-winning documentary film *Bowling for Columbine*, Michael Moore attempted to identify the cause of America's pattern of violence against itself. By comparing Canada, which has an almost negligible rate of murder and violent crime, with the United States, he was able to dispose quickly of a few popular straw men: guns and violent media. He discovered that Canada has a high rate of per capita gun ownership and its citizens watch the same violent movies and video games that Americans watch. What, then, can account for the dramatic difference in violent behavior? Moore concluded that it is fear. Americans are not just frightened of foreigners. They are terrified of other Americans. Canadians show no such anxiety.

The terrorism of 9/11 has had its intended consequence, leaving terror in its wake, exacerbating an already tense social and political climate in the United States. The FBI now proudly proclaims that it has changed from a "reactive" to a "proactive" law enforcement organization. The agency will no longer focus on arresting and punishing criminals and terrorists but will identify those with such an inclination and apprehend them before any illegal act is committed. This requires massive, pervasive profiling of American citizens, data mining endless amounts of personal information, and recruiting a national cadre of citizen snitches to ferret out "suspicious" people, including those who read "suspicious" books.

Supreme Court Justice William O. Douglas said in 1973, "If the lady from Toledo can be required to disclose what she read today and what she will read tomorrow, fear will take the place of freedom in the libraries, bookstores and homes of the land."[2]

In case you thought the Douglas quote was out of date, it was cited in 2002 by a judge who ruled against the police seizure of local library computers without a warrant.

Library surveillance has a sordid history, and the FBI's purposes in that regard have been consistent: to control information available to and disseminated by libraries; to acquire personal information about library patrons; and to recruit librarians to spy on patrons, particularly foreigners. These purposes were made evident in the FBI's ill-fated Library Awareness Program conducted during the 1970s and 1980s, and they represent an even greater danger in the post-9/11 climate of fear.

As we shall see in Chapter 1, FBI surveillance under the Library Awareness Program focused heavily on foreigners. Agents went to libraries at places like the University of Maryland asking library staff to report "anyone with a foreign-sounding name or foreign-sounding accent." Hard as it is to believe, the Patriot Act has raised the level of xenophobia far beyond what was displayed in the Library Awareness Program, and Muslims are the target of choice.

The story of Tarik Al Basi and his wife, Carolyn, is a good case in point. Tarik is a naturalized American citizen, born in Egypt, who met his American wife in Cairo where she was pursuing her degree in Arabic Studies. The two married and moved to the United States, where they began a restaurant, the Crazy Tomato, in Evansville, Indiana. Tarik's employees were friends from his rowing team at the American University in Cairo.

One night in October 2001, Tarik called Carolyn to tell her that the FBI had come to his restaurant and he would not be coming home. Tarik and all of his friends had been served with a warrant and arrested as "material witnesses" after the FBI had received a "tip" that they were involved in a terrorist plot to fly a plane into the Sears Tower in Chicago. Wearing striped prison jumpsuits and shackled hand and foot, the nine men were secretly taken to the federal detention center in Chicago, where neither their families nor their attorneys could find them. Tarik's wife told Public Television's Gwen Ifill, "Being an American citizen means nothing. It means nothing."

Fortunately, Tarik's lawyer, Ken Cuniff, knew the prosecutor and was able to arrange access to his client. "If it were any other prosecutor, I probably would never have been allowed to talk to my client," he said. "Tarik still might have been in custody."

Eventually, all of the men were released. The FBI's tip was bogus. The FBI's chief investigator in Indiana later took the extraordinary step of publicly apologizing to the men, but the false arrest and detention remained on Tarik's record. In 2002 he was questioned for five hours at Kennedy International Airport after his name appeared on an airline warning list. Tarik's restaurant is not doing much business anymore, because people still think he is a terrorist.

In Durham, North Carolina, A.J. Brown, a college freshman, was searched for an hour by secret service officers who thought she had pro-Taliban propaganda in her apartment. The officers found no such material.

A student teacher in Maine was fired for giving a lesson on Islamic culture to her 10th-grade world history class.

Even libraries are becoming anti-Muslim battlefields. A *St. Petersburg Times* editorial describes a library incident at Edison Community College in which campus security was contacted about three "Middle-Eastern-looking men" who were whispering as they used library computers to look up Arabic language newspapers. The Collier County Sheriff's Office promptly sent deputies to seize the library's computer hard drives. The *Times* editorial concluded,

> [T]he situation raises disturbing questions. What exactly was suspicious about the behavior of these men: Whispering in a library? Reading newspapers in their native language? Being Middle Eastern? The Patriot Act is trying to make librarians into citizen spies. . . . Do you suddenly feel a chill in our public libraries?[3]

Because this book focuses on government surveillance, with emphasis on libraries and bookstores, it leaves a gap in our coverage of the Patriot Act. Many provisions of the Patriot Act concern the prosecution, detention, and punishment of foreigners for a variety of newly defined crimes and under substantially lowered legal standards. Thousands of foreigners have been detained since the passage of the Patriot Act, many without charges or without the right to legal representation. Many remain detained, either in Guantanamo, Cuba, or in the United States; even their names have been kept secret from the American public.

The Justice Department's own inspector general has issued semiannual reports since the passage of the Patriot Act, each documenting violations of the civil rights and civil liberties of Muslims by federal employees enforcing the Patriot Act. One of the complaints in the June 2003 report concerned an immigration officer threatening a Muslim detainee by holding a loaded gun to his head. Another concerned a prison doctor who treated Muslim inmates "in a cruel and unprofessional manner."[4] The Patriot Act does not authorize such abuses, but its provisions are clearly directed at foreigners, and in the post-9/11 political climate, that means Muslims.

A number of the Patriot Act's more punitive provisions apply only to "non-U.S. persons" or specify constitutional protections only for "U.S. persons." The most publicized constitutional safeguard in the Patriot Act allows surveillance of U.S. persons "provided that the investigation is not conducted *solely* on the basis of First Amendment activities." We shall see that, even for U.S. persons, this is a hollow protection, but even this feeble safeguard is denied to non-U.S. persons.

It will be the job of other authors and researchers to examine in detail the provisions of the Patriot Act that allow virtually unrestrained prosecution and detention of foreigners. Our job in this book is to shed light on the dangers of domestic surveillance under the Patriot Act, whether it be directed at foreigners or U.S. persons and whether it occurs specifically in libraries and bookstores or in the broader society as well. Librarians have learned from history that when government surveillance powers are expanded generally, libraries will suffer in particular.

My first book, *Surveillance in the Stacks* (1988), chronicled the FBI's Library Awareness Program, an ill-conceived war on library confidentiality. Nationwide criticism and ridicule of this unlikely war eventually led the Bureau to seek a strategic withdrawal from and armistice with America's libraries. By the time of that book's publication, the program had seemingly ended with a whimper. The FBI, while defending its right to prowl the unclassified collections of America's libraries, claimed to have put its Library Awareness Program on hold.

Who would have guessed that little more than a decade later, the excesses of the Library Awareness Program would pale in comparison to a new federal assault on libraries built upon a succession of draconian laws, executive orders, and administrative guidelines passed in the wake of the 9/11 terrorist attacks on the World Trade Center and Pentagon. The new war on intellectual freedom and library confidentiality is led by the controversial Patriot Act, which represents a broad assault on the Bill of Rights that goes far beyond libraries, all in the name of anti-terrorism.

Herbert S. White, dean and professor at the Indiana University School of Library and Information Science, has noted, "The confrontation between librarians, who seek to assume the maximum use of information, and security officials, for whom the ideal state may be one in which material is destroyed before anyone can read it, is as natural and instinctive as between the mongoose and the cobra. It is not only a natural conflict but perhaps a necessary one."[5]

The confrontation is unavoidable because of a simple truth: Whenever the protection of our rights prevents their exercise, there will be fundamental and principled conflict. I believe that the growing federal policy to restrict information and monitor those who would use it is anti-intellectual, xenophobic, and ultimately injurious to our national security.

Among the new wrinkles in library surveillance introduced by the Patriot Act and revised FBI guidelines are expanded authority to monitor the use of the library's public computer terminals, new authority to seize "any tangible thing" in a library without probable cause and without an adversarial court procedure, and new FBI authority to post undercover agents routinely in libraries. We know the chilling possibilities that these new authorities represent, but they will be more difficult to document and assess because of the unprecedented "gag order" that the Patriot Act imposes on librarians, booksellers, and others served with the newly authorized secret warrants. Any librarian who reveals the very existence of library surveillance under the Patriot Act is subject to fines and imprisonment.

My first book relied heavily upon the personal accounts of librarians who dealt with FBI agents under the Library Awareness Program. Any librarian who provides me with similar accounts of FBI visits under the Patriot Act risks serious prison time. As a result, firsthand reports on library surveillance will be relatively rare in this book, often replaced with more subtle acknowledgments of FBI visits supplemented with descriptions of library strategies to protect patron confidentiality. During the heavily publicized Library Awareness Program, a public image of librarians emerged that was bold, outspoken, and ultimately successful. Under the Patriot Act, librarians will have a strong but relatively silent image, and the outcome of their battle with government agents may not be determined for years.

Chapter 1 of this book summarizes twentieth-century government surveillance of libraries, with emphasis on the FBI's Library Awareness Program, conducted from 1976 to about 1990. Chapter 2 examines the USA PATRIOT Act, its passage, its general provisions, and its threat to libraries and bookstores. Chapter 3 documents federal incursions on libraries since the passage of the Patriot Act and describes library attempts to deal with this new threat. Chapter 4 describes the web of new legislation, executive orders, and administrative guidelines assembled by the Justice Department and its congressional allies to fortify and extend the Patriot Act. Chapter 5 tells of the response of libraries, bookstores, civil rights organizations, and members of Congress who are attempting to expose the dangers of the Patriot Act and, if possible, repeal the most repressive sections of the Act. A brief Conclusion assesses Attorney General Ashcroft's recent characterization of critics as "hysterics" and his claim that Section 215 of the Patriot Act—the most controversial of its provisions—has never been used.

One must ask, how did America come to this sorry state of First Amendment decline represented by the Patriot Act? First, our freedoms were cast aside by craven politicians in both parties who exploited the post-9/11 fears and confusion to accomplish an agenda they had sought long before terrorism became a buzzword. The shameful legislative process by which the Patriot Act was passed, described in detail in Chapter 2, reveals the arrogance of Republicans and the servility of Democrats. Party leaders colluded to pass this monstrous threat to the Bill of Rights without meaningful debate. Most members of Congress who voted for the 342-page bill had never read it. No matter. It was the patriotic thing to do, and its passage made the halls of Congress the last refuge of scoundrels.

Today's media coverage is less consistent and less effective in informing and protecting the public against the Patriot Act than it was against the Library Awareness Program. Why? First, the Library Awareness Program was an isolated FBI program operating in peacetime. With minimal political or national security cover, it stood out like a sore thumb. Today's library surveillance is only one part of the massive and complex Patriot Act, which is itself only one component of the ubiquitous international war on terrorism. Second, the compelling personal stories of librarians whose opposition to the Library Awareness Program made the FBI seem foolish are missing from today's news, thanks to the unprecedented gag order surrounding the Patriot Act. Third, the Patriot Act has succeeded in wrapping library surveillance in the flag, shielding it from the ridicule that greeted the Library Awareness Program. Fourth, Attorney General Ashcroft's success in muzzling the Freedom of Information Act has kept the public ignorant of the dangers of the Patriot Act, whereas the Library Awareness Program was revealed in depth by the FOIA release of hundreds of previously secret FBI documents. Finally, whereas Rep. Don Edwards (D-CA), himself a former FBI agent, used his Subcommittee on Civil and Constitutional Rights to reveal the danger posed by the Library Awareness Program, today's compliant Congress pays homage to its biggest mistake, the USA PATRIOT Act.

The post-9/11 media have been intimidated into acquiescence. Columnists and political cartoonists have been fired for an alleged lack of patriotism, and the American people have been largely silent. The 2002 survey of the State of the First Amendment, conducted by the Freedom Forum's First Amendment Center, suggests an answer. Executive Director Ken Paulson explains, "[T]he stakes have risen. In the wake of September 11, Americans are afraid of more than just being offended. The results of our 2002 survey suggest that many Americans view these fundamental freedoms as possible obstacles to the war on terrorism."[6]

Among the key findings of the 2002 survey:

1. For the first time in the annual polling, almost half of those surveyed said that the First Amendment goes too far in the rights it guarantees.

2. Forty-two percent of respondents said the press in America has too much freedom. More than 40% said newspapers should not be allowed to freely criticize the U.S. military about its strategy and performance.

3. More than four in ten said they would limit the academic freedom of professors and bar criticism of military policy.

4. About half of those surveyed said government should be able to monitor religious groups in the interest of national security, even if that means infringing upon religious freedom.

5. More than 40% said the government should have greater power to monitor the activities of Muslims living in the United States than other religious groups.[7]

In these trying times, is it asking too much of Congress and the American people that they maintain their support for freedom, or must we rely on the U.S. Supreme Court to reverse legislation like the Patriot Act? Senator Russ Feingold (D-WI), the only member of the Senate to vote against the Patriot Act, told his colleagues, "We cannot simply rely on the Supreme Court to protect us from laws that sacrifice our freedoms. We took an oath to support and defend the Constitution of the United States. In these difficult times that oath becomes all the more significant. . . . There is no doubt that if we lived in a police state it would be easier to catch terrorists. . . . [But] it would not be a country for which we could, in good conscience, ask our young people to fight and die. In short, that country would not be America."[8]

Some members of Congress have recognized the disastrous consequences of the Patriot Act and are doing their best to rein it in. Rep. Bernie Sanders (D-VT) has introduced the Freedom to Read Protection Act, which would remove the new powers of the Patriot Act to intrude on the confidentiality of library and bookstore records. In a speech made to the American Library Association's June 2003 conference he explained,

> Neither you nor I nor the American people want to see a slow but sure chilling impact on intellectual curiosity. We do not want to see young people, or any person, hesitate to take out a book on politics, on religion, on history or science because someone in the government might think that the person reading that book might have terrorist tendencies. The truth about the U.S.A. Patriot Act, Mr. Ashcroft, is that this is an extremely dangerous piece of legislation that strikes at the heart of what freedom is about and, in fact, allows government agents, in unconstitutional ways, to snoop and spy on the American people and certainly does allow law enforcement agencies virtually unfettered access to libraries and bookstores.[9]

Despite growing support for the Freedom to Read Protection Act and other legislation proposed to reverse the more egregious provisions of the Patriot Act, secrecy and surveillance grow apace in our society. Dr. David Cole, professor of law at Georgetown University, has described this new era: "[J]ust as we did in the McCarthy era, we have offset the decline of traditional forms of repression with the development of new forms of repression. A historical comparison reveals not so much a repudiation as an evolution."[10]

Susan Chamberlin of the conservative/libertarian Cato Institute describes that evolution:

> You're never going to have the day come when Congress passes a law that says, "Okay, starting now, we're a police state, and law enforcement has every power we can think of." Instead, what we see is incremental upward adjustments in the power of law enforcement and the power of our military such that somebody born in the United States last week is born into a considerably less free, and arguably not more safe, United States than his parents.[11]

Notes

1. "Insatiable Appetite: The Government's Demand for New and Unnecessary Powers after September 11," ACLU Report, April 2002, American Civil Liberties Union, Washington, D.C., p. 14.

2. Kate Riley, "The Lady from Toledo Has Friends in the Library," *Seattle Times*, April 28, 2003, 4th Edition, p. B4

3. "A Chill in the Library: A Times Editorial," *St. Petersburg Times*, July 23, 2002, p. 1. www.sptimes.com/2002/07/03/Opinion/A_chill_in_the_library.shtml.

4. Susan Schmidt, "IG Probes Patriot Act Charges," *Washington Post*, July 22, 2003, p. A15.

5. Herbert S. White, "Librarians and the FBI," *Library Journal*, October 15, 1988, p. 54.

6. "State of the First Amendment 2002," First Amendment Center, New York, 2002, p. 2.

7. Ibid., pp. 2–3.

8. *Congressional Record—Senate*, October 11, 2001, p. S10570.

9. "Statement of Congressman [Bernie] Sanders on 6/23/2003 Regarding: Freedom to Read Protection Act," bernie.house.gov/statements/20030623160151.asp.

10. John W. Dean, "Hearing Transcripts Invaluable after Charges of 'New McCarthyism,' " CNN.com/Law Center, May 9, 2003, p. 1. www.cnn.com/2003/LAW/005/09/findlaw.analysis.dean.mccarthy/index.html.

11. Grant Gross, "Civil Liberties Advocates Question Patriot Act," *InfoWorld*, April 14, 2003, p. 1. www.infoworld.com/article/03/04.14/HNpatriot_1.html.

Chapter 1

A Recent History of Library Surveillance

Background

This opening chapter will summarize details from my first book, *Surveillance in the Stacks: The FBI's Library Awareness Program*, which surveys the recent history of library surveillance. The FBI's practice of surveillance of libraries, their employees, and their users is a long-standing one. The Library Awareness Program, the Bureau's first coordinated attempt at library surveillance, was regarded as part of the broader counterintelligence effort. The FBI's earlier interest in libraries seemed more focused on civil disturbances and campus unrest.

The first well-publicized government confrontation with the library profession came at the hands of the U.S. Internal Revenue Service (IRS). In 1970 Senator John L. McClellan's Subcommittee on Investigations requested that the Alcohol, Tobacco and Firearms (ATF) Division initiate a broad program to investigate suspected users of explosives. The ATF thought it might be useful to examine library borrower records to see who was reading any material related to explosives or guerrilla warfare. Their investigations took them to urban centers across the country, cutting a swath so wide as to reveal the names of teenagers working on term papers.

In one case a librarian who refused to provide information to ATF agents was forced to comply by the city attorney's office. As in their subsequent response to the Library Awareness Program, the American Library Association (ALA) and the National Education Association both passed resolutions denouncing the ATF investigations and called on all librarians to report any further federal requests for library records and to defend library confidentiality and intellectual freedom.

On July 29, 1970, the Secretary of the Treasury, David M. Kennedy, announced a change of policy: Agents would no longer be permitted to make a general search of libraries to find out who read certain books but would be allowed to investigate what books were checked out by a particular suspect. On July 16, 1970, the American Library Association issued an advisory statement warning that

> the Internal Revenue Service of the Treasury Department has requested access to the circulation records of public libraries in Atlanta, Georgia, and Milwaukee, Wisconsin, for the purposes of determining the identity of persons reading matter pertaining to the construction of explosive devices. The Association is further advised that such requests were not based on any process, order, or subpoena authorized by federal, civil, criminal, or administrative discovery procedures.[1]

The ALA's statement claimed that "the efforts of the federal government to convert library circulation records into 'suspect lists' constitute an unconscionable and unconstitutional invasion of the right of privacy of library patrons, and, if permitted to continue, will do irreparable damage to the educational and social value of the libraries of this country."[2] The statement concluded by recommending that each U.S. library adopt a confidentiality policy, advise all library employees that library records not be released except pursuant to a court order, and resist the issuance or enforcement of such an order until a proper showing of good cause had been made in a court of competent jurisdiction. The ALA's Intellectual Freedom Committee subsequently used the Advisory Statement in the introduction to its Policy on Confidentiality of Library Records, which was formally endorsed by the ALA Council during its midwinter meeting in 1971.

In July 1970 Senator Sam Irvin (D-NC), on behalf of librarians, sent a letter to the secretary of the treasury expressing concern over these untoward government inquiries. Ervin wrote, "Throughout history, official surveillance of the reading habits of citizens has been a litmus test of tyranny." The secretary of the treasury answered Irvin's letter on July 29, 1970, claiming that the inquiries had been made "to determine the advisability of the use of library records as an investigative technique to assist in quelling bombings. That survey . . . has terminated and will not be repeated." The secretary concluded ominously that "it is our judgement that checking such records in certain limited circumstances is an appropriate investigative technique." On July 31, 1970, the *New York Times* wrote, "To its watchful librarians the country owes a vote of thanks. To itself it owes an alertness against any repetition of the IRS's deplorable venture."[3]

On August 5, 1970, representatives of the ALA and IRS met in Washington, D.C. and issued a joint statement on guidelines acceptable to both organizations. The statement concluded,

In reaching this accord, the principals recognized that due notice will have to be taken of the individual's right to privacy as well as the agency responsibility to administer the statutes. In the work ahead, an attempt will be made to identify areas of reconciliation that would give the Government access to specific library records in justifiable situations but would unequivocally proscribe "fishing expeditions" in contradistinction to the investigation of a particular person or persons suspected of a criminal violation.[4]

The Library Awareness Program

On September 18, 1987, a front-page article in the *New York Times* described an FBI visit to Columbia University in June of that year. The ALA had provided information on the Columbia incident to the *Times* after receiving a letter from Paula Kaufman, director of Academic Information Services at Columbia, complaining of that visit. In her letter Kaufman stated, "They explained that they were doing a general 'library awareness' program in the city and that they were asking librarians to be alert to the use of their libraries by persons from countries 'hostile to the United States, such as the Soviet Union' and to provide the FBI with information about these activities."[5]

The *New York Times* article paraphrased the FBI's description of the Columbia visit as "a Library Awareness Program that is part of a national counterintelligence effort," but this claim seemed to contradict the visiting agent's description of a "program in the city."

On July 1, 1987, Judith Drescher, chairperson of the ALA's Intellectual Freedom Committee, wrote the FBI to inquire about its program. In his July 31 response, FBI Assistant Director Milt Ahlerich stated, "You wrote seeking information regarding what you call the FBI's library awareness program." Ahlerich acknowledged that the Bureau's New York Office (NYO) had been contacting area libraries to reduce the availability of unclassified technical information and added,

We have programs wherein we alert those in certain fields of the possibility of members of hostile countries or their agents attempting to gain access to information that could be potentially harmful to our national security. In this regard, our New York Office has contacted staff members of New York libraries to alert them to this potential danger and to request assistance. . . . The FBI relies in great measure on the willingness and cooperation of the American people to assist us in fulfilling our responsibilities, and we have found programs of these types helpful.[6]

On August 3, 1987, the New York Library Association (NYLA) wrote the FBI expressing support for library confidentiality and opposing "the use of intimidation by government officials as a means of obtaining information about library users." The letter concluded, "In light of these standards we are concerned about the 'library awareness' program being conducted by the FBI in New York City."[7] The NYLA formally condemned the program in an October 1987 statement: "The Library Awareness Program jeopardizes the rights to confidentiality of library patrons in violation of the Library Bill of Rights and New York State Law, and . . . the New York Library Association . . . calls on the Bureau to desist from any further attempts to involve library staffs in reporting on library users."[8]

In October 1987 the ALA's Intellectual Freedom Committee released a lengthy advisory statement outlining the threat posed by the FBI's program and recommending a firm response based on existing ALA policy. The advisory warned that libraries are not "extensions of the long arm of the law or of the gaze of Big Brother," and it defined the role of libraries "to make available and provide access to a diversity of information, not to monitor what use a patron makes of publicly available information."[9]

Throughout this period the FBI offered confusing and contradictory descriptions of the program. Quinlan Shea of the National Security Archive, a Washington-based research organization, stated,

> In September [1987], Deputy Assistant Director Fox of the New York Office called this a national counter-espionage program. In January, Deputy Assistant Director DuHadway of the Intelligence Division at Bureau Headquarters said it was limited to three cities: New York, Washington, and San Francisco. That same statement was made by Director Sessions in April, before the Senate Appropriations Committee. In May, however, before the Senate Judiciary Committee, he changed his position and said it was only in New York.[10]

During the 1988 congressional hearings on the Library Awareness Program, Rep. Don Edwards (D-CA) expressed similar confusion: "We had testimony from both the director and somebody else in the FBI that the program was also taking place in San Francisco and Washington, D.C. . . . He [the Director] said it is actually restricted to New York City although there have been other activities in connection with San Francisco and Washington. Now what do you suppose the Director meant by that?"[11]

Librarians like myself found the FBI's explanations unsatisfactory, especially the suggestion that the Bureau had been targeting only New York libraries. Two of my own branch libraries at the University of Maryland at College Park had been visited by the FBI in May 1986, and one had been the subject of FBI surveillance years before. Did the FBI have separate program names for each state? Or were they all part of a master program?

Origins in the New York Office

In July 1988, after twice denying the existence of the Library Awareness Program, the FBI responded to a Freedom of Information Act (FOIA) request from the National Security Archive by releasing thirty-seven heavily excised pages describing counterintelligence activities in New York City's libraries. At the same time, Assistant Director James Geer told Congress:

> FBI investigations since the early 1960s have thoroughly documented SIS [Soviet Intelligence Services] contacts with librarians in specialized science and technology libraries, SIS instructions to develop sources to steal microfiche containing specific technical reports from those libraries, SIS targeting of libraries for clandestine meetings, and SIS efforts to recruit the librarians and students associated with these libraries. In response to this effort, the New York Office (NYO) initiated an awareness program, which has come to be known as the Library Awareness Program.[12]

All pages were unnumbered and stamped "SECRET" or "TOP SECRET," and all names and dates were expunged throughout. However, in a subsequent meeting with the ALA's Intellectual Freedom Committee, FBI spokesmen revealed that the Library Awareness Program functioned from 1973 through 1976 and from 1985 to date [1988]. The pastiche of information in the released FBI documents revealed a program proposed by the New York Office, considered skeptically by FBI headquarters, but nonetheless implemented off and on in the New York City area. A heavily censored FBI document described the program as follows:

> The librarians are apprised of this Bureau's responsibilities with regard to the protection of the U.S. They are further apprised that the technical needs of the Soviet Union can frequently be derived from any variety of publications regarding current and "cutting edge" technologies that can be located in their facilities. If the librarian is cooperative and pursue[s] other countries of interest, the Soviet bloc countries will also be included.[13]

The final pages of the NYO documents revealed that the operation described was the Library Awareness Program: "Columbia University, Manhattan, New York, was contacted by [deleted] and advised of this program. [deleted] indicated it was Columbia University's policy not to divulge any information which would impinge on the right to privacy of any individual who might utilize their library system. [deleted] stated that neither she nor any librarian employed at Columbia would be able to assist the FBI."[14] The name excised in the first sentence is that of the FBI agent. The name excised in the final two sentences is recognizable as Paula Kaufman, the librarian at Columbia who blew the whistle on the Library Awareness Program, resulting in the September 1987 expose in the *New York Times.*

On March 22, 1988, Special Agent in Charge (SAC) William Warfield sent a secret memo to Bureau supervisors stating,

> Recent media attention has been focused on the NYO's Library Awareness Program, a program designed to alert librarians of scientific and technical libraries of the interest of hostile intelligence services in their holdings. . . . Supervisors are instructed to inform all personnel that no public comment is to be made on this program, and any requests for a speaker to address library groups, classes, etc., should be forwarded to ADIC [Assistant Director in Charge] Fox without any commitment made to the requestor.[15]

In February 1988 the Bureau was invited to serve as a panel member at the Nassau Library System's April 11 trustee workshop. The Bureau declined. In May 1988 the FBI rejected a formal request from the ALA for a briefing on the Library Awareness Program and in December it declined an invitation to attend a New Jersey Library Association workshop on the program.

A September 21, 1988, FBI memo described authorization for an agent to deliver a prepared speech to the Special Libraries Association, but the memo warned, "FBIHQ advised that the speech must not address or reference the subject of the FBI 'Library Awareness Program.' In accordance with the above advisement, SLA representative . . . was telephonically advised instant date of the above conditions, and that no question-and-answer period would follow the presentation. . . . Speaker will depart immediately following presentation."[16]

The FBI Meets Congress

Shortly after the Library Awareness Program was publicly exposed, the NYLA wrote to Rep. Edwards, chairperson of the House Subcommittee on Civil and Constitutional Rights, warning,

> Should the citizens of this nation perceive the library and its staff as a covert agency of government watching to record who is seeking which bits of information, then the library will cease to be creditable as a democratic resource for free and open inquiry. Once the people of this country begin to fear what they read, view or make inquiry about may . . . be used against them or made the object of public knowledge, then this nation will have turned away from the very most basic principle of freedom from tyranny which inspired this union of states.[17]

Representative Edwards, himself a former FBI agent, spoke skeptically of the Bureau's purposes: "They think they can learn what the Russians are doing scientifically if they know what they are reading. But turning librarians into agents is terribly chilling. It's reminiscent of the domestic intelligence files the FBI kept for many years. I thought those bad old days were gone."[18] Edwards reflected, "One wonders what's going to happen to people who write controversial, creative works if they think they are going to be looked at by an FBI agent . . . or be reported by library employees who are working for the FBI."[19]

Indeed, as librarians criticized the Bureau's program, they recognized that the public's judgment of the FBI might have less ultimate impact on society than the public's altered image of libraries. What good social purpose would be served if, as the result of public debate over the Library Awareness Program, the FBI were seen as a sinister intruder on library confidentiality, while librarians were seen as weak and possibly obliging collaborators? The traditional relationship of trust and confidence between librarians and library users is so long-standing that we tend to overlook its obvious fragility. Library users take it on faith that their reading habits will not be used to judge or embarrass them. But that faith, nurtured by a century of unwavering library ethics, can be eroded quickly, perhaps irrevocably, by even the perception of library complicity in federal surveillance such as the Library Awareness Program.

In April 1988 the American Civil Liberties Union (ACLU) wrote to the Senate Select Committee on Intelligence "to express our concern about the FBI's counterintelligence activities focused on the library community." The ACLU recommended, "At minimum, the Committee should request that the FBI produce guidelines and procedures on the Library Awareness Program and related activities. In addition, the existence and implementation of this FBI Program suggests that it is time for Congress to act to preserve the integrity of certain institutions, such as libraries, by imposing appropriate restrictions on intelligence gathering."[20]

In June 1988 the ACLU wrote to Rep. Edwards urging that he initiate an investigation of the Library Awareness Program for the purpose of requiring the FBI to (1) provide guidelines and procedures on their programs in libraries, (2) abide by state law, (3) honor the professional and ethical codes of the library community, and (4) circumscribe the scope of intelligence-gathering activities in libraries. Similarly, People for the American Way asked Edwards to request that the Bureau end its program: "In the event that the FBI refuses to comply, we would urge the Congress to take measures through the authorization and appropriations process to limit the scope of FBI intelligence gathering in our nation's libraries."[21]

By summer 1988 Edwards had succeeded in organizing hearings on the Library Awareness Program before his subcommittee. Shortly before the first day of hearings, a secret FBI memo was sent to Director Sessions:

For all practical purposes, Capitol Hill itself is an open area for Soviet officials, but a restricted one for FBI agents intent on continuing physical surveillance or pursuing the identity of Soviet contacts. . . . Of concern is the possibility these pending hearings will result in new guidelines restricting investigative contacts in libraries. . . . If aggressively handled, perhaps hearings and resultant publicity could serve as a platform from which to alert all librarians nationwide of the threat faced by the U.S. from hostile intelligence services.[22]

On June 20, the first day of hearings, Chairman Edwards stated that "this is a matter important enough for Judge Sessions to not only attend in a subsequent hearing, but to announce a whole program that would extirpate this noxious activity completely out of the FBI, to repudiate it in the widest audience possible." Edwards said the Library Awareness Program "is simply a witch hunt for—they don't even know what." Rep. John Conyers (D-MI), a member of the subcommittee, described the program in the context of other questionable FBI activities: "We are being beset upon by an intelligence agency that has gone far, far afield, and in my judgment has never come back to limiting these excesses. . . . When you take it in conjunction with all of the excesses, it seems to me that we have a very, very serious situation."[23]

Witnesses testifying against the Library Awareness Program included C. James Schmidt from the ALA, David Bender from the Special Libraries Association (SLA), and Duane Webster from the Association of Research Libraries. Paula Kaufman and I were the witnesses representing particular libraries visited by the FBI. Schmidt told the subcommittee: "The requests of the FBI that library staff monitor and report the use of the library by any patron chills the First Amendment freedoms of all library and database users. The Library Awareness Program is a threat to the fundamental freedom of this nation. If continued, it will seriously and unnecessarily invade the intellectual life of citizens."[24]

Duane Webster characterized the Library Awareness Program as "a deliberate effort to control and intimidate library staff to cooperate in monitoring library use." He claimed, "Even the suggestion of library manipulation by such Government requests will have a frightening effect on library-users. . . . Such perceptions profoundly inhibit the freedom of citizens to receive and exchange ideas." Webster said that the FBI's program would require librarians to "ascribe motives to the use of library resources and then report their judgments to the FBI. In effect the FBI is asking librarians to police the use of libraries."[25] Webster rejected this information-policing role as the antithesis of a librarian's professional code of ethics and urged Congress to take prompt action to stop the program's abuses.

Chairman Edwards told Geer:

What disturbs some of us about this program is the FBI's apparent failure to recognize the special status of libraries in our society . . . the FBI should recognize that libraries and books and reading are special. In our nation libraries are sacred institutions, which should be protected and nurtured. Going into libraries and asking librarians to report on suspicious users has ominous implications for freedom of speech and privacy. Everybody in this country has a right to use libraries and they have the right to do so with confidentiality.

Edwards concluded, "I would hope that the FBI would reconsider this program, admit that it is over-broad, and get on to more productive work. . . . [T]he word should certainly go from Headquarters . . . that before they get permission to move ahead with a program that has caused this much anguish . . . they had better have a very carefully, narrowly drawn charter of some sort that protects the agents, protects the office, and protects the rights of privacy and State laws." Geer answered, "Agreed."[26]

Edwards concluded by warning Geer, "You have not measured what you are doing to freedom of speech and privacy and so forth against the panic that you are causing in this country. And it is real. [A]ll kinds of imagining and fear is going to run through the libraries of this nation. . . . [O]nce something like this starts, there is no end to the panic that overtakes our precious libraries, and that is what is going on today."[27]

The Controversy Escalates

The FBI tried to put the best face on it, but the Library Awareness Program had been a public-relations disaster. Judith Keogh of the Pennsylvania Library Association wrote FBI Director Sessions to protest the FBI's program, stating: "Free access to information is one of the fundamental principles of a free society. Libraries must uphold the rights of patrons to pursue information without the fear that library staff will 'spy' on them to any government agency . . . Librarians are employed to serve the needs of their patrons, not to act as agents for the government." Keogh quoted from an editorial in the *Philadelphia Daily News*: "Setting up a network of informants alerted to report anyone they consider 'suspicious' encourages the kind of paranoia and divisiveness which inspire just the kind of environment we deplore in countries whose 'spies' we are supposed to be protecting ourselves against—an environment in which neighbor informs against neighbor and child informs against parent." Keogh concluded succinctly, "The 'Library Awareness Program' must be ended."[28]

The Association for Research Libraries issued a statement on "Library Users' Right to Confidentiality" condemning "the efforts of any government agency to violate the privacy of library users, to subvert library patron records, and to intimidate or recruit library staff to monitor so-called 'suspicious' library patrons or report what or how any individual uses library resources. Such actions are an affront to First Amendment freedoms, individual privacy, and all citizens' right to know."[29]

On July 8, 1988, the ALA's Resolution in Opposition to FBI Library Awareness Program called for the immediate cessation of the program "and all other related visits by the Bureau to libraries where the intent is to gain information, without a court order, on patrons' use."[30] The resolution was sent to President Ronald Reagan, FBI Director Sessions, the National Commission on Libraries and Information Science, and appropriate Senate and House subcommittees.

At the conclusion of its 1988 annual conference, the Special Library Association Board of Directors, under pressure from its membership, endorsed a statement opposing the Library Awareness Program. At its 1988 business meeting, the Society of American Archivists passed a resolution condemning the Library Awareness Program. The Medical Library Association affirmed its commitment to the unrestricted access to information by the general public and condemned any efforts of the FBI to compromise the ability of the public to exercise its right to free access to information. Other library organizations, including the American Association of Law Libraries, passed similar resolutions.

Margaret Truman told the 1988 ALA conference that her father, former President Harry S Truman, had little use for J. Edgar Hoover, but that no president dared fire him. She saw the Library Awareness Program as a "distinctly dubious surveillance operation" reminiscent of the Hoover era, and declared, "These intelligence people, whether in the CIA or FBI, never give up. They are forever trying to make informers out of us. They don't seem to understand that a country in which every citizen informs on every other citizen, and every citizen reports to the authorities, is nothing more than a police state."[31]

Margaret Chisholm, former president of the ALA, wrote, "The specter of having the FBI, or its surrogates, gazing over one's shoulder, following one through the stacks and to the photocopy machine, and making reports on database searches of items requested through interlibrary loan, must, perforce, have a chilling impact on the First Amendment rights of each and every one of us."[32] *Library Journal* presented a similar indictment: "The FBI has hampered the free exchange of ideas by creating an unwholesome climate of fear and mistrust. The Bureau must bear the burden of having hindered intellectual advancement and slowed the enrichment and diversity of human culture."[33]

The *Wilson Library Bulletin* stated,

Libraries have a much more complicated view of the world than does the bureau. We believe in building bridges, opening communications, revealing secrets. We want as much as possible known. We think it would be progress if KGB agents checked out armloads of books and kept them overdue. The KGB doesn't understand our historic role or contemporary position. We're here to divulge information, to educate, enlighten, change, and alter. We're here to scatter knowledge. Not to spy on our users but to help them surveil life.[34]

It Only Hurts When We Laugh

Unlike previous assaults on library confidentiality, the Library Awareness Program seemed less fearsome than ridiculous. A joke made the rounds in 1988 that described an FBI agent's report to Director William S. Sessions that the Bureau had successfully apprehended six Libyans, to which the disappointed Sessions responded, "No, no! I said librarians."

Cartoons caricaturing the Library Awareness Program have appeared throughout the national and local press, with Herblock, the dean of political cartoonists, actually lampooning the program in two consecutive months. One cartoon shows FBI Director Sessions hiding on a library shelf among the Russian literature collection; the other pictures a menacing FBI agent spying in the stacks while a librarian complains to the police that he was "lurking around here . . . acting kind of un-American"[35] Larry Wright, in the *Detroit News,* drew a picture of three elderly, bespectacled female librarians converging on a reader and announcing, "You're busted Mr. Foreigner! We're librarians for the FBI!"[36]

Political satirist Mark Russell ridiculed the FBI's paranoia about library users with foreign names and accents, claiming, "So far they've arrested Henry Kissinger, Zbigniew Brzezinski, and Michael Dukakis." Russell then paid a musical tribute to the Library Awareness Program with a ditty entitled, "We're the Library Hit Squad of the FBI."[37]

The *Miami Herald* wrote, "It's just absurd for anyone to think that spies are infesting Broward's West Regional Library . . . its shelves laden with best sellers and Winnie the Pooh. . . . If it weren't so serious, the FBI's Library Awareness Program would be ridiculous."[38]

Rick Horowitz wrote in the *Philadelphia Inquirer*: "The FBI has put together a cheery little something called the 'Library Awareness Program' . . . designed to step up America's effort against foreign espionage by bringing in the big guns—librarians. Chortle all you want to . . . The FBI is not amused. They may not see foreign agents lurking under your bed anymore—they're all hiding in the stacks."[39]

One writer in the *Baltimore Sun,* seeing the dubious success of the FBI's program in libraries, offered some equally absurd hunting grounds for spies, including ballet schools, barber shops, and the Daughters of the American Revolution: "There is as yet no hard evidence of a KGB presence in the DAR, but if it could become a Russian target, why shouldn't the FBI extend its vigilance there as well?"[40]

The *Atlanta Constitution* editorialized, "The FBI's Library Awareness Program was always slightly absurd. No, the Bureau didn't dispatch agents to reading rooms to spy on patrons by peeking through holes cut in newspapers—but the project wasn't much more sophisticated."[41]

Anne Hagedorn of the *Wall Street Journal* stated, "If Big Brother isn't watching you, that may be because he's spending a lot of time at the library. But Big Brother, a.k.a. your friendly FBI agent, isn't brushing up on Shakespeare. . . . [Y]our FBI in peace and war has leapt into action trying to enlist patriotic librarians in the War Against Illicit Research."[42]

Time magazine declared that the name Library Awareness Program "sounds like a high-minded effort to get kids to check out *Huckleberry Finn*," but instead it is "spy vs. spy in a battle of the bookshelves."[43]

A *New York Times* editorial ridiculed the FBI's "spooks in the stacks" program but concluded, "Sensible librarians protest such subversion of their profession and they're right."[44]

Even the library profession was unable to overlook the comic aspects of the Library Awareness Program. Gregg Sapp, writing for the *Idaho Librarian,* reported, "Ever since the FBI alerted librarians to be aware of Soviet spies in the stacks, I've been suspicious of anybody who looks just a little too Ukrainian. . . . In my library, I've launched an operation that I call 'Assignment Rasputin.' Our entire right-minded reference staff has agreed to deliberately give incorrect answers to anybody suspected of being, having been, or having ever known a Communist." Sapp described a phone call from someone requesting the name of the U.S. secretary of state. "When I considered the potential havoc that the Soviets could wreak with such delicate strategic information, I answered without hesitation: 'Sylvester Stallone.' J. Edgar Hoover, God rest that noble man's soul, would have been proud."[45]

In summing up the FBI's struggle with librarians, Herbert S. White claimed that "this particular battle makes the FBI look not so much nasty as silly, and that is bad for the country. We need an effective FBI, one we can rely upon." But White urged librarians and the public at large not to take the Library Awareness Program lightly, warning, "Stupidity should not be allowed to masquerade as security."[46]

A Selective Survey of Library Visits

When the *New York Times* broke the story on the Library Awareness Program in September 1987, Columbia University was represented as the battleground on which librarian Paula Kaufman confronted the FBI. The *Times* story quoted from Kaufman's letter, which concluded, "I explained that we were not prepared to cooperate with them in any way, described our philosophies and policies respecting privacy, confidentiality and academic freedom, and told them they were not welcome here."[47]

This dramatic confrontation had occurred on June 7, 1987, when two female agents from the FBI's NYO approached a clerk at Columbia University's Mathematics and Science Library, asking that he report on the activities of foreigners who use that library. A professional librarian who overheard the conversation directed the agents to Paula Kaufman, the university librarian. Kaufman has speculated that had her reference librarian not discovered the initial contact, the clerk might have cooperated with the agents, who were trying to make him violate the New York State law protecting the privacy of borrower records.

An FBI memo recounts, "Kaufman informed the agents that if the FBI wanted any information from Columbia University regarding its library users, a court order would be necessary. . . . While Kaufman was not rude or hostile to the agents, she was emphatic that she was not willing to cooperate with the FBI . . . The agents felt that continuing the interview would serve no useful purpose at that time."[48]

During the July 1988 hearings before the House Subcommittee on Civil and Constitutional Rights, Paula Kaufman described the behavior of the FBI agents during their Columbia visits:

> They asked us to report on who was reading what, and I refused to coop-erate with them. . . . They explained that libraries such as ours were of-ten used by the KGB and other intelligence agents for recruiting activities. . . . [T]he agents warned that students and librarians, "who are traditionally underpaid," are the primary targets of these recruiting ef-forts. I continued to refuse to spy on our readers.[49]

Kaufman reflected on the ethical quandary posed by the Bureau's inquiries:

> The FBI's request to me to report on foreigners using our libraries is one with which I could not practically comply, even if our institution sup-ported such cooperation, which it does not; even if such a request did not contravene my professional ethics, which it does; even if it did not infringe upon the First Amendment and privacy rights of all library pa-trons, which it does; and even if it does not violate the laws of the State of New York, which it does. The academic community, indeed, Ameri-can society, includes persons with a variety of backgrounds, interests, and nationalities. The FBI's definition of "foreigners" is sufficiently vague, and the environment at Columbia is sufficiently international, that it becomes patently absurd to even think about how one is to iden-tify possible spies from among our general population. Zbigniew Brzezinski, for example, who is a member of our faculty . . . could eas-ily fit that definition. . . . We should be looking for ways to acquire more materials on our shelves, rather than for ways to interfere with the use of what we already own.[50]

Kaufman's brief but resolute encounter with the FBI earned her unexpected notoriety in the press and the well-deserved applause of librarians and libertari-ans. While serving as a heroine to her peers, she was every bit the villain in the eyes of the intelligence community and its supporters. During his briefing with the National Commission on Libraries and Information Science, Deputy As-sistant Director Tom DuHadway claimed that the FBI's library visits had been received very favorably by librarians, "with one exception." That one exception was, apparently, Paula Kaufman. DuHadway said, "[W]e evidently struck a chord with one librarian who thought this was atrocious and said she would not cooperate, and she said it's a violation of the First Amendment and I'm going to call the Intellectual Freedom Committee at the American Library Association and she's gotten on a letter writing campaign." DuHadway referred to Paula Kaufman as "that person who wrote these letters," and he insisted that "we're not going to back away . . . at Columbia University." DuHadway attributed the FBI's lack of success at Columbia to Kaufman's bad temper and the consequent difficulty in "talking to people like that" who are "not going to make a whole lot of sense."[51]

The FBI intrusion on Columbia University captured most of the New York headlines, but there were other visits to libraries in the Big Apple. Nancy Gubman, head librarian at New York University's Courant Institute of Mathematical Sciences Library, told me, "In the spring of 1986, an FBI man came in and told me they were looking at the technical libraries in New York. He said one of every three U.N. delegates from the Soviet Union are spies, and wanted to know if any Soviets have come in asking for sensitive information, unusual database searches or large photocopying requests."[52] Gubman said she was stunned and told the agent that she would not monitor library users and therefore could not help him.

The agent claimed that, though the materials in question were unclassified, some items might be "more sensitive than general library materials," particularly when organized through database searches. Gubman advised him that the Courant Institute only did database searches for its students and faculty, and in any case, the databases contained only publicly available information. When the agent asked about photocopying, Gubman told him it was self-service and coin-operated, adding, "Anyone who can use the library can use the photocopier, and we're not going to place a camera under it."[53]

Perhaps because the NYU visit predated the incident at Columbia University, the visiting agent made no mention of the Bureau's program name, but the visit was later acknowledged as part of the Library Awareness Program. Gubman told me, "About two months later I received a call from another FBI agent asking if I had anything to report on 'you know what.' That was the expression he used. I said no, there's nothing to report, and there won't be anything. That was the last I heard from them."[54]

In May 1988, shortly before the congressional hearings on the Library Awareness Program, Nancy Kranich, director of public and administrative services at NYU, wrote subcommittee chairman Don Edwards recounting the incident at NYU:

The agent asked the librarian if there were members of the Soviet mission to the United Nations who requested sensitive information available through online databases or copied large amounts of unusual types of information. . . . The librarian responded . . . by explaining that the administration, faculty, and students of New York University are outraged at this incident and the prospect of future FBI visits. We simply do not wish to have our readers feel that they may be under surveillance by intelligence agents. Furthermore, we want to assure all library users of their right to read freely and to explore ideas without question of their motives. At New York University we believe this type of invasion into the privacy of the American public is an unwarranted threat to our civil liberties.[55]

Joseph Murphy, chancellor of the City University of New York, condemned the Library Awareness Program in a press release, stating, "Covert surveillance activities have no place in college libraries or any other library. I share the outrage of the city's librarians who regard it as unconscionable that they should be asked to serve as informants for the FBI as part of their professional duties."[56]

After the *New York Times* expose, it was learned that in the spring of 1987 an FBI agent had visited the New York Public Library (NYPL) and inquired about a particular library user. Two agents returned on November 24, this time inquiring about former NYPL employees. The Bureau's investigative interest in employee Fernando Clark began after Clark discussed the library's ongoing exchange program with a Cuban diplomat. One member of the library's senior policy group was quoted as saying, "The FBI was told not to contact anyone, and they went ahead and did it anyway. They are escalating this awareness thing." The head of the library then met with James Fox of the FBI's NYO, and a library official later said of the meeting, "Its purpose was to say we felt we were being harassed."[57]

Director Vartan Gregorian said, "We thought it was an unwarranted intrusion into the private affairs of a member of our library . . . and that's against our rules, regulations, and expectations." On the general issue of library surveillance, Gregorian stated, "We consider reading a private act, an extension of freedom of thought. And our doors are open to all."[58]

Across town in Brooklyn, FBI agents warned the Brooklyn Public Library that "persons acting against the security of the United States" might be using their library. One agent told a librarian "to look out for suspicious looking people who wanted to overthrow the government." The librarian said there was nothing secret there to protect, but the agent nonetheless urged him to report such people to the Bureau.[59]

Larry Brandwein, director of the Brooklyn Public Library, reported:

In terms of how it affects the actual, day-to-day running of the library, such a visit isn't of much consequence, for the agent was just told that we do not give out any information of any kind regarding individual use of the library. But the fact of such a visit is clearly an attempt to invade the privacy of the public in general. Libraries, as I have understood them, are nonpartisan organizations. The people using them have always assumed, and assumed correctly, that their rights to privacy are protected.[60]

An internal FBI memo gave the Bureau's view of the December 1, 1987, Brooklyn visit:

> The attitude exhibited by Brandwein is much more prevalent among librarians associated with publicly accessible institutions than within private organizations. However, this attitude has increasingly been encountered as a direct result of the publicity surrounding the incident at Columbia University and subsequent involvement of the Intellectual Freedom Committee of the American Library Association, and it should not remain unchallenged.[61]

Public libraries outside of New York were also targeted by the FBI. In a 1988 memo to Director Sessions, FBI Newark stated,

> A contact at "Princeton Municipal Library," circa 1978, did result in a less than cooperative encounter. . . . A library employee became rather indignant and proved to be most uncooperative. The employee summoned his supervisor, who was equally uncooperative. Even after a thorough explanation of the FBI's role in FCI investigation, both remained adamant in their non-cooperation.[62]

In Fort Lauderdale, Florida, Selma Algaze, head of the Broward County Public Library, said that an FBI agent tried to appeal to her "sense of patriotic duty." She said that there was "an implied threat that I should do what he asked." The agent claimed that there were "agitators" in the area who were using the library for information. When Algaze asked the agent for specifics, she was told that it was privileged information. When the agent asked to look at the library's computer records, Algaze said, "What you're asking is privileged information to us, too."[63]

A memo from the Bureau's Miami office to the director of the FBI described how an FBI agent contacted Algaze in December 1986,

> According to Selma Algaze an unidentified FBI Agent identified himself to her with a display of credentials and requested her assistance in identifying "unsavory types, subversives, to see the circulation database, individuals looking at books on bombs, guns and armaments, appealing to her sense of patriotism." Algaze . . . denied the Agent any access, stating there was a Florida statute protecting the privacy of records . . . and alleged the Agent requested she bypass this procedure to which she replied, "You don't want me to break the law, do you?"[64]

One of the more mysterious of the documented FBI visits to libraries outside of New York, and therefore allegedly outside the Library Awareness Program, occurred during the 1970s at the University of Maryland at College Park, where I worked until 1996. The employee approached by the FBI did not report the incidents until she left the university several years later. What we do know is the following.

In 1982, when the technical reports librarian at the University of Maryland's Engineering and Physical Sciences Library retired from service, I conducted an exit interview with the employee, who revealed that "a few years earlier" FBI agents had questioned her about the use of our Technical Reports Center. She told me that the FBI had asked her to monitor the use of certain technical reports and to report to the FBI the names of any persons reading or requesting such reports. When I asked why she had not reported these incidents to me earlier, she said that she had felt intimidated by the Bureau's inquiries, particularly since she was a foreign national.[65]

Only in January 1989 did I receive official confirmation of those early FBI visits to my library. FBI Assistant Director Milt Ahlerich acknowledged the FBI contact "several years before 1980 regarding specific individuals in whom we had investigative interest." Ahlerich told me that because of the Privacy Act and the classified nature of the Bureau's investigation, he could provide no further information.[66]

In April 1986, another agent returned to the same Technical Reports Center and again approached the librarian, though now a new incumbent, Hugh O'Connor, held the position. O'Connor described a female FBI agent who approached him, flashed a badge, and asked if he had observed anything unusual that should be reported to the FBI. When O'Connor said that he had seen nothing out of the ordinary, the agent inquired about library users with foreign names or accents who might have used the Technical Reports Center. O'Connor told the agent that he was unable to identify such library users and suggested that the agent speak to me as head of the library. The agent declined and departed.

The agent then went to the adjoining White Memorial Library (WML), which houses the chemistry materials, and approached Sylvia Evans, a reference librarian, displayed her badge, and spoke about national security. She described her presence as part of an effort "to discover if people from Soviet-bloc countries were using our libraries." According to librarian Evans, the agent also wanted to know what kinds of materials these Soviet-bloc nationals were reading or requesting. Evans recalls, "I explained to the agent that all of our libraries had open stacks and were available to anyone. It would therefore be impossible to identify our users unless they asked for a particular service, like database searching."[67]

The agent immediately asked if Evans had ever done a database search for a Soviet national. Evans said that she recalled doing a MEDLINE search a few years earlier for a person identifying himself openly as a Soviet physician. Evans advised the agent that since the records of database searches were kept at the main library she could be of no further assistance.

Evans said, "There was something intimidating about the agent's attitude. For example, she emphasized that I should not feel obliged to protect library users who were not American citizens." Evans said she did not believe that the FBI agent was investigating the Soviet physician or anyone else in particular. "The impression I had was that it was a generalized fishing expedition."[68]

I alerted the University of Maryland Libraries' associate director for public services, Danuta Nitecki, to these FBI visits, and she subsequently spoke by phone with FBI agent Kathryn Kaiser, presumably the agent who made the original inquiries. When Nitecki questioned the appropriateness of revealing confidential information, agent Kaiser said that she could understand the university's concern if a Maryland student were involved, but, after all, "The person in question was not a U.S. citizen."[69]

Nonetheless, after review with the library director, Nitecki expressed the libraries' support for the principle of protecting the privacy and confidentiality of library use, "regardless of user status or origin."

In July 1988, James Geer appeared on television's *MacNeil-Lehrer Report* and acknowledged that general questions about foreigners were asked at the April 1986 visit to College Park, but he claimed that there was a good purpose behind such questions: "Quite frankly, that was no more than a pretext, because we knew the person we were interested in. We knew what name we were trying to get at."[70]

The FBI gave the same explanation during its September 9 meeting with the ALA's Intellectual Freedom Committee. According to Geer,

> Mr. Foerstel and [I] discussed about an agent coming in and asking a librarian about anyone who was perhaps frequenting there with some kind of foreign-sounding name. That sounds absurd on the face of it, even to me, if I did not know the circumstances. . . . The agent knew full well who and how many times this individual had been in contact with this specific employee of the library. He used a pretext to try to avoid getting into our sources and methods and what have you. He used a pretext to get that employee to come up with the name. . . . But he didn't know at that point what had developed between this employee and this person who happened to be a known intelligence officer.[71]

Earlier, Deputy Assistant Director Thomas DuHadway said of the Maryland visit:

> That was not a contact made under the Library Awareness Program. It was a specifically directed investigation to a specific individual. . . . We had very good information, which we won't go into, as to what the Soviet was trying to do. . . . The least intrusive method we could utilize was to go talk to the individual with whom we knew the Soviet to be in

contact. . . . It was a contact made in the investigation of a known intelligence officer . . . The agent was trying to elicit information about that contact specifically with that person. Not the intelligence officer's use of the library, not what he was doing in other instances, but what was his association with her.[72]

The FBI commentary refers to "a specific library employee" who had been contacted by "a specific individual . . . a known intelligence officer." Why then did the agent interrogate librarians from two different libraries? Which one contained the specific employee? Also, in describing the library contact, DuHadway referred to the intelligence officer's "association with *her*." Was this an inadvertent identification of Sylvia Evans as the library employee?

In the fall of 1986 an FBI agent visited the Lockwood Memorial Library at the State University of New York at Buffalo. SUNY Buffalo spokesman Dave Webb said that "the FBI came to the library and asked to see research reference requests made by a specific foreign student. They wanted to see library records, databases he's searched. The University refused."[73]

According to the SUNY campus newspaper, the FBI agents claimed that an Iraqi student was involved in activities that would endanger the national security. Stephen Roberts, associate director of libraries, said that the FBI "wanted to use the library records to corroborate their evidence," but Roberts informed the agents that the library's user records were confidential and could not be divulged. He later explained, "If somebody shows up with a badge, we don't just pass information across the counter."[74]

The FBI subsequently obtained the records in compliance with a subpoena from a local federal grand jury, naming a graduate student from Iraq as the target of the investigation. The library was forced to turn over the records of all searches requested by the Iraqi student, but as a result of FBI inquiries, SUNY Buffalo library officials reconsidered the nature and detail of user records maintained there. Associate Director Roberts commented, "It's interesting that the FBI has become aware of this whole new fact of information gathering. . . . But we don't want to be gathering information that puts us at odds with the people we serve. We have to look at what we're keeping and how we're keeping it."[75]

On January 23, 1986, the FBI came to Virginia's George Mason University, asking Head Librarian Charlene Hurt to suspend borrowing privileges for a Soviet patron who was said to be reading materials on missiles. Librarian Hurt explained, "Many of our contributors are those who would say we should have cooperated. I told the FBI about the library's confidentiality policies and Virginia's confidentiality statute, but I said I would confirm my decision with the administration. Then I told my secretary to tell the FBI I wasn't in every time they called."[76] Hurt said that, after the FBI's initial visit, the agent called every day for a month and eventually told the librarian's secretary, "It sounds like she'll never be in." The secretary replied, "You're right."[77]

The FBI's request to see the Soviet patron's circulation records was denied, as is required by Virginia's library confidentiality statute. The FBI's account of its visit to George Mason was as follows:

> There was no violation of the Virginia state statute restricting disclosure of library records since no requests for records were made. [T]he FBI's contact at George Mason University was in response to a telephone call placed by a staff member of the library who was concerned about defense documents being checked out by an individual the librarian believed to be a Soviet. These contacts were initiated by the *library,* and not the FBI.[78]

Hurt told me that the staff member who called the FBI was not a librarian and was new to the country. When a Soviet national approached him and identified himself, the new employee first called the FBI and then his supervisor. Hurt explained, "He just became nervous when he heard the Russian name. He probably was trying to be a good American, but he really didn't understand the library's rules or ethics. Since then we've established a training program on this issue for all employees."[79]

Hurt said the FBI was concerned that the Soviet was using the government documents collection, yet Hurt was amazed that the agents were completely ignorant of such *documents.* "When I told them about the government documents program, they seemed to know nothing about it. I said these are documents made public by the United States Government, and if the Government doesn't want people to see them, they won't publish them. I told them about the depository program and NTIS [National Technical Information Service], and they took notes. I thought, good heavens, what am I dealing with here?"[80]

Over a year later, the FBI called Charlene Hurt once more, asking if it could send some agents around to question the library staff. Hurt recalls: "I said, 'You know the answer to that.' The agent said, 'No I don't,' and I said, 'Well you ought to.' " Hurt told me, "I think overall they wasted their time, and they didn't get any information. Still, I would say we are not overwhelmingly proud of the events in our little confrontation." Hurt added, "I haven't checked for a long time to see if our 'spy' still has a library card, and without his name I guess we can't."[81] As far as she knows, the Russian may have renewed his Friends of the Library Card, perhaps continuing to function as a borrower in good standing.

FBI agents visited the University of Cincinnati in 1976 or 1977, where, according to one librarian, they made inquiries about a Polish student. The Bureau maintained its interest there and in 1985 requested records of library use by a Soviet citizen. An FBI agent claimed that the Soviet's proper field of interest should have been mining engineering, but he had instead borrowed a book on robotics. FBI agents returned to the University of Cincinnati in 1986 with similar inquiries about another Soviet scholar. Dorothy Byers, head librarian at the University of Cincinnati, described a "pushy" agent who attempted to convince one of her clerks of the excitement and mystery of library surveillance. Byers refused to cooperate, and she recalls, "I resented being pulled into this. The information community shuts down if we try to limit it."[82]

Charles Osburn, former dean of libraries at Cincinnati, recalls, "I had the FBI come into my office one day. They wanted us to report the names of people who asked for certain engineering journals. They were real stony-faced—I couldn't make them laugh—and I told them we could not comply with their request." Osburn concluded, "It's not our job to be the policemen. They're the policemen."[83]

A recently released FBI memo admitted that "through historic memory and review of files, two substantive cases were located." Most of the seven-page memo was blacked out, but one portion stated, "Cincinnati, FBI, has made contact with university library employees under proper predication and with specific investigative targets in view, of which specific intelligence was known or suspected." After emphasizing the university's strength in aerospace engineering and its ties to General Electric and the National Aeronautics and Space Administration (NASA), the FBI's memo concluded,

> Cincinnati [FBI] further has concerns that the U.S. private sector and government sector affords the capital, resources and investment for research and development in technology applicable to matters falling within the purview of national security. A considerable source of this research and development would be conducted in an unclassified mode at various universities. The HIS [Hostile Intelligence Services], by penetrating this veil of educational endeavor, are capable of obtaining the research and development without exorbitant expenditure of capital, resources or investment.[84]

In 1987 FBI agents journeyed to the University of Wisconsin's library, still seeking Soviet scholars. Alexander Rolich, the library's Soviet and East European bibliographer, told of teams of agents who would watch a Soviet national while he read *Pravda.* "They wanted to know if the newspaper he was reading looked funny, or like it had been marked up."[85]

At the University of Michigan, Maurita Holland, head of the Engineering Library, described how two FBI agents showed her a magazine article describing the role librarians might play in protecting scientific information. Holland recalled that there was a heavy patriotic theme, as the agents expressed concern that a visiting Russian mathematics professor was spending a suspicious amount of time at the photocopy machines. "They appealed to my feelings about being a good citizen," said Holland.[86]

In 1988 the FBI visited the University of Utah's Marriott Library and attempted to monitor library use by a Soviet citizen working in the United States. The Soviet had written a letter to the library inquiring about the National Technical Information Service (NTIS), and the FBI justified its intervention by claiming that the Soviet was attempting to "use the library to gain access to the NTIS." James Geer, the FBI's assistant director, summed up the Utah case: "The Soviet did not identify himself as such, attempting to conceal his true background. After learning of the Soviet's activity, the FBI contacted the library and received information which helped identify Soviet methodology and clandestine activity."[87]

When FBI agents visited the University of Houston, they asked the library to monitor interlibrary loans and computerized literature searches by foreigners, justifying the request by claiming that certain Russians were acquiring "economic materials" that could benefit them. The librarian told the agent that such precautions were preposterous, since these databases could be dialed up from Moscow. Counsel Scott Chafin explained, "If they have a problem with Soviet scientists, they should not let them in. Librarians are not going to do the work of the F.B.I."[88]

In 1987 two FBI agents visited the Engineering Library at the University of California at Los Angeles and asked the librarians about the reading habits of a visiting Russian student. In addition, they asked the librarians to inform the Bureau of anyone else similarly suspicious in nature, saying it was the librarians' duty to cooperate. The librarians explained that they could not cooperate with the agents because the information they sought was confidential.

Winding Down a Troubled Program

FBI Director William Sessions continued to defend the Library Awareness Program, despite public demands for its cessation. First Amendment advocate Nat Hentoff advised, "Sessions can begin to show the back-room boys - and the public—that he is indeed the captain and the quarterback by simply announcing that the Library Awareness Program was stupid and has now been shelved."[89] Rep. Don Edwards (D-CA), a former FBI agent, made a similar suggestion in a letter to Director Sessions: "Given the limited results compared with the confusion and concern that it has generated, I think the Bureau would be best served by strictly limiting the program or curtailing it altogether."[90]

In July 1988, Assistant Director Milt Ahlerich was asked for the current status of the Library Awareness Program. He answered, "The Soviet threat hasn't gone away, and we are therefore bound to carry out our duties here."[91] Another Bureau spokesperson suggested the permanence of the Library Awareness Program by claiming, "There's no logical end as long as there's something out there to be aware of."[92] But a New York agent gave a clearer picture of the continuing confrontation between the FBI and the library profession: "We can't let organizations like the American Library Association affect our internal policies." He referred to the hundreds of university and public libraries in the New York City area and said, "We will try to hit all of them."[93]

David Atlee Phillips, a former CIA agent, said that even though the Library Awareness Program had been ineffective in detecting foreign spies, most of the intelligence community believed it would be unwise to curtail it in the face of public opposition. Phillips himself said that "although the FBI operation was clearly legal and the counterintelligence program important, FBI management should recognize that the *prudent* course would be to postpone the operation and take another look at it a few years down the road."[94]

A September 14, 1988, letter from Director Sessions to Rep. Edwards seemed to suggest a willingness to scale back the Library Awareness Program, but an FBI spokesperson said Sessions' letter was intended only to dispel the myths about the program. The letter began, "When deemed necessary, the FBI will continue to contact certain scientific and technical libraries (including university and public libraries) in the New York City area concerning hostile intelligence service activities in libraries." The letter reaffirmed the FBI's desire that librarians report any library users who identify themselves as Soviets or Soviet bloc nationals who (a) seek assistance in conducting library research, (b) request research assistance from students or faculty, (c) remove materials from libraries without permission, or (d) seek biographical information from librarians. Sessions concluded, "[T]he FBI is completely uninterested in the library activities of anyone other than those persons who meet these specific criteria."[95]

Representative Edwards was not completely reassured by Sessions' new guidelines. In a letter he sent to me and other interested parties, Edwards declared that "it is disappointing to see that the FBI continues to defend its library visits. . . . You will see from the Director's letter that the FBI intends to continue asking without a warrant for library borrowing records of individuals who have been identified as hostile intelligence officers and their co-optees."[96]

Though Sessions' letter was characterized as conciliatory by many, C. James Schmidt, chairman of the ALA's Intellectual Freedom Committee, said, "I do not regard it as so. While Director Sessions says he 'shares concerns' about public and university libraries, he states that agents will continue to visit them. While he says that the Bureau will not ask for circulation lists, he states that they will 'inquire further' about what certain Soviet or Soviet bloc nationals are reading."[97] Schmidt communicated his skepticism in a letter to Rep. Edwards, "I am greatly disheartened that the FBI has reiterated its intention to make requests for confidential information on library patrons. . . . This intent demonstrates that the Bureau does not understand, or has chosen to ignore, that however important its duties may be, they are subordinate to the First Amendment rights of patrons using a library or to state confidentiality laws."[98]

On November 29, 1988, Director Sessions sent an eight-page memo to all SACs defending all Bureau activities in libraries. In a significant extension of the concept of proactive "awareness" programs, the memo stated, "Nothing in the above guidelines precludes any other Field Division from implementing a Library Awareness Program if a demonstrated need exists for the establishment of such a program."[99]

This invitation to FBI offices across the country to implement their own Library Awareness Programs was undoubtedly the Bureau's policy from the beginning.

The Role of Librarians in FBI Surveillance

Representative Edwards summed up the broader motivation for the Library Awareness Program: "The recent controversy over FBI visits to libraries highlights the continuing debate over government information controls. The controversy also underscores the need for a new approach to information policy." Edwards claimed, "The library visits were tied to the troubling, though sometimes fitful, government effort to control unclassified information. . . . We must reexamine the basic laws that govern dissemination and access to information."[100]

C. James Schmidt, chairman of the ALA's Intellectual Freedom Committee, agreed: "The FBI's visits to libraries are part of a systematic, coordinated interagency effort to prevent access to unclassified information. This effort is coordinated by the interagency Technology Transfer Intelligence Committee—a group representative of 22 agencies and hosted by the CIA."[101]

In January 1988 the FBI's deputy assistant director, Thomas DuHadway, claimed that "90 percent of what the Soviets collect in this country is free, available, and unclassified." He warned, "There are certain sections of specialized libraries that are supposed to be restricted, and those are some of the areas that we find our Soviet friends mucking about in. They really shouldn't be there."[102] Where? What unclassified collections within technical libraries should have excluded Soviet citizens? The only example the FBI offered was the NTIS material, which we shall see is not off limits to Soviet citizens or anyone else.

Director Sessions had stated that "for several years now—maybe as many as ten years—we have sought the assistance of librarians in connection with specialized libraries where there are people who come to gather technical research. Believe it! That these are places where foreign, hostile intelligence persons seek both to gather information and to recruit people who will be their agents in this country! . . . We expect librarians to be aware of things that in their minds are in fact foreign, hostile intelligence gathering efforts."[103]

Similarly, Assistant Director James Geer told the ALA that the Soviets hope "to glean all the information from libraries they can and to recruit as many librarians as they could."[104]

In January 1988 the Bureau's position paper *The KGB and the Library Target* claimed that the FBI must pursue any contact by an American with a Soviet citizen. Quinlan Shea of the National Security Archive expressed the opinion of most librarians: "I don't believe that I've ever had a 'contact' with a Soviet, but if I ever do, that contact is not any of the FBI's business. . . . As far as I'm concerned, the FBI should not go into a church, or a library or a newsroom or ask about a 'contact' between a Soviet and an American—unless they have reasonable grounds for suspecting that unlawful activity has occurred, is occurring, or is about to occur."[105]

The FBI was claiming that the SIS sought to identify America's emerging technologies before their components became classified or restricted and to identify selected librarians, students, or professors to assist in this unclassified information gathering. In his 1988 letter to Rep. Edwards, FBI Director Sessions explained that the purposes of the FBI's library contacts were twofold: "[T]o inform these libraries that hostile intelligence services attempt to use libraries for intelligence gathering activities that may be harmful to the United States, and to enlist their support . . . in helping the FBI identify those activities."[106]

The Bureau's DuHadway lamented, "The U.S. government and our society don't have the manpower . . . for surveilling all of these people 24 hours a day to find out what they're doing. We just don't do that, we don't have enough money, we don't have enough manpower and it's impossible to do."[107] All the more reason why librarians were regarded as an essential cadre in the full-time effort to restrict unclassified information.

On what authority could librarians actually prevent foreigners or undesirables from accessing unclassified and unrestricted technical information? There have been a number of formal federal attempts to create a structure within which librarians would deny access to such information. The Unclassified Controlled Nuclear Information (UCNI) regulations were intended for just that purpose, and only after lengthy and emotional public hearings, at which librarians refused to collaborate in denying such information to "unauthorized" readers, did the Department of Energy agree to remove access restrictions on UCNI information.

Similarly, the concept of "sensitive but unclassified" was intended precisely for the purpose of citizen complicity in information control. Librarians were also pressured by government agencies to remove unclassified materials from their open shelves on the basis of vaguely worded export controls. Now, under the Library Awareness Program, librarians were not only expected to implement restrictive government policies, but to infer their own, acting as information vigilantes with federal sanction.

Early in 1987 the FBI began claiming in reports, public interviews, and congressional testimony that librarians were required to prevent Soviet citizens from "accessing" documents issued by the NTIS. This completely spurious claim, declared gravely by FBI spokespersons, deserves further discussion.

The NTIS, operated under the U.S. Department of Commerce, collects, archives, and openly disseminates research publications originating in 400 federal agencies. In February 1985, Commerce Secretary Malcolm Baldridge described a hemorrhage of information through NTIS to foreign governments and proposed tighter screening of what goes into NTIS, requiring that unclassified but potentially sensitive documents be withheld. During this same period the FBI had been visiting private database vendors, expressing its concern about open access to NTIS and other databases.

The FBI study, *The KGB and the Library Target,* states the following:

Unclassified and nonrestricted DOD technical reports are made available to the general public through the National Technical Information
Service (NTIS), Springfield, Virginia. The Soviets were embargoed
from directly accessing materials through NTIS on January 8, 1980
when former President Jimmy Carter sent a letter to the U.S. Secretary
of Commerce captioned "Policy on Technology Transfer to the USSR."
One of the specific purposes of this executive order was to prevent the
"USSR, its entities or agents," from accessing information through
NTIS.[108]

An FBI internal memo, written in anticipation of the 1988 congressional
hearings on the FBI's library activities, drew an explicit connection between
NTIS access and the Library Awareness Program: "Some predicate for the FBI's
Library Awareness Program may be found in SIS officers attempting to recruit
librarians to check out NTIS materials for them."[109]

On July 13, 1988, when Geer testified before the House Subcommittee on
Civil and Constitutional Rights, he told Assistant Counsel James Dempsey:

Geer: . . . [W]hat they [the Soviets] have asked for is accessed in the National Technical Information System, [to] which they are denied access by executive order which was instituted during President Carter's
Administration.

Dempsey: Denied direct access.

Geer: Denied direct access, which is an attempt to deny them access obviously.

Dempsey: And obviously, as well, they continue to have access to that material.

Geer: By going to a library in some cases, yes, and asking that it be provided to them.

When counsel Dempsey asked how the FBI could prevent anyone in a library from reading unclassified material, NTIS or otherwise, Geer was even
more explicit, "I certainly would not hesitate to point out to the librarian that this
request for information accessing through the . . . National Technical Information Service was prohibited."[110]

On the morning of Geer's congressional testimony, I discussed the Library
Awareness Program on ABC TV's *Good Morning America* with George Carver,
former deputy director of the CIA, who warned that the Soviets were not sup-
posed to use NTIS materials. That same night, on Public Television's
MacNeil-Lehrer Report, I debated the Library Awareness Program with James
Geer himself, who once more described Soviet attempts "to access the National
Technical Information Service, which they are prohibited by executive order
from accessing."[111]

In a July 1988 discussion on American University's Public Radio station, FBI Assistant Director Ahlerich told me that NTIS was "embargoed information which intelligence officers and foreign nationals from other countries were not allowed access to. And that is exactly the type of information that the intelligence officers are obtaining."[112]

I told Ahlerich, "There has been some confusion about what the executive directive really requires of NTIS or of the materials. The National Technical Information Service is prevented from selling their documents to the Soviet Union, but the materials themselves are in no way restricted. . . . That would mean that NTIS documents in the University of Maryland Libraries or elsewhere can be . . . 'accessed' by anyone." In the course of our radio discussion, Ahlerich once more stated, "We've learned that they [the Soviets] have been trying to get information through the NTIS, or access to the NTIS." Again I pointed out, "That is not illegal. There is nothing illegal about anyone reading the unclassified NTIS documents. That, once again, is a misinterpretation of the executive order . . . The materials themselves are as unclassified and readily available as any other book or journal on our shelves." Ahlerich simply responded, "I wouldn't argue the point with you. It's certainly subject to legal interpretation."[113]

In reality, the mysterious Carter "executive order" invoked in all FBI statements was a memo, not a numbered executive order, and it did not even mention the NTIS. Clearly, Soviet access to NTIS documents was not one of its "specific purposes," as claimed in the 1988 FBI report. The January 8, 1980, Carter memo simply states,

> Pending review, no validated export licenses for shipment of goods or technical data to the Soviet Union are to be approved. This review is to reassess what exports will make a significant contribution to the military potential of the Soviet Union and therefore prove detrimental to the security of the United States in the light of the Soviet intervention in Afghanistan.[114]

The day after his initial memo, President Carter sent another memo to the secretary of commerce directing him immediately to suspend all export licenses to the Soviet Union pending the earlier-mentioned review. Only on January 25 did the issue of the NTIS enter the picture, when Francis Wolek, deputy assistant secretary for science and technology, wrote to the director of the Office of Export Administration describing the routine Soviet subscriptions to NTIS reports and asking "whether the continuation of these sales is appropriate in the light of the President's restrictions on export licenses of high technology items to the Soviet Union." Wolek admitted that it might be difficult to include the NTIS in these export restrictions: "As we know, NTIS technical information is openly published material which is exported under a general export license which does not require special review by the Office of Export Administration." The assistant general counsel for science and technology responded in a February 12 memo:

"[I]n the light of President Carter's restrictions on export licenses for high technology to the USSR, NTIS . . . can be directed to suspend its sales to USSR organizations here and abroad."[115] This option to restrict "sales" was simply *offered*, not required, by the Commerce Department (DOC).

Finally, on February 20, 1980, Jordan J. Baruch, assistant secretary for productivity, technology, and innovation, acting on the Commerce Department's opinion, wrote Melvin Day: "I have decided as a matter of policy to direct you to suspend all sales of NTIS materials to the Union of Soviet Socialist Republics."[116]

Baruch's directive was again a DOC policy decision, not an implementation of any particular portion of President Carter's original memo. In any case, no memo, response, or interpretation from the president or anyone else bore any relevance to Soviet "use of" or "access to" NTIS materials, as claimed in the various FBI statements. The only matters addressed by the Commerce Department were "export licenses" and "sales," and because NTIS material is openly published, its export did not even require review by the Office of Export Administration. In fact, Section 6 of the Export Administration Act of 1979 states that export controls applied for foreign-policy purposes require annual extension, and no such extension appears to have occurred. Dr. Robert Park, the scientific community's most influential opponent of information control, has succinctly summarized the matter: "In short, the Carter 'executive order,' which may no longer be in force, did not even indirectly apply to NTIS. An eight-year-old Commerce Department policy on NTIS subscription sales to the Soviets has no bearing on library use."[117]

By the fall of 1988 I assumed that the FBI's NTIS campaign had run its course, but during the FBI's September meeting with the ALA's Intellectual Freedom Committee, Assistant Director James Geer again presented the spectre of supposedly illegal access to NTIS reports: "[A Soviet] may just be using that library, which is true in probably four of five of the instances here, to circumvent the ban on accessing the National Technical Information Service. He can't do it directly. . . . So he goes through a library or an employee of a library, asking that library to access documents from the National Technical Information Service for him and return them to him. That's been done. We don't try to enforce an Executive Order that bans that: we can't."[118]

C. James Schmidt, chair of the ALA's Intellectual Freedom Committee, asked Geer, "Jim, is there an Executive Order that prohibits access to the NTIS reports by Russian nationals?" Geer answered, "I wish I had brought a copy with me." I wish he had too. It might have stopped this NTIS charade once and for all. But Geer continued, "I can't remember exactly how it's worded . . . but it may say 'representatives of the Soviet Union.' . . . I can't speak to the wording, but I certainly can speak to the intent. The intent is to deny them access to it."[119]

Why would allowing foreign nationals to read unclassified, publicly available materials be harmful to the United States? Hugh O'Connor, at the University of Maryland's Engineering Library, explained, "One gets the impression that it is not just microcomputers and better aircraft that ought to be kept out of Soviet hands, but odorless cat boxes and pop-up toasters as well."[120]

In addition to restricting access to unclassified technical information, the Library Awareness Program sought to recruit librarians as assets for use in gathering positive intelligence. Director Sessions stated that the program would use librarians in the "initial identification process" of suspected foreign agents. But there is considerable evidence that the Bureau's desire to use librarians as "assets" is directly related to the federal goal of information control, inasmuch as it allows the identification of those scientific subjects and materials that are in demand by foreign nationals. Information is flagged for future classification or designated as "sensitive" simply because it is requested by Americans through the FOIA or by Soviets at an American technical library. Information in demand is information to be denied, and librarians could be most useful in this delicate and contradictory process.

Late in 1989 the first hard evidence of FBI assets in libraries was acquired through an FOIA request that produced about forty reports itemizing Bureau contacts from March 1986 through June 1989. These reports provided the name of the asset, the date of contact, the contacting agent, and the reliability of the asset. Were these "assets" librarians? Library clerks? Student assistants? FBI plants? Given the Bureau's semantic license in these matters, these assets may have had a tenuous connection with libraries.

David Atlee Phillips, a former CIA operative who had frequently recruited agents abroad during his clandestine career, met with a dozen of his retired colleagues to discuss the Library Awareness Program's use of librarians as assets. Phillips described the role of librarians in the FBI's program as "benign supporting players in a legitimate counterintelligence operation. The librarians were to be, in intelligence jargon, spotters, assessment agents or access agents." Phillips wondered why journalists and librarians, "consenting adults" as he called them, should be off limits: "Are librarians, too, to be prevented by some sort of blanket restriction from cooperating with their own security services . . . ? Sometimes, intelligence professionals feel, they are expected to seek recruits only among pimps and whores."[121]

Phillips described the FBI's use of librarians as proper but temporarily awkward. "The FBI proposal to use librarians as support agents is not, in my mind, immoral. But it is unwise. The timing is wrong." Phillips advised FBI Director Sessions to avoid outraging civil libertarians with "operations that do not promise a major counterintelligence breakthrough" and concluded, "FBI recruitment of New York City librarians is an example of what Webster was sensitive to during his tenure, and of what Sessions can now do without, given the temper of the times."[122]

James Geer described the broad range of intelligence information that librarians could acquire: "Some of it is obviously positive intelligence. And whether it is of any use to the FBI or not, it could well be of use to other parts of the intelligence community."[123]

The FBI's report *The KGB and the Library Target* emphasizes that a librarian or library user who has had contact with a Soviet citizen can provide the FBI with personality assessment data impacting upon the subject's recruitment or defection potential. In a closed briefing, Deputy Director DuHadway revealed, "We do like to know what it is they're collecting because that gives us an idea . . . as to what their intelligence needs are, where they're going, what industries they're developing, what technologies we may even need to suggest become classified." DuHadway also described how librarians can assist in "identifying intelligence officers so we can then run a double agent case or try to develop other assets, informants if you will, against them."[124] Patricia Berger, then ALA president, complained, "Some of us believe that an unstated objective of the FBI's Library Awareness Program was and is to use the staffs of America's scientific libraries to identify persons who can later be 'turned' by the FBI to become double agents. The FBI has been less than candid regarding this matter."[125]

The Special Libraries Association

Despite overwhelming rejection of the Library Awareness Program by the library profession, the FBI continued to claim that librarians were "cooperating." The Bureau told author Natalie Robins: "Librarians can't admit they're cooperating with us, due to the program's controversial and confidential nature. Plus there's the risk of alienating people. A librarian won't say; it would make them suspect."[126]

In discussing that matter with me on a Public Radio station, Assistant Director Ahlerich claimed, "We've had lots of success. Librarians are cooperating with us despite the position that's taken by their national organizations." I expressed my doubts to Ahlerich that librarians were "cooperating," but Ahlerich persisted, "This is a positive intelligence program, and librarians have significantly assisted the FBI in fulfilling our counterintelligence responsibilities. . . . We've learned about the methodology, the tradecraft and tasking of intelligence officers of the Soviet Union as the result of these contacts with selected libraries."[127] He expressed the belief that only a small element within the library profession was protesting the Library Awareness Program, a conclusion at odds with all available evidence.

The SLA, an organization representing virtually all government and corporate libraries, has been at the center of an embarrassing controversy surrounding FBI "assets" in libraries. Despite the SLA's official resolution opposing the Library Awareness Program, there have been unverified charges, many of them originating within the Bureau itself, that the SLA leadership has been working with the FBI. The transcript of a January 14, 1988, meeting between the FBI and the National Commission on Libraries and Information Science revealed FBI Deputy Director DuHadway's claim that "we went to the president of the New York chapter of the Special Libraries Association and explained to her what we intended to do. She, in turn, contacted the Executive Director of the Special Library Association in Washington, D.C." When DuHadway was asked how these special libraries responded to the FBI overtures, he answered, "Very favorable, fine."[128]

The most serious charges against the SLA were made by author Natalie Robins, who revealed the FBI's claim that the head of one particular library association was coordinating FBI visits to libraries. An unidentified source told Robins that "the Bureau was working with two executives in a single library association, one of whom was based in New York and the other in Washington." When Robins asked the FBI to identify the cooperating association, she was told, "We have coordinated the program with the Specialized Library Association, but we can't say who we are dealing with there." There is no "Specialized Library Association," but doubts were raised because of the name's similarity to that of the Special Libraries Association. After hearing denials from the SLA, Robins returned to the FBI, where a spokesperson told her that "Specialized Library Association" was just a generic name, and the Bureau could not reveal the real name. Another FBI source insisted that "the head of the association has endorsed the program. There's probably not an association that would say they are it." Still another FBI source told Robins that the mysterious association was very probably the SLA, and that the collaboration with the FBI "was coordinated mostly through the New York Office." When Robins contacted an SLA chapter president in New York, he was evasive about the SLA's cooperation with the FBI.[129]

The SLA's board of directors first discussed the Library Awareness Program in October 1987 and chose not to take a position one way or another. David Bender, the SLA's executive director, complained, "I can't get a firm stand. I'm governed by the Board of Directors. We are remaining neutral on what the FBI is doing." Still, Bender claimed, "We're working toward the same end as the A.L.A., but just using different means."[130] In April 1988 the board again maintained its official neutrality, saying that this was "due to the diversity of libraries and information centers in which the Association's membership is employed."[131]

Finally, on June 17, 1988, the SLA board of directors adopted a policy statement endorsing access to information and confidentiality of library records. It concluded, "The Association opposes the activities of the FBI Library Awareness Program."[132]

In his June 20, 1988, testimony before Congress, David Bender, executive director of the SLA, complained more of the allegations of SLA complicity with the FBI than of the Library Awareness Program itself. Bender expressed concern over the "conflicting and misleading reports" issued by the FBI and said that such reports "serve only to unfairly implicate SLA of wrongdoing." Along with his testimony, Bender submitted copies of three letters dealing with charges of SLA complicity. On April 21, 1988, Bender had written to FBI Director Sessions complaining that "the media has construed our position as one of supporting the FBI's program." Bender pressed Sessions to reveal whether the SLA really was the mysterious association that had allegedly endorsed the Library Awareness Program, stating, "First, the reputation of SLA has been cast in doubt. Secondly, accurate information should be provided to the media."[133]

On May 23, SLA President Emily Mobley also wrote to Sessions: "Recent reports from the FBI imply that SLA is the association cooperating with the Library Awareness Program. Although you have not replied to Dr. Bender's letter of April 21 requesting that the FBI confirm or deny SLA's endorsement of the Library Awareness Program, it seems unlikely and contradictory that SLA would cooperate."[134]

On June 7, Director Sessions finally wrote to Bender, saying that he was, deeply disturbed by public comments that would portray cooperation with the FBI in a negative light. As for questions about SLA collaboration with the Bureau, Sessions simply reiterated his claim that "the term specialized libraries association was used by the FBI in a 'generic' sense."[135]

Librarians as Potential KGB Agents

The FBI adhered to its belief that some librarians were serving the SIS and that the Library Awareness Program discouraged their recruitment by the KGB. Because these claims were ambiguous and unverifiable, they were usually dismissed as nothing more than a public relations image of a paternal Bureau protecting a naive and vulnerable library profession. The first source of confusion is the FBI's inclusive definition of the term "librarian." For example, in his meeting with the ALA's Intellectual Freedom Committee, FBI Assistant Director Geer was asked, "Are you calling everybody that works in a library a librarian?" Geer answered, "Well, I can be, yes. I'm using it in a very broad context." A second FBI semantic problem concerns its definition of a KGB "source" to include anyone providing unclassified information, such as NTIS reports, to a Soviet citizen. For example, Assistant Director Geer stated, "The Soviets recruit sources that they use to collect unclassified information all over the country, simply because they don't want to be seen doing it themselves."[136] This description of a "source" would, of course, fit almost any American reference librarian, making it logical to claim that librarians are being recruited successfully each day by the KGB.

Curiously, the SLA has been alleged by the Bureau to be both an FBI "asset" and a KGB "source." The "asset" charge was covered earlier in this chapter, and the "source" allegation seems equally questionable. After the FBI charged that the SIS had acquired valuable information from the SLA's office, the association's president wrote to the Bureau to dispute the claim. Director Sessions responded,

> You take strong exception to the statement that "The SIS has utilized clandestine means to obtain large volumes of documents from the Special Libraries Association" and you assert that the statement is false. . . . No one in the FBI has ever suggested that any librarian would knowingly provide such documents. Intelligence officers are highly trained

and use covert and seemingly innocent means to accomplish their goals. They, little by little and with apparently innocuous materials, obtain significant intelligence when the information is added together.[137]

The SLA tried to explain to the FBI that not only had nothing been taken from its office, but there was nothing there to take other than the most trivial and tedious materials on library management. Nevertheless the FBI remained convinced that the SLA was an unwitting "source." In January 1988, FBI Deputy Director DuHadway stated, "We've had Soviets tell us that they think it's better to recruit two librarians in a science and technological library than it would be to recruit three engineers . . . , because those librarians have access to people, places and things that can front for the Soviet. . . . They think it's extremely important to have sources in libraries."[138]

James Geer warned of hostile intelligence officers utilizing America's technical libraries "to develop sources, train agents, and obtain information vital to their government's needs." Geer claimed that the Soviets "utilize unsuspecting employees and patrons of these libraries." He declared that payments or other inducements have been offered by the SIS to librarians "in an effort to recruit these individuals as agents, either wittingly or unwittingly."[139] Again, in the context of unclassified libraries, the notion of "unsuspecting" librarians serving "unwittingly" as KGB agents was equivalent to librarians providing normal reference service to Soviet nationals.

The Bureau described the Library Awareness Program as "a very measured response to a well planned and organized effort . . . to exploit our specialized scientific and technical libraries and recruit our citizens."[140] In May 1988 Assistant Director Ahlerich claimed, "the Soviet Union routinely attempts to develop librarians as sources of information or recruit them as agents."[141] He later discussed this issue with me on Public Radio, claiming that "the Soviet intelligence services are actually involved in recruiting librarians." When I asked if he could be more specific, Ahlerich answered, "Not other than to say it has occurred. We know for a fact that librarians have been recruited by the intelligence services of hostile countries. . . . We think it is incumbent on the FBI to let librarians know that they are the targets of recruiting efforts . . . and that success has occurred, with the Soviets then going to certain scientific libraries and extracting information." By describing "recruitment" in terms of "extracting information," Ahlerich implied that any librarian providing normal service to a Soviet national was a co-optee of the SIS.[142]

On a subsequent radio show out of Chicago, Ahlerich again told me that the Soviets had frequently recruited librarians as KGB spies. "We know they have done this, and they have successfully recruited librarians in the past." Ahlerich further claimed, "We know the Soviets and their surrogates are in these libraries, recruiting the librarians and using it to their advantage. And that does not seem to meet with any objections from the librarians, yet the FBI's interest in trying to counter this threat does."[143]

On August 24, 1988, I wrote to Ahlerich that I was unaware of any librarians being recruited by the SIS and asked for details. Ahlerich assured me that he did not believe that librarians were less loyal or less concerned about our nation's security than other Americans. He said that he wished it were possible to reveal the details of instances where librarians had been successfully recruited by the SIS, but such information was classified and could not be divulged.[144]

Paint the Critics Red

Documents released through the FOIA revealed the depth of the FBI's paranoia and the shocking extent of its "index checks" on librarians. A February 6, 1989, memo from the FBI's New York ADIC to Director Sessions described a sixteen-month investigation of librarians: "After a review of 266 New York indices checks conducted on the names of individuals since 10/87 in an attempt to determine whether a Soviet active measures campaign had been initiated to discredit the LIBRARY AWARENESS PROGRAM (LAP), only the following eight references were noted. All other indices checks were either negative or of no significance to this study."[145]

The "active measures campaign" referred to in the FBI's memo is intelligence jargon for any effort made by hostile intelligence to influence popular opinion through disinformation, propaganda, or front groups. The memo withheld the eight names allegedly involved with a Soviet campaign to discredit the Library Awareness Program, but any of the librarians who have spoken publicly against the program could be on the list. The most disturbing aspect of the Bureau's investigation of librarians was its Hoover-era assumption that any domestic criticism of an FBI program must have been Soviet-instigated. In reality, the library profession's opposition to FBI intrusions on libraries was homegrown, motivated only by grassroots outrage. To suggest that foreign subversion was necessary to "discredit" a program that had been rejected and ridiculed by the public is to ignore the painful lessons of the Bureau's past.

Throughout the 1,200 previously secret FBI documents released on October 30, 1989, there was other evidence of continuing FBI investigations of librarians. Even when the FBI withheld documents, there were frequent exemption forms stating, "The withheld pages are copies of search slips on individual(s) associated with a library or library organization." The exemption forms indicated that approximately 450 such "search slips" were withheld, at least 266 of them since October 1987. FBI Director Sessions initially said he was unaware of the FBI's background checks on librarians, but he said he would have approved such checks had he been asked. "It is natural for us to check," he said. "It is routinely done."[146]

Representative Edwards said that his subcommittee had no information to support the FBI's suspicions about a Soviet influence campaign. "There is absolutely no evidence to support this theory either in any of our private briefings or public testimony by the F.B.I. on this program," said Edwards. "It's very dismaying that the F.B.I. so failed to understand what was the source of this criticism."[147]

Joseph S. Murphy, chancellor of the City University of New York, asked Congress to look further into the Bureau's investigations of librarians, stating that the FBI had questioned the loyalty of librarians who wrote letters critical of the Library Awareness Program. The ALA's Office for Intellectual Freedom also protested the FBI's actions: "It's not consistent with First Amendment principles to investigate somebody on the basis of what he reads, nor to investigate somebody because he stands up to defend a First Amendment principle."[148]

A *New York Times* editorial stated, "Declassified documents show that the F.B.I. conducted cursory investigations of librarians and others who publicly criticized its program." The editorial asked Director Sessions to repudiate the Bureau's meddling in libraries, concluding, "If his agents fear spies in the stacks, let them get a court order to check it out. His main mission ought to be to end this offensive encroachment of the rights of library workers and users."[149]

John Berry, *Library Journal*'s editor in chief, wrote, "It hurt when the FBI director impugned the patriotism of librarians who wouldn't enlist in the Bureau's Library Awareness Program. It angered us to find out that the FBI was investigating the nearly 250 librarians who refused to take part in the program. . . . Fixated on communist subversion, the FBI tends to see all dissent as emanating from Moscow. It was predictable, alas, that agents would search for links between the suspicious librarians and the USSR. . . . The FBI nearly always sees something subversive in any opposition to its efforts to protect the 'secrets' of our government or to limit access to our libraries." Berry concluded, "We the people plant the seeds of subversion. They are there in our Bill of Rights, our elections, our free press, and, of course, in our libraries."[150]

The Law and Library Surveillance

The Library Awareness Program was created within the FBI's bureaucracy. It was authorized by no federal law, nor did it represent any clear violation of federal law. As a result, the constitutional challenges offered to the Library Awareness Program on the basis of freedom of speech and inquiry were tentative at best. In 1988 the Freedom to Read Foundation considered a direct confrontation with the Library Awareness Program through an injunction to force the Bureau to cease and desist, but its July 1988 report explained the legal difficulties involved. When the governmental purpose is to suppress speech, the courts will almost always find a violation of the First Amendment, but if the government claims another purpose, such as enforcing the criminal laws preventing espionage, "any *incidental* suppression of speech that results from governmental efforts to achieve that other purpose will not violate the First Amendment, unless these government efforts are 'wholly gratuitous.' " Since the FBI denied that the purpose of the Library Awareness Program was to suppress free speech, the foundation concluded that to win a suit against the FBI, we would have to prove either that FBI contacts with libraries are so unrelated to preventing espionage that such contacts are gratuitous and unreasonable; or that the FBI's real purpose is to deter patrons from using libraries or . . . librarians from providing information to patrons. Either type of proof would be what attorneys call fact-intensive, and therefore "very expensive," and the final result of such a suit is very uncertain.[151]

The IFC's chair, C. James Schmidt, agreed:

[A] lawsuit directly challenging the FBI Library Awareness Program would almost certainly be unsuccessful and might be strategically damaging. . . . To succeed in a lawsuit, we would have to sustain challenges to our standing and prove that the purpose of the FBI Library Awareness Program is to stifle or limit speech. The record as we now know it would make supporting this claim difficult. Second, strategically, if we were to file a lawsuit with a low prospect for success, we run the risk of establishing negative precedent on the issue of our *standing* to sue. We also risk undermining the credibility of the library profession's opposition to the FBI Library Awareness Program, because a government victory in court even if only on standing rather than the merits, might be seen by the public as a judicial endorsement of the Program.[152]

Faced with likely defeat in federal courts, the library profession turned to state law. Although state library confidentiality laws could not control the behavior of federal agencies like the FBI, they *could* control the behavior of libraries themselves, prohibiting them from revealing patron information at the bidding of the FBI, or anyone else, unless served with a properly drawn and tested subpoena. Today, forty-eight of our fifty states have library confidentiality statutes, and the other two states, Kentucky and Hawaii, have state attorney general guidelines that provide similar protection. Despite their limitations, state confidentiality laws can provide important protection from federal intrusion on libraries because many FBI visits continue to occur without a warrant or subpoena and without the explicit authorization of laws like the USA PATRIOT Act (the Uniting and Strengthening America by Providing Appropriate Tools to Intercept and Obstruct Terrorism). Under state confidentiality laws, such requests for information *must* be denied.

Because I was privileged to play a major role in the passage of the Maryland confidentiality statute and because it was introduced in direct response to the Library Awareness Program, it may be useful to describe its history briefly. Maryland Delegate Samuel (Sandy) Rosenberg, who, with cosponsor Nancy Kopp, introduced the Maryland bill, told me how he first learned of the Library Awareness Program: "I've always been very interested in First Amendment issues," he said. "In January [1988] I saw an advertisement by the National Emergency Civil Liberties Committee in the *New York Times,* with the heading, 'The FBI Invades U.S. Libraries.' I was appalled by this blatant invasion of privacy."[153]

He sent letters of concern to Maryland's state superintendent of education, the head of the State Board of Higher Education, and the president of the University of Maryland, who offered his full support for the bill. I was soon called to testify before the Maryland House of Delegates in support of the Rosenberg-Kopp Bill (H.B. 1239) and in opposition to the Library Awareness Program. Together with representatives of organizations such as the Maryland Library Association, the American Library Association, and Common Cause, we succeeded in convincing the Maryland House of Delegates to vote 133 to 0 in favor of the bill. I then testified before the Maryland Senate's Economic and Environmental Affairs Committee, and the full Senate subsequently approved the bill, again unanimously.

H.B. 1239 not only extended confidentiality protection to any "free association, school, college or university library," but it broadened the protected data to include any "item, collection or grouping of information about an individual . . . [that] identifies the use a patron makes of that library's materials, services or facilities." The latter was particularly important because it brought Maryland confidentiality law into the computer age, covering database searches.

In discussing the successful campaign for H.B. 1239, Rosenberg told me, "That no one opposed this legislation is encouraging. . . . I just hope that other states will now see fit to follow Maryland's lead."[154] In a letter to the *Baltimore Evening Sun,* Rosenberg stated, "Citizens using any library in Maryland will be safe from the unwarranted snooping of FBI agents under legislation enacted by this year's General Assembly. Circulation records, as well as computer database searches, are protected from the Bureau's invasion of free expression and privacy rights under House Bill 1239." Rosenberg described the FBI's visits to two University of Maryland libraries and concluded, "The fortitude of Herbert Foerstel, the libraries' administrator, in thwarting this witch hunt is now bolstered by state law."[155]

As noted earlier, new federal laws such as the Patriot Act override *all* state confidentiality laws while imposing a gag order on librarians. Today, the only iron-clad protection for libraries lies in more careful records-retention policies. No government agency can abscond with patron records if the library does not maintain them, and Georgetown law librarian Bruce Kennedy has strongly urged his colleagues, "The Church Report condemned the federal intelligence community for collecting too much data and holding it for too long. Some libraries can be similarly condemned. . . . Libraries should become information storage centers for their patrons and not *about* their patrons."[156]

Notes

1. "Memo to Members," *American Libraries*, July–August, 1970, p. 658.

2. Ibid.

3. Kathleen R. Molz, *Intellectual Freedom and Privacy* (Washington, D.C.: NCLIS, 1974), pp. 25–26.

4. "Memo to Members," *American Libraries*, September–October, 1970, p. 771.

5. "Libraries Are Asked by FBI to Report on Foreign Agents," *New York Times*, October 18, 1987, p. 22.

6. Letter from Milt Ahlerich, FBI Assistant Director, to Judith A. Drescher, Chairperson, ALA Intellectual Freedom Committee, July 31, 1987. October 30, 1989, FOIA release to National Security Archive.

7. Letter from Helen F. Flowers, President, New York Library Association, to John Otto, Acting Director, FBI, August 3, 1987. October 30, 1989, FOIA release to National Security Archive.

8. "The Talk of the Town," *New Yorker*, May 30, 1988, p. 24.

9. ALA Office for Intellectual Freedom, "Intellectual Freedom Committee Advises Librarians on FBI 'Library Awareness' Program," October 1987, p. 3.

10. Quinlan J. Shea, Speech Before the American Society of Access Professionals, July 28, 1988, p. 2.

11. U.S. Congress, House Committee on the Judiciary, *FBI Counterintelligence Visits to Libraries*, 100th Cong., 2d Sess., June 20 and July 13, 1988 (Washington, D.C.: GPO, 1989), p. 125.

12. Ibid., pp. 110–11.

13. Ibid., p. 301.

14. Ibid., p. 320.

15. Memo from SAC William H. Warfield to all Supervisors, March 22, 1988. October 30, 1989, FOIA release to Nation Security Archive.

16. Memo from FBI Cleveland to Director, FBI, September 21, 1988. October 30, 1989, FOIA release to National Security Archive.

17. *FBI Counterintelligence Visits to Libraries*, pp. 348–49.

18. Anne Hagedorn, "FBI Recruits Librarians to Spy on 'Commie' Readers," *Wall Street Journal*, May 9, 1988, p. 32.

19. "Librarians Challenge FBI on Extent of Its Investigations," *Publishers Weekly*, July 9, 1988, p. 11.

20. Letter from Morton Halperin, Director, ACLU, to Senate Select Committee on Intelligence, April 21, 1988.

21. *FBI Counterintelligence Visits to Libraries*, pp. 327, 329.

22. Memo from FBI Los Angeles to Director, FBI, May 27, 1988. October 30, 1989, FOIA release to National Security Archive.

23. *FBI Counterintelligence Visits to Libraries*, pp. 64–67.

24. Ibid., p. 13.

25. Ibid.

26. Ibid., pp. 105, 160–61.

27. Ibid., p. 121.

28. Letter from Judith L. Keogh, Pennsylvania Library Association, to William S. Sessions, Director, FBI, April 4, 1988. September 1989, FOIA release to National Security Archive.

29. *FBI Counterintelligence Visits to Libraries*, p. 17.

30. *Memorandum*, ALA Office for Intellectual Freedom, July–August 1988, Attachment II.

31. "Margaret Truman Looks Back," *Newsletter on Intellectual Freedom,* September 1988, p. 182.

32. "People for the American Way Suit Against FBI Library Informant Plan," *Publishers Weekly,* June 17, 1988, p. 16.

33. "Library Directions in 1988," *Library Journal*, January 1989, p. 55.

34. "The World Is a Dangerous Place, Etc.," *Wilson Library Bulletin*, October 1988, p. 4.

35. Herblock cartoons, *Washington Post*, June 7, 1988, p. A22 and July 24, 1988, p. C6.

36. Larry Wright cartoon, *Detroit Press*, July 24, 1988.

37. From *Mark Russell's Comedy Special*, Public Television Series, 1988. (Permission by Dan Ruskin).

38. "Read It and Weep," *Miami Herald*, April 22, 1988, p. 24A. Emphasis in original.

39. Rick Horowitz, "When the FBI Decides to Go by the Books," *Philadelphia Inquirer*, March 9, 1988, p. 13A.

40. Victor T. Levine, "On the Trail for the FBI," *Baltimore Evening Sun*, July 27, p. A13.

41. "A New Chapter for FBI Library Gumshoes," *Atlanta Constitution*, November 18, 1988, p. 22A.

42. Ann Hagedorn, "FBI Recruits Librarians to Spy on 'Commie' Readers," *Wall Street Journal,* May 19, 1988, p. 32.

43. "Spying in the Stacks," *Time*, May 30, 1988, p. 23.

44. "Librarians as Counterspies," *New York Times*, September 8, 1987, p. A24.

45. Gregg Sapp, "Some Editorial Thoughts . . . on Libraries and Espionage," *Idaho Librarian*, July 1988, p. 50.

46. Herbert S. White, "White Paper," *Library Journal*, October 15, 1988, pp. 54–55.

47. "Libraries Are Asked by FBI to Report on Foreign Agents," *New York Times*, September 18, 1987, p. 1.

48. Memo from FBI New York to FBI Headquarters, September 21, 1987. September 1989, FOIA release to National Security Archive.

49. *FBI Counterintelligence Visits to Libraries*, pp. 77–78.

50. Ibid., pp. 81–82.

51. FBI presentation to U.S. National Commission on Libraries and Information Science by Thomas DuHadway, San Antonio, Texas, January 14, 1988, pp. 32–33.

52. From my interview with Nancy Gubman, June 1989.

53. Ibid.

54. Ibid.

55. *FBI Counterintelligence Visits to Libraries*, p. 345–46.

56. "Academic Libraries Must Oppose Federal Surveillance of Their Users," *Chronicle of Higher Education*, March 23, 1988, p. A48.

57. Natalie Robbins, "The FBI's Invasion of Libraries," *Nation*, April 9, 1988, p. 501.

58. *Nightline*, ABC TV, July 13, 1988.

59. People for the American Way, *The FBI's Library Awareness Program Background Report* (Washington, D.C., 1988), p. 3.

60. "The Talk of the Town," *New Yorker*, May 30, 1988, p. 2–3. Emphasis in original.

61. Undated memo from FBI New York to FBI HQ concerning December 1, 1987, visit to Brooklyn Public Library. September 1989, FOIA release to National Security Archive.

62. Memo from FBI Newark to Director, FBI, May 27, 1988. October 30, 1989, FOIA release to National Security Archive.

63. Robbins, "The FBI's Invasion of Libraries," p. 499.

64. Memo from SAC Miami to Director, FBI, April 22, 1988, pp. 2–3. September 1989, FOIA release to National Security Archive.

65. From my 1982 exit interview with the retiring head of the Technical Reports Center.

66. Letter from Milt Ahlerich, Assistant Director, Office of Congressional and Public Affairs, FBI, to Herbert Foerstel, University of Maryland, January 30, 1989, p. 2.

67. From my interview(s) with Sylvia Evans, September 1989.

68. Ibid.

69. From my interview with Danuta Nitecki, June 27, 1988.

70. *MacNeil-Lehrer Report*, Public Television, July 13, 1988.

71. Transcript of meeting of FBI and ALA Intellectual Freedom Committee, September 9, 1988, p. 22.

72. Ibid., p. 32.

73. "FBI Asks Libraries to Help It Find Spies on Campuses," *College Press Service*, January 18, 1988, p. 3.

74. "Sensitive but Unclassified: Government Threatens Access to Data Bases," *Crab*, May 1987, p. 1.

75. Ibid.

76. Interview(s) by Herbert Foerstel with Charlene Hurt, June 1989.

77. Robbins, "The FBI's Invasion of Libraries," p. 500.

78. *FBI Counterintelligence Visits to Libraries*, p. 158. Emphasis in original.

79. From my interview(s) with Charlene Hurt, June 1989.

80. Ibid.

81. Ibid.

82. Robbins, "The FBI's Invasion of Libraries," p. 499.

83. "FBI Asks Libraries to Help It Find Spies on Campuses," p. 3.

84. Memo from FBI, Cincinnati, to FBI, New York and the Director, FBI, May 27, 1988. September 1989, FOIA release to National Security Archive.

85. Robbins, "The FBI's Invasion of Libraries," p. 500.

86. Hagedorn, "FBI Recruits Librarians," p. 32.

87. *FBI Counterintelligence Visits to Libraries*, pp. 117–18.

88. Robbins, "The FBI's Invasion of Libraries," p. 499.

89. Nat Hentoff, "The FBI in the Library," *Washington Post*, July 23, 1988, p. A23.

90. ALA Office for Intellectual Freedom, *Memorandum*, October 20, 1988, p. 4.

91. *Page Two*, WBEZ-Public Radio, Chicago, Illinois, July 19, 1988.

92. Robbins, "The FBI's Invasion of Libraries," p. 502.

93. "FBI Asks Librarians to Help in the Search for Spies," *Philadelphia Inquirer*, February 23, 1988, p. 17A.

94. David Atlee Phillips, "FBI's Timing Is Questionable, Not Its Morals," *Newsday*, October 16, 1987, p. 83.

95. *FBI Counterintelligence Visits to Libraries*, p. 151.

96. Letter from Rep. Don Edwards, Chairman Subcommittee on Civil and Constitutional Rights, U.S. House of Representatives, to Herbert Foerstel, University of Maryland, October 12, 1988.

97. Memo on Library Awareness Program from C. James Schmidt, Chair, Intellectual Freedom Committee, to ALA Executive Board/Council, January 8, 1989, p. 2. Reprinted by permission of the American Library Association.

98. "FBI to Limit Probes of Library Users," *Washington Post*, November 15, 1988, p. A3.

99. Memo from Director, FBI, to all SACs, November 29, 1988. October 30, 1989, FOIA release to National Security Archive.

100. Rep. Don Edwards, "Government Information Controls Threaten Academic Freedom," *Thought and Action: The NEA Higher Education Journal*, Spring 1989, p. 87.

101. Memo on Library Awareness Program from C. James Schmidt, Chair, Intellectual Freedom Committee, to ALA Executive Board/Council, January 8, 1989, p. 4. Reprinted by permission of the American Library Association.

102. FBI presentation to U.S. National Commission on Libraries and Information Science by Thomas DuHadway, San Antonio, Texas, January 14, 1988, pp. 7, 40.

103. Robbins, "The FBI's Invasion of Libraries," p. 498.

104. Transcript of meeting of FBI and ALA Intellectual Freedom Committee, September 9, 1988, p. 7.

105. Quinlan J. Shea, speech before the American Society of Access Professionals, Washington, D.C., July 28, 1988, p. 4.

106. *FBI Counterintelligence Visits to Libraries*, p. 150.

107. FBI presentation to U.S. National Commission on Libraries and Information Science by Thomas DuHadway, p. 18.

108. FBI Headquarters, Intelligence Division, *The KGB and the Library Target*, p. 15

109. Memo from SAC, WMFO, to Director, FBI, June 1988. October 30, 1989, FOIA release to National Security Archive.

110. *FBI Counterintelligence Visits to Libraries*, p. 144.

111. *MacNeil-Lehrer Report*, Public Television, July 13, 1988.

112. *The Diane Rehm Show*, WAMU Public Radio, Washington, D.C., July 19, 1988.

113. Ibid.

114. *FBI Counterintelligence Visits to Libraries*, p. 129.

115. Ibid., pp. 407–8.

116. Ibid., p. 131.

117. Ibid., p. 406.

118. Transcript of meeting of FBI and ALA Intellectual Freedom Committee, September 9, 1988, p. 43.

119. Ibid., p. 44.

120. Hugh O'Connor, "America Becomes Aware of FBI in Libraries (pt. 2)," *Crab*, November 1988, p. 8.

121. David Atlee Phillips, "FBI's Timing Is Questionable, Not Its Morals," *Newsday*, October 16, 1987, p. 83.

122. Ibid.

123. *FBI Counterintelligence Visits to Libraries,* p. 144.

124. FBI presentation to U.S. National Commission on Libraries and Information Science, pp. 8, 30.

125. Letter from Patricia W. Berger, ALA, to Jerald C. Newman, Chairman, NCLIS, September 8, 1989, p. 2.

126. Robbins, "The FBI's Invasion of Libraries," p. 501.

127. *The Diane Rehm Show*, WAMU Public Radio, Washington, D.C., July 19, 1988.

128. FBI presentation to U.S. National Commission on Libraries and Information Science by Thomas DuHadway, p. 32.

129. Robbins, "The FBI's Invasion of Libraries," pp. 501–2.

130. Natalie Robbins, "Library Follow-Up," *Nation*, June 25, 1988, p. 886.

131. "SLA Reluctantly Joins Fray in FBI 'Awareness Battle,' " *School Library Journal*, August 1988, p. 14.

132. "SLA Board Acts to Oppose FBI Library Awareness Program," *Specialist*, August 1988, p. 1.

133. *FBI Counterintelligence Visits to Libraries*, pp. 42, 51.

134. Ibid., p. 53.

135. Ibid., p. 57.

136. Transcript of meeting of FBI and ALA Intellectual Freedom Committee, September 9, 1988, pp. 8, 44.

137. Letter from William S. Sessions, Director, FBI, to Emily R. Mobley, President, Special Libraries Association, July 11, 1988. October 30, 1989, FOIA release to National Security Archive.

138. FBI presentation to U.S. National Commission on Libraries and Information Science by Thomas DuHadway, p. 25.

139. *FBI Counterintelligence Visits to Libraries*, pp. 111–13, 119–20.

140. "Librarians Tell Congress FBI Is Spying on Readers," *News Media and the Law*, Summer 1988, p. 38.

141. Milt Ahlerich, "Soviets Are Exploiting USA's Libraries," *USA Today*, May 28, 1988, p. 10A.

142. *The Diane Rehm Show*, WAMU Public Radio, Washington, D.C., July 19, 1988.

143. *Page Two*, WABE Public Radio, Chicago, Illinois, July 19, 1988.

144. Letter from Herbert Foerstel to Milt Ahlerich, Assistant Director, FBI, August 24, 1988, and reply to Foerstel, September 12, 1988.

145. Memo from ADIC, New York, to Director, FBI, February 6, 1989. October 30, 1989, FOIA release to National Security Archive.

146. "Documents Disclose F.B.I. Investigations of Some Librarians," *New York Times*, November 17, 1989, p. A1.

147. Ibid.

148. "Reports That FBI Checked on Librarians Prompt Call for Congressional Hearings," *Chronicle of Higher Education*, November 15, 1989, p. A3.

149. "Card-Carrying Librarians," *New York Times*, November 17, 1989, p. A38.

150. John N. Berry III, "Editorial: Little Shops of Subversion," *Library Journal,* December 1989, p. 6.

151. "President's Report to Council," *Freedom to Read Foundation News* 15, no. 4 (1989): p. 1. Emphasis in original..

152. Memo on Library Awareness Program from C. James Schmidt, Chair, Intellectual Freedom Committee, to ALA Executive Board/Council, January 8, 1989, p. 3. Reprinted by permission of the American Library Association.

153. From my interview with Del. Samuel Rosenberg, September 24, 1989.

154. Ibid.

155. Samuel I. Rosenberg, "Library Snoops," letter to the editor, *Baltimore Evening Sun*, August 24, 1988, p. A15.

156. Bruce Kennedy, "Confidentiality of Library Records," *Law Library Journal*, Fall 1989, p. 766. Emphasis in original.

Chapter 2

The USA PATRIOT Act

Passage of the Bill

The September 11, 2001, attacks on New York's World Trade Center set in motion an intense political conflict within the United States over the proper balance between governmental power and personal privacy. Only days after the attacks, the FBI reportedly began installing its "Carnivore" system at some Internet providers to monitor electronic communications. The government also wanted unfettered access to telephone records, e-mail, library records, and the ocean of data assembled by corporations each day about individuals' personal lives, all to assist in the hunt for potential terrorists. To accomplish this task, the White House, the Department of Justice, and their allies in Congress wanted to remove the restraints on governmental power that had been imposed in the wake of such scandals as Watergate and COINTELPRO,[1] as well as the shocking revelations of the earlier Church Committee.[2]

A particular focus of the new anti-terrorist coalition was to rewrite the law regarding the Foreign Intelligence Surveillance Act (FISA), which was originally created to *restrain* government authority to conduct domestic surveillance when seeking foreign intelligence information. This original purpose of the FISA now seemed to be an impediment to the Bush administration's desire to expand domestic surveillance.

"It's the beginning of a different epoch," explained award-winning journalist Scott Armstrong. "It's a conceptual shift in the way government and First Amendment Freedoms interact. We are now in a period where civil liberties get put to the side while we fight this war against terrorism. And since it is a war of ideas, it has all of the problems one would associate with a war against ideas."[3]

In the fear and confusion immediately following 9/11, there was a legislative stampede to reduce American civil liberties to a degree unimagined before the terrorist attacks, and civil libertarians seemed powerless to bring Congress to its senses. As we shall see, the Patriot Act became the primary weapon in a legislative and administrative assault on the Bill of Rights. It was the realization of intelligence agency plans conceived long in advance of 9/11 and having nothing to do with terrorism.

The morning after the 9/11 attacks, Assistant District Attorney Viet Dinh, Attorney General John Ashcroft's take-charge-guy, convened a meeting with Justice Department policy specialists in Dinh's suite of offices. Ashcroft did not attend. He was in hiding, along with other top government officials, but he had conveyed all of his desires to Dinh.

"Beginning immediately," Dinh told the attending policy advisors, "we will work on a package of authorities. . . . The charge [from Ashcroft] was very, very clear: 'all that is necessary for law enforcement, within the bounds of the Constitution, to fight this war against terror.'"[4]

Dinh and his colleagues proceeded to catalogue their complaints about restraints on police and intelligence agency authority, complaints that had been heard in Washington for years. But now the political climate was right for radical change.

On September 12, as Dinh and his Justice Department zealots were working on a plan to expand federal surveillance powers, an equally committed group of civil libertarians was bracing for the government's assault. Morton Halperin, former head of the Washington office of the American Civil Liberties Union (ACLU), sent out a warning to colleagues on his computer. Anticipating a Justice Department call for broad authority to conduct electronic and other surveillance and to investigate political groups, Halperin issued his own call for a defense of American civil liberties. Within hours, people like Jim Dempsey from the Center for Democracy and Technology and Marc Rotenberg of the Electronic Privacy Information Center joined Halperin in creating a manifesto: "In Defense of Freedom at a Time of Crisis."

On the Friday after the terrorist attacks, the ACLU's townhouse on Capitol Hill was flooded with people responding to Halperin's e-mail. In addition to liberal activists like Dempsey and Rotenberg, there were libertarians from the conservative Free Congress Foundation and the Eagle Forum. "I had never seen that kind of turnout in 25 years," said Laura Murphy, director of the ACLU's national office. "I mean, people were worried."[5]

Eventually the group hammered out a ten-point statement expressing faith in the Constitution and appealing for a legislative process that would protect both the freedom and security of all Americans. The document was signed by representatives of more than 150 groups ranging from religious organizations to gun owners to police. When the joint statement was released at a press conference a few days later, it was uniformly ignored. White House and Justice Department officials later admitted that they had never even heard of the statement.

Meanwhile, the attorney general transmitted to Congress a proposal containing his wish list of expanded police powers, including new authority to obtain sensitive personal information about individuals, eavesdrop on conversations, monitor computer use, and detain suspects without probable cause, all with minimal judicial oversight. To make matters worse, Ashcroft demanded that his proposal be enacted within three days, and he suggested publicly that Congress would be responsible for any subsequent terrorist attacks if it did not meet his deadline.

Under growing public pressure and strident demands from Ashcroft, Senate Judiciary Committee Chairman Patrick Leahy (D-VT), a long-time First Amendment champion, was faced with the responsibility for crafting the Senate version of anti-terrorism legislation. The ranking Republican on Leahy's Judiciary Committee, Orrin Hatch (R-UT), proposed a floor amendment to a routine spending bill that would expand the government's authority to intercept oral and electronic communications. Senator Leahy wanted to follow a more deliberative process in considering major changes to America's civil liberties, but Senator Jon Kyl (R-AZ) declared, "Our constituents are calling this a war on terrorism. In wars, you don't fight by a Marquis of Queensberry rules."[6]

Hatch's amendment passed quickly, and the floodgates were opened. The Senate was now faced with Ashcroft's omnibus Patriot Act. Leahy held a perfunctory hearing at which Ashcroft appeared for only about an hour. Then, in an effort to avoid being labeled an obstructionist by the White House, Leahy made the mistake of agreeing to negotiate his bill directly with the Bush administration, bypassing the normal committee approval process.

Jim Dempsey was disappointed by Leahy's capitulation on procedure, but he understood the difficult political environment in which Congress was forced to work. "A crisis mentality emerges," he said. "The push for action, the appearance of action, becomes so great."[7]

Just a few days after the 9/11 attacks, a number of senators introduced legislation that had been proposed and rejected years earlier because of constitutional concerns. Now the senators could represent these same questionable bills as appropriate anti-terrorism legislation. The resurrected Combating Terrorism Act, a Clinton-era attempt to expand FBI surveillance powers, proposed new authority to trace telephone and e-mail communications. The act had originally been rejected by Congress as an infringement on civil rights. Now it was approved in minutes.

Morton Halperin, senior fellow for the Council on Foreign Relations, recognized the opportunistic nature of these recycled proposals for increased government surveillance. "Washington is a town with people with solutions looking for problems," he remarked.[8] "Now these old, discredited solutions could be brought out and applied arbitrarily to the problem of terrorism."

On September 19, leaders from Congress, the White House, and the Justice Department met in the Capitol to share their legislative proposals. Leahy, Hatch, and Richard Shelby (R-AL) led the Senate delegation. House Majority Leader

Richard Armey (R-TX) and John Conyers (D-MI) led the House delegation. White House Counsel Alberto Gonzales was accompanied by Ashcroft, Dinh, and the Justice Department entourage.

Dinh handed out copies of his own forty-page proposal and Leahy did the same with his draft. Both bills updated pen register and "trap and trace" laws, extending them to e-mail and the Internet, and they strengthened wiretap laws as well. But Dinh's bill went much farther, modifying the FISA law to authorize domestic surveillance whenever foreign intelligence is "a" purpose of an investigation, rather than "the" purpose. It also permitted the unrestricted sharing of grand jury and eavesdropping information throughout the government and encouraged Internet providers to tap e-mail "voluntarily." It even called for the indefinite detention of any noncitizen the attorney general has reason to believe might further or facilitate acts of terrorism.

Leahy and other congressional representatives at the meeting felt that Dinh's changes would erode constitutional safeguards against unreasonable searches and seizures, and even Richard Armey, one of the more conservative members of Congress, expressed concern. "There were a lot of people in the room, both Republican and Democrat, who were not about to give the unfettered power the attorney general wanted," said Leahy, who later told reporters, "We do not want the terrorists to win by having basic protections taken away from us."[9]

Late in September, Jim Dempsey was invited by Beryl Howell, Leahy's senior adviser, to a legislative briefing. Howell wanted Justice Department officials and civil libertarians like Dempsey to share their thoughts with Senate staffers. When the Justice Department officials arrived, they refused to accept the presence of Dempsey and his colleagues. "They were livid," recalls Dempsey. "They explicitly said, 'We don't think outsiders should be here, and we won't talk unless they leave the room.' "[10]

It was decided that Dempsey and his colleagues could stay to hear Justice's proposal, but they could say nothing. The Justice delegation made their presentation, then promptly rose and departed. Within a few days, Howell met with White House Deputy Counsel Timothy Flanigan to negotiate some of the wording in Leahy's bill. Flanigan, representing the views of Bush and Ashcroft, reached agreement with Howell on a number of issues, including an understanding that a court would review the results of surveillance before that information was shared among law enforcement and intelligence agencies.

Leahy believed he had reached a final agreement that would provide a degree of oversight of domestic surveillance and intelligence gathering. On October 2, he met with Ashcroft, Hatch, Michael Chertoff, chief of the Justice Department's criminal division, and Alberto Gonzales, the White House counsel, to sign off on the deal. Ashcroft quickly made it clear that he would no longer abide by the agreements negotiated with Flanigan.

A shocked and disconsolate Leahy told Ashcroft, "John, when I make an agreement, I make an agreement. I can't believe you're going back on your commitment." Ashcroft would not budge. After he left Leahy's office, he held a press conference at which he declared, "Talk won't prevent terrorism." Ashcroft then chided Congress, saying he was "deeply concerned about the rather slow pace" of the legislative process.[11]

Leahy had been blindsided and was left with little political leverage. It seemed now that only the House could fight the battle with the administration on matters such as court scrutiny of the government's new surveillance powers. This was particularly true of Section 215 of the government's bill, the section that would greatly expand the power of the FISA to gain access to business records from libraries, book stores, Internet providers, grocery stores—virtually anybody. Under the Patriot Act, the target of a records search was not required to be "an agent of a foreign power."

Civil libertarians like Jim Dempsey were disappointed that Leahy and his allies were unwilling or unable to stand up to the administration on these matters of privacy and confidentiality. Leahy's bill, introduced in the Senate just two days after his hostile meeting with Ashcroft, had given the government much more power than he had intended.

On October 11, the Senate convened to vote on the USA Patriot Act. Leahy warned, "I have deep concerns that we may be increasing surveillance powers and the sharing of criminal justice information without adequate checks on how information may be handled and without adequate accountability in the form of judicial review."[12]

As we saw earlier, the Justice Department led Leahy to believe that his proposals for judicial review of the new executive powers were acceptable to the Bush administration. A gloomy Leahy seemed resigned to the administration's heavy-handed tactics as he told his Senate colleagues, "[T]he Administration agreed to my proposal on Sunday, September 30, but reneged within two days. . . . Frankly, the agreement of September 30, 2001 would have led to a better balanced bill. I could not stop the Administration from reneging on the agreement. . . . In these times we need to work together to face the challenges of international terrorism. I have sought to do so in good faith."[13]

Leahy said he was still unsure of the administration's reasons for reneging on their agreement, but he explained his own position: "I am the old style Vermonter: When you make an agreement, you stick with it."[14]

Under heavy political pressure, Leahy and Senate Majority Leader Tom Daschle (D-SD) had decided that since every Republican senator had committed to support the act, they would pressure their fellow Democrats to vote unanimously for it as well. Only Russ Feingold (D-WI) refused to accede to his party's demands. Feingold was particularly worried about the sweeping surveillance powers given to the government in Section 215, and he expressed a desire to introduce amendments to protect personal privacy. Furious with Feingold's refusal to fall in line, Daschle cornered him in the back of the Senate floor just before the vote and insisted that the bill would only become worse if it were opened up to debate and amendments. Feingold insisted on offering his amendments, but, as the result of Daschle's lobbying, they were quickly tabled with only a few votes of support.

In a subsequent interview, Feingold described the hostile pressure he received from Daschle, his own majority leader, who supported all the onerous provisions of Ashcroft's original bill. When asked to characterize Daschle's treatment of him, Feingold said, "Fairly brutal."

Feingold, who had been hopeful that the Ashcroft bill could be improved by principled compromise and appropriate amendments, expressed his disappointment in his own party:

[S]omething happened in the Senate, and I think the Democratic leadership was complicit in this. . . . I was told that a unanimous consent agreement was being offered with no amendments and no debate. . . . I refused. The majority leader came to the floor and spoke very sternly to me, in front of his staff and my staff, saying, you can't do this, the whole thing will fall apart. I said, what do you mean it'll fall apart, they want to pass this, too. . . .

He was on the belligerent side for Tom Daschle. And everybody said they were surprised at his remarks. Reporters thought it was so unlike him. . . . What happened in the Senate was that even though the Attorney General was going to allow these changes to make it moderately better, the Administration insisted, and Daschle went along with pushing this through. I finally got to offer the amendments late at night. . . . And a lot of senators came around to me, who, of course, voted for the bill, and said, you know, I think you're right. Then Daschle comes out and says, I want you to vote against this amendment and all other Feingold amendments; don't even consider the merits. This was one of the most fundamental pieces of legislation relating to the Bill of Rights in the history of our country! It was a low point for me in terms of being a Democrat and somebody who believes in civil liberties.[15]

That evening, Feingold spoke on the Senate floor:

If we lived in a country where the police were allowed to search your home at any time for any reason; if we lived in a country where the government was entitled to open your mail, eavesdrop on your phone conversations, or intercept your e-mail communications; if we lived in a country where people could be held in jail indefinitely based on what they write or think, or based on mere suspicion that they were up to no good, the government would probably discover and arrest more terrorists. . . . But that would not be a country in which we would want to live. . . . Preserving our freedom is the reason we are now engaged in this new war on terrorism. We will lose that war without a shot being fired if we sacrifice the liberties of the American people in the belief that by doing so we will stop the terrorists.[16]

Feingold attempted three times to introduce amendments to moderate the Patriot Act's assault on civil liberties, but each time Majority Leader Daschle rose to oppose them. In fact, Daschle opposed Feingold's right to introduce *any* amendments, and he urged his colleagues to ignore the merits of the amendments. "[M]y argument is not substantive, it is procedural," said Daschle. "We have a job to do. The clock is ticking. The work needs to get done. . . . I hope my colleagues will join me tonight in tabling this amendment and tabling every other amendment that is offered, should he choose to offer them tonight. Let's move on and finish this bill."[17]

After Leahy spoke in favor of Daschle's motion to table the amendment, Feingold objected to the ramrod procedure.

[O]n this bill there was not a single moment of markup or vote in the Judiciary Committee. I accepted that because of the crisis our Nation faces. This is the first substantive amendment in the Senate on this entire issue, one of the most important civil liberties bills of our time, and the majority leader has asked Senators to not vote on the merits of the issue. I understand the difficult task he has, but I must object to the idea that not one single amendment on this issue will be voted on the merits on the floor of the Senate. What have we come to when we don't have either committee or Senate deliberation on amendments on an issue of this importance?[18]

Feingold's second amendment was tabled without debate. When Feingold introduced his final amendment, Daschle quickly responded, "I am sympathetic to many of these ideas, but I am much more sympathetic to arriving at a product that will bring us to a point where we can pass something into law. . . . For that reason I move to table this amendment."

The vote was 90 to 7 in favor of tabling Feingold's last amendment. At this point, Senator Arlen Specter (R-PA) felt the need to question the procedural irregularities:

I am concerned about the procedures on establishing a record which will withstand constitutional scrutiny. . . . I wrote the chairman of the committee two letters urging hearings, and there was ample time to have hearings to find out about the details of this bill. . . . This bill was negotiated between the chairman and ranking member and the White House. The Judiciary Committee did not take up the bill. . . . But when the majority leader says he is concerned about procedure and not about

> substance, we are regrettably establishing a record where we have not
> only not shown the deliberative process to uphold constitutionality, but
> we are putting on the record a disregard for constitutionality and elevat-
> ing procedure over substance, which is not the way you legislate in a
> constitutional area where the Supreme Court of the United States bal-
> ances law enforcement's needs with the incursion on privacy.[19]

Needless to say, the Patriot Act was overwhelmingly passed by the Senate, without debate or amendments. Feingold cast the only nay vote.

Now it was up to House to face the stampede. Ironically, the Republi-can-controlled House soon showed itself to be much more responsible and colle-gial in addressing the delicate issues of security and civil liberties than had the Democratic-controlled Senate. When the Judiciary Committee's Republican chairman, F. James Sensenbrenner, Jr. (R-WI), indicated his intention to follow normal committee procedure in approving the Patriot Act, he came under imme-diate attack by the Bush administration and by conservative newspaper colum-nists including Robert Novak. Novak had complained that the government's attempt to pass anti-terrorist legislation quickly was being "slowed down by se-nior members of Congress." In particular, Novak faulted House Judiciary Chair-man Sensenbrenner for slowing down the process by insisting on "the regular legislative procedure."[20]

Sensenbrenner's committee took just two weeks to mark up and *unani-mously* approve the gigantic and complex bill. On October 3, when its Republi-can and Democratic members ordered it favorably reported to the House, Sensenbrenner could not resist reminding columnist Novak:

> When I first announced that I wanted the regular order to prevail in
> Committee consideration of this bill, Columnist Robert Novak took a
> shot at me, saying that all I wanted to do was slow it down and goof it
> up. Mr. Novak, we have shown that you are wrong, and I think that this
> shows that with respect to conflicting viewpoints and a bipartisan ap-
> proach, the legislative process works, and everybody who has partici-
> pated in this deserves the credit. We are all the winners. The terrorists
> are the losers.[21]

John Conyers, the ranking Democrat on the House Judiciary Committee, congratulated Chairman Sensenbrenner for preserving the regular committee process in considering the Patriot Act and joined him in praising the final bill:

> My friends in law enforcement tell me that they can be trusted not to
> abuse the sweeping new powers that they have requested. . . . I wish I
> could be confident that that would occur, but history has proven other-
> wise, regardless of what political party might have been in charge.
> Chairman Sensenbrenner and I have both fought to expedite the process

as much as possible. At the same time, the Founding Fathers did not intend the Congress to be a passive part of government, especially in times of crisis when the Bill of Rights may be threatened. So as much as I want to help John Ashcroft do his job as effectively as possible, it would be irresponsible to give him a blank check.[22]

Chairman Sensenbrenner described the committee's bill as follows:

> The united efforts of this country are reflected in the bipartisan efforts of this bill, which I was pleased to introduce with the Ranking Member, Mr. Conyers, along with the cosponsorship of 18 bipartisan Members of this Committee. The bill represents the essence of compromise. The left is not completely happy with this bill, and neither is the right, but [it] certainly does not represent the Justice Department's wish list. I think it means we have got it just about right. . . . [T]he bill does not do anything to take away the freedoms of innocent civilians. Of course we all recognize that the fourth amendment to the Constitution prevents the government from conducting unreasonable searches and seizures, and that is why the Patriot Act will not change the United States's Constitution or the rights guaranteed to citizens of this country under the Bill of Rights.[23]

Indeed, the bill approved by a 36–0 vote in the House Judiciary Committee was too good, too balanced, too constitutionally sound to be acceptable to the Bush administration. It had to be headed off at the pass before it reached the House floor. The arm-twisting used by the Senate leadership to pass the Patriot Act there would not work in the House. A more devious strategy would be required. The Justice Department persuaded the House leadership to rewrite the bill in the middle of the night before the floor debate, making it conform to Ashcroft's specifications.

In a discussion with National Public Radio host Marc Steiner on August 21, 2002, Conyers explained the bizarre procedure followed to ensure that the government's wish list would prevail in the House bill:

> What you need to know is that the Patriot Act that I sponsored is not the Patriot Act that was passed. After the chairman of the Judiciary Committee and I had worked to get a unanimous Committee vote in favor of the original version of the Act, it went before the leadership on the way to the Rules Committee. At that point, the bill was scrapped and replaced by a bill written by the staff of the Attorney General's office. So it was a bill that was foreign to all of us on the Committee. It was quite different, and it was a bill that I voted against.[24]

When Conyers was asked why he voted against the bill, he responded,

First of all, I voted against the procedure. For Attorney General Ashcroft, a former United States Senator, to throw out the unanimous work product of a congressional committee and substitute his own bill, that alone would have prevented me from voting for it. We had very carefully crafted a bill that did not ignore constitutional questions in the way the present Patriot Act did. How, in a time of urgency and crisis, could the Attorney General decide to become a legislative member and replace all 43 members of the House Judiciary Committee? It was so arrogant, so uncalled for. We were not consulted. We came the next morning to go to the Rules Committee, and there was a different document in front of us. Nobody had read it, nobody knew about it, but we had to vote out the administration's bill. It was a usurpation of the congressional prerogative.[25]

Laura Murphy, head of the ACLU's Washington Office, recalls, "When we found out the bill was being introduced, we went to Conyers and Sensenbrenner and begged them not to push it through in three days, as the attorney general was urging. They agreed, and their committee rewrote the bill to accommodate some of our concerns. The revised bill cleared the House Judiciary Committee by a vote of 32 to zero. Then in the middle of the night—it was reprinted at 3:30 A.M.—the bill was rewritten again to get all the troublesome stuff back in. When the members voted the following day, hardly anyone except a few staffers had actually seen the bill they were voting on."[26]

And so on October 12, thanks to a little slight of hand and the complicity of the Senate and House leadership, the House passed a version of the Patriot Act that was very similar to the Senate's bill. The bill was passed by large majorities in both houses, but Conyers later explained, "Nearly everybody in both houses voted for the Patriot Act. But they voted for it not knowing what was in it and under a great fear of being considered unpatriotic if they didn't vote for it. Were there hearings held today and the bill brought to a vote, the Patriot Act would be defeated."[27]

There was no official conference committee meeting to reconcile the differences between the House and Senate bills. Instead, on October 17, Leahy, Daschle, Flanigan, Dinh, and others assembled behind closed doors in House Speaker Dennis Hastert's office to negotiate the final package. The House bill included two-year sunset provisions that were not in the Senate bill, and in the discussion over reconciling the House and Senate bills, Flanigan expressed his concern about any provisions that would set an expiration date for certain sections. "We're feeling very strongly about the sunsetting," he told the assembled lawmakers. "This is not a war of a fixed duration."[28]

Eventually, a four-year sunset agreement was reached on several sections of the bill, far less than the sunsetting built into the original Sensenbrenner/ Conyers bill. The result was a Patriot Act, signed into law by President George Bush on October 26, which contained virtually all of the domestic surveillance powers requested by Bush, Ashcroft, and Dinh.

Only after the bill became law did a modicum of debate surface among members of Congress, many of whom felt demeaned by the bizarre process of its passage. Rep. C.L. Otter (R-ID), one of three Republicans to oppose the Patriot Act, said, "[S]ome of these provisions place more power in the hands of law enforcement than our Founding Fathers could have dreamt and severely compromise the civil liberties of law-abiding Americans."[29]

Rep. Ron Paul of Texas, another of the three Republicans to stand up to the House leadership and vote against the Patriot Act, said, "It's my understanding the bill wasn't printed before the vote—at least I couldn't get it. They played all kinds of games, kept the House in session all night. . . . [T]he bill definitely was not available to members before the vote."[30]

When asked what the nation's Founding Fathers would have thought of the Patriot Act, Paul responded, "Our forefathers would think it's time for a revolution. . . . They revolted against much more mild oppression."[31]

General Provisions

The 342-page bill that became law on October 26, 2001, had an elaborate title and a self-righteous acronym: the Uniting and Strengthening America by Providing Appropriate Tools to Intercept and Obstruct Terrorism Act (the USA PATRIOT Act). This awkward attempt to cloak the bill in the flag was offensive to many in Congress, including those who voted for it. When Rep. Barney Frank (D-MA) supported the original Patriot Act in the House Judiciary Committee, he felt the need to distance himself from the awkwardly constructed acronym.

It is entirely legitimate for those of us who are proud of America to reaffirm our patriotism at a time when enemies of freedom attack us. But invoking the word PATRIOT in the context of this bill gives the unfortunate impression that those who disagree with it are not patriots. I voted for the bill, and I am pleased with the work that we did collectively to provide for enhanced law enforcement powers in a way that I believe is consistent with American liberty and privacy. But I fully respect those who disagree with our work, and I wish we had not chosen a title for the bill that in any way reflects on their good faith in expressing that disagreement.[32]

As we saw in the preceding section, it was the Bush administration, not the civil libertarians, who effectively scrapped the original Patriot Act, making good use of the stirring acronym in gaining passage of their own bill.

The massive Patriot Act, among the most wide-ranging laws ever passed by Congress, has created new federal offices and new crimes, substantially amended at least twelve federal statutes, mandated dozens of new reports and regulations in four Cabinet departments, and directly appropriated $2.6 billion while frequently "authorizing" unspecified additional amounts.

The act has had three fundamental effects on American government and society: (1) it has introduced unprecedented government secrecy; (2) it has removed checks and balances within our governing system, specifically weakening the judicial oversight of the Executive branch; and (3) it has eroded the civil liberties of citizens and noncitizens alike, allowing secret arrests and detention of persons based solely on their country of origin, race, religion, or ethnicity.

The Patriot Act is structured in ten titles that indicate its broad scope:

Title I: Enhancing Domestic Security Against Terrorism

Title II: Enhanced Surveillance Procedures

Title III: International Money Laundering Abatement and Anti-Terrorist Financing Act of 2001

Title IV: Protecting the Border

Title V: Removing Obstacles to Investigating Terrorism

Title VI: Providing for Victims of Terrorism, Public Safety Officers, and Their Families

Title VII: Increased Information Sharing for Critical Infrastructure Protection

Title VIII: Strengthening the Criminal Laws Against Terrorism

Title IX: Improved Surveillance

Title X: Miscellaneous

Within these ten titles are numerous sections, the more prominent of them being:

Section 101: Establishes a new counterterrorism fund without fiscal year limitation and of unnamed amount, to be administered by the Justice Department.

Section 103: Re-invigorates the Justice Department's Technical Support Center and gives it $200 million for the years 2002 through 2004.

Section 105: Establishes a "national network of electronic crimes task forces" to be set up by the Secret Service throughout the country to prevent, detect, and investigate various electronic crimes.

Section 203: Mandates the sharing of "foreign intelligence" information between numerous federal agencies. The broad definition of "foreign intelligence" includes virtually anything related to national defense, national security, or foreign affairs. All such information in the possession of any federal investigative or law enforcement officer may be shared with any other federal "law enforcement, intelligence, protective, immigration, national defense, or national security officer." No court order is necessary and the information is not limited to the person being investigated

Section 206: Provides "roving wire tap" authority to FISA.

Sections 207 and 208: Increase the duration of FISA warrants and increases the number of FISA court judges.

Sections 209 and 212: Enact numerous technical changes and enhancements to standard surveillance techniques, including the authorization of the government's controversial "Carnivore" electronic surveillance programs.

Section 213: Allows delayed notification of "non-physical search warrants," known as "sneak and peek" warrants.

Section 214: Allows pen/trap orders concerning foreign intelligence information. The target of such an order may be a U.S. person, provided that the investigation is not conducted *solely* upon the basis of First Amendment activities.

Section 215: Allows federal investigators to seize "any tangible thing" in FISA type investigations by showing only that the items sought are "relevant" to an ongoing investigation related to terrorism or intelligence activities. The court *must* grant the warrant to the requesting agency, even if the judge believes the request is without merit.

Section 216: Explicitly places access to Internet information, including e-mail and Web browsing information, within the reach of pen/trap orders, without need to show probably cause. Again, law enforcement need only certify that what they seek is "relevant" to an ongoing terrorism investigation.

Section 217: Allows any government employee to conduct electronic content surveillance of U.S. persons.

Section 218: Lowers the standard for obtaining FISA warrants.

Sections 219 and 220: Establish single jurisdiction search warrants and nationwide service of warrants.

Sections 311, 312, 316, and 319: Allow federal investigators to impose "special measures" upon any domestic bank or financial institution and impose new due diligence requirements upon such institutions as a way of revealing terrorist financing. Set a 120-hour deadline for financial institutions to respond to information requests by federal investigators. Create new forfeiture provisions for those charged or convicted of certain terrorist crimes. Permit access by federal investigators to records of certain "correspondent" accounts in foreign banks.

Section 326: Establishes new or expanded requirements to track identities of persons opening new bank accounts and authorizes a study to track aliens or foreign nationals by a numerical system similar to social security numbers.

Section 358: Allows government investigators access to consumer records without a court order.

Section 403: Mandates a new information system to allow State Department access to certain criminal files kept by the FBI and requires a new technology standard to be applied to all visas and all border checkpoints.

Section 411: Creates a new definition of terrorism, establishing three types of "terrorist organizations," with wide latitude for federal investigators to identify such groups.

Section 412: Provides for mandatory detention of suspected aliens, allowing a person to be held for seven days without charge and possible indefinite detention for aliens deemed not removable. Requires a biannual report to Congress on aliens detained, but the report need not contain fundamental information like names, when seized, where detained, or nature of charges.

Sections 414–417: Establish new standards for entry and exit systems and data systems for border entry points. Expand the foreign student monitoring program.

Section 503: Greatly expands the DNA information bank on criminals.

Section 504: Links the investigation of any crime with the search for foreign intelligence, including information sharing.

Section 505: Amends three statutes to facilitate the FBI's use of "National Security Letters," a form of administrative subpoena that allows the FBI to seek information from libraries and other institutions without the need for a court order. (See later discussion of National Security Letters.)

Sections 507 and 508: Allow government investigators access to educational records without a court order.

Section 701: Establishes a major initiative for a "secure information sharing system" to investigate and prosecute multi-jurisdictional terrorist activities.

Section 802: Creates a new crime called "domestic terrorism," defined as "activity that involves acts dangerous to human life that violate the laws of the United States or any state and appear to be intended: (i) to intimidate or coerce a civilian population; (ii) to influence the policy of a government by intimidation or coercion; or (iii) to affect the conduct of a government by mass destruction, assassination or kidnapping."

Section 803: Expands the crimes of harboring, concealing, or providing material support for terrorists.

Section 808: Expands the list of "federal crime of terrorism."

Sections 809–812: Allow increased penalties for certain terrorist crimes, with no statute of limitations.

Sections 901 and 905: Mandate information sharing by the CIA with the Justice Department and by the Justice Department with the CIA.

Section 903: Deputizes all "officers and employees" of the "intelligence community" and authorizes them to investigate terrorism.

Section 908: Establishes a cross agency training program for law enforcement officials and agencies, including state and local, so they can better handle "foreign intelligence" investigations.

Section 1005: Provides grants for state and local fire and emergency service departments.

Section 1016: Establishes new programs for critical infrastructure protection.

Most of the provisions of the Patriot Act go well beyond terrorism offenses, applying instead to all federal investigations. Among the sweeping provisions in the new law are the following:

1. It permits the attorney general to incarcerate or detain noncitizens for engaging in speech protected by the First Amendment.

2. It severely restricts the power of the courts to prevent illegal telephone and Internet surveillance of American citizens.

3. It expands government authority to use "sneak and peek" or "black bag" searches without notification of the person being searched.

4. It grants the FBI, law enforcement, and intelligence agencies broad access to personal medical, financial, mental health, and student records with minimal judicial oversight.

5. It allows law enforcement to investigate American citizens on criminal matters without the need for a showing of probable cause.

6. It allows the CIA to spy on American citizens by giving the Agency broad authority to target individuals for surveillance.

7. It allows the attorney general to detain a noncitizen for seven days before criminal or deportation charges are brought and to detain that suspect indefinitely thereafter, without meaningful judicial review.

8. It chills constitutionally protected speech by defining "domestic terrorism" so loosely that it would allow the government to designate lawful advocacy groups as terrorist organizations subject to surveillance, wiretapping, harassment, and criminal penalties. The definition of domestic terrorism would apply to many forms of civil disobedience, including those practiced by organizations like Greenpeace or Operation Rescue.

The loss of judicial oversight of executive power is one of the more troubling effects of the Patriot Act. Under many of the act's provisions, the court exercises no review function whatsoever. For example, the court is often required to grant government access to sensitive personal information upon the mere request by a government official. The act also provides only a minimal standard of review for Internet communications, allowing law enforcement agents to acquire such information by merely certifying that it is "relevant" to an investigation. The court must accept such a claim, and the judge must issue the order even if he or she finds the certification unpersuasive.

Provisions Directly Affecting Libraries

The Patriot Act expanded the authority of the FBI and law enforcement generally to gain access to "business records," including medical records, educational records, library records, and stored electronic data and communications. These sweeping new surveillance procedures represent a major challenge to privacy and confidentiality in the library.

Sections 214 and 216 concern pen register and "trap and trace" telephone devices, and new authority in this regard can have grave implications for library privacy and confidentiality. Section 216 extends telephone monitoring laws ("pen register" and "trap and trace") to include routing and addressing information for all Internet traffic, including e-mail addresses, IP addresses, and URLs of Web pages. Since virtually all libraries now provide public Internet terminals, they will become targets of these new surveillance powers and will be required to cooperate in the monitoring of a user's electronic communications sent through the library's computers. State law enforcement may also apply for and obtain an order under Section 216, which is not limited to the investigation of terrorism or foreign intelligence matters.

Section 216 compels a recipient of a monitoring order to provide all necessary cooperation to law enforcement authorities to facilitate the installation of the monitoring device, or to provide the information to the investigating officer from their own records. The recipient of the order cannot disclose that communications are being monitored. Federal agents can obtain a *nationwide* court order for a wiretap from any federal court having jurisdiction over the offense under investigation. The officers and agents seeking warrants under the pen register statute need only affirm that the information sought is relevant to a criminal investigation.

Section 214 is similar to Section 216, applying to "pen register" and "trap and trace" authority under the FISA. Because Section 214 concerns the secret FISA court, an agent acting under that section need only claim that the records he seeks may be related to an ongoing investigation related to terrorism or intelligence activities, a very low legal standard. Again, the FBI's monitoring authority extends to routing and addressing information for all Internet traffic, and the libraries that provide such service may become the target of a court order.

Perhaps the greatest potential danger to libraries, publishers, and booksellers in the Patriot Act comes from Section 215: Access to Records Under Foreign Intelligence Security Act (FISA). This section allows an FBI agent to obtain a search warrant for "any tangible thing," which can obviously include books, circulation records and other data, floppy discs, data tapes, and computer hard drives. The generality of "any tangible thing" allows the FBI to compel the library or bookstore to release virtually any personal information it has maintained, including Internet records and registration information stored in any medium.

The Freedom to Read Committee of the Association of American Publishers complains that the Patriot Act "contains provisions that threaten the First Amendment-protected activities of book publishers, book sellers, librarians and readers." In its statement on "The Patriot Act and the First Amendment," the organization warns, "Section 215 . . . threatens the privacy and First Amendment rights of library patrons and bookstore customers whose reading choices and Internet usage patterns may be subject to disclosure despite existing protections for the confidentiality of library readership records and customer records in bookstores."[33]

Attached to the Freedom to Read Committee's statement was a form letter which supporters could send to Senator Leahy and Rep. Sensenbrenner urging them to hold hearings on the Patriot Act. The letter concluded with the warning: "If people come to believe that the government can readily obtain access to their library and bookstore records, they will no longer feel free to request the books and other materials they want and need out of a fear that they might become a target of government surveillance."[34]

There are a number of aspects of this new government surveillance of libraries and bookstores under Section 215 that make it far more onerous than what was endured in the past. As with Section 214, the FBI agent does not need to demonstrate "probable cause," that is, facts to support the belief that a crime has been committed or that the data sought are evidence of a crime. Instead, the agent only needs to claim that the records sought are "relevant" to an ongoing investigation related to terrorism or intelligence activities, a very low legal standard.

Past FBI requests for library records have required a court-ordered subpoena, which can be challenged in open court by the library. Under the Patriot Act, a "warrant" issued by a secret FISA court is sufficient to require the immediate release of library records, and no court review or adversarial hearing is available to challenge the process. To make matters worse, libraries or librarians served with such a warrant may not disclose, under penalty of law, the existence of the warrant or the fact that records were produced in response to it.

Another discouraging aspect of library surveillance under Section 215 of the Patriot Act is the fact that state library confidentiality laws, passed in forty-eight of our fifty states, are overridden by these new FBI warrants. Thus, years of hard work by librarians and state legislators throughout the land to protect the privacy of library patrons have been undone by a single federal law.

During the brief and fruitless Senate debate over Russ Feingold's amendment to Section 215, he explained that his amendment would maintain all existing federal and state statutory protections for the privacy of personal information:

> My State of Wisconsin, along with many other States, has very strong library confidentiality laws which requires a court order for disclosure of public library system records. . . . [M]y fear is that what section 215 does is effectively trump any and all of these State and Federal privacy protections. I think that is a result that most of our citizens and their State representatives would not countenance. . . . To the extent that the records sought have no such statutory protection, the only effect this amendment would have is to ensure that the records actually pertain to the target.[35]

Senator Maria Cantwell (D-WA) was the only senator to support the Feingold amendment:

> I have heard from many in my state, including my State librarian, consumers and businesses that are concerned that this provision is far too broad. . . . The bottom line is this legislation could circumvent or supercede Federal and State privacy laws that protect student records, library records, and health records not previously admissible under FISA.[36]

Despite Majority Leader Daschle's attempt to silence him, Feingold tried to convince his Senate colleagues of the danger posed to American civil liberties by Section 215:

> Under current law, the FBI can seek records from only a limited set of businesses—from public accommodations, such as hotels and motels, car rental companies, storage facilities, and travel records, such as those from airlines. . . . But under section 215 of this bill, all business records can be compelled to be produced, including those containing sensitive personal information such as medical records from hospitals or doctors, or educational records, or records of what books someone has taken out of the library. This is an enormous expansion of authority, compounded

by the elimination of the requirement that the records have to pertain to an agent of a foreign power. Under this provision, the Government can apparently go on a fishing expedition and collect information on anyone—perhaps someone who has worked with or lived next door to or has been seen in the company of, or went to school with, or whose phone number was called by the target of an investigation. . . . All the FBI has to do is allege in order to get the order that the information is sought for an investigation of international terrorism or clandestine intelligence gathering. . . . On that minimal showing in an ex parte application in a secret court, the Government can lawfully compel a doctor or a hospital to release medical records or a library to release circulation records. This is truly a breathtaking expansion of the police power, one that I do not think is warranted.[37]

Daschle was more perturbed than convinced, and he quickly moved to table Feingold's amendment. The motion to table was approved by a vote of 89 to 8.

Another provision of the Patriot Act that directly threatens library confidentiality is Section 217, which adds a new form of government surveillance, allowing *any* government employee, not just a law enforcement officer, to conduct content surveillance of U.S. persons. This can occur whenever a computer owner and operator "authorizes" surveillance and a law enforcement officer "has reasonable grounds to believe contents of a communication will be relevant" to an investigation of computer trespass. The section allows interception of messages sent through a computer without "authorization," a term that is not defined, thus leaving the owner/operator and government agent dangerous discretion in determining a violation. Indeed, a librarian would be authorized under this section to conduct surveillance of the use of a library computer if a minor technical infraction such as incorrectly filling out a computer sign-up sheet should occur, and that surveillance could continue *forever*.

In his lonely but impassioned opposition to Section 217, Senator Feingold tried to introduce an amendment that would protect libraries from this dangerous provision.

[T]his provision could allow universities, libraries, and employers to permit government surveillance of people who are permitted to use the computer facilities of those entities. Such surveillance would take place without a judicial order or probable cause to believe that a crime is being committed. Under the bill, anyone accessing a computer "without authorization" is deemed to have no privacy rights whatsoever, with no time limit. . . . [T]his provision completely eliminates fourth amendment protection for a potentially very large set of electronic communications. . . . People who don't own home computers use computers at libraries. Students use computers at school in computer labs or student centers. Without my amendment, these innocent users could become subject to intrusive government surveillance merely because they disobeyed a rule of the owner of the computer concerning its use.[38]

Senator Cantwell, again a lonely supporter of Feingold's amendments, added,

> For those who may be reviewing this legislation for the first time . . . as they go to their workplace, or as they go to their educational institution, or as they go to their library to enhance their education, they could be under surveillance for a very long and indefinite period of time without their knowledge. Thus, once authorized by a computer systems operator, the Government could intercept all communications of a person forever without a proper search warrant.[39]

The pleas of Feingold and Cantwell went unheeded, especially by their own majority leader, Tom Daschle, who again rose to table the amendment. The motion to table was passed by a vote of 83 to 13.

Feingold would try one more amendment, this one concerning Section 206, the roving wiretap provision. He explained, "The amendment simply provides that before conducting surveillance, the person implementing the order must ascertain that the target of the surveillance is actually in the house that has been bugged, or using the phone that has been tapped."[40]

On a vote of 90 to 7, Feingold's amendment was tabled once more. The Senate's version of the Patriot Act was left essentially as submitted by the Justice Department, and the final bill was passed overwhelmingly on a perfunctory vote. In a series of back room deals, the House and Senate reconciled their bills without debate, and the final law emerged as the monster faced by libraries today.

National Security Letters and Emergency Foreign Intelligence Warrants

One of the sources of confusion in attempting to itemize the provisions of the Patriot Act that affect libraries is the fact that the act amended many other statutes to facilitate their use in acquiring library records. When the FBI employs one of those statutes under the new Patriot Act guidelines, it will claim that it is not using the Patriot Act. A good example can be found in the use of National Security Letters (NSLs).

The Justice Department has consistently refused to make public any data on the number of times the Patriot Act, NSLs, or any other anti-terrorism tools have been used in libraries, but it has indicated which tool it would prefer to use to acquire electronic library records. In his July 26, 2002, letter to Sensenbrenner, the chairman of the House Judiciary Committee, Assistant Attorney General Daniel J. Bryant avoided a specific answer to the committee's question about the number of times Section 215 of the Patriot Act had been used to acquire library or bookstore records, but he noted in passing, "If the FBI were authorized to obtain the information the more appropriate tool for requesting electronic communication transactional records would be a National Security Letter (NSL)."[41]

Just what are these NSLs? First, they are a form of Justice Department "administrative subpoena," meaning that they may be issued by Attorney General Ashcroft, his designee, or even field offices, without the need for a court order and without judicial oversight. The only way a judge would see an NSL would be if it were subsequently challenged in court. There are three types of NSLs:

1. Pursuant to the Electronic Communications Privacy Act, the FBI can issue NSLs for (a) telephone subscriber information (limited to name, address, and length of service); (b) telephone local and long-distance toll billing records; and (c) electronic communication transactional records (e.g., e-mail and Web usage).

2. Pursuant to the Right to Financial Privacy Act, the FBI can issue NSLs to obtain financial records from banks and other financial institutions.

3. Pursuant to the Fair Credit Reporting Act, the FBI can issue NSLs to obtain consumer identifying information and the identity of financial institutions from credit bureaus.

The first category of NSL is clearly the most likely to be served on libraries and bookstores, and the frequency with which they are used is the result of amendments effected by the Patriot Act on the three statutes listed above. Section 505 of the Patriot Act amended these three statutes in a way that is similar to the changes introduced in Section 215. That is, Section 505 eliminated the requirement that before issuing an NSL the FBI must demonstrate reason to believe that the person whose records are sought is a "foreign power" or an "agent of a foreign power." Now, as a prerequisite to FBI issuance of an NSL, the three amended statutes require only that the records sought are "relevant" to an investigation "to protect against international terrorism or clandestine intelligence activities." In addition, each of the three statutes authorizing NSLs includes a gag order preventing the recipient of the NSL from disclosing to anyone that the FBI has sought or obtained the information.[42]

The Patriot Act prohibits the issuance of an NSL in an investigation of a "United States person" conducted "solely upon the basis of activities protected by the First Amendment to the Constitution." This purported reassurance is hollow, since it allows investigations of individuals "primarily" or even "overwhelmingly" on the basis of protected activities. Nor does it cover investigations of third parties to which the records of a United States person may be relevant.

After the passage of the Patriot Act, the FBI quickly communicated its new power to issue NSLs through memos to all offices and field agents. According to an internal FBI memo dated November 28, 2001, the Patriot Act "greatly broadened the FBI's authority" to gather information through NSLs. The memo goes on to say, "The USA PATRIOT Act has greatly simplified the NSL process. The FBI official authorizing the issuance of an NSL is no longer required to certify that there are specific and articulable facts giving reason to believe that the information sought pertains to a foreign power, or an agent of a foreign power. NSLs may now be issued upon a certification of relevance to an authorized investigation to protect against international terrorism or clandestine intelligence activities."[43]

National Security Letters can be used as part of criminal investigations and preliminary inquiries involving terrorism and espionage, according to FBI officials and internal guidelines. They are being used to obtain records about people living in the United States, including American citizens, without probable cause that these people have committed any crime. FBI spokesperson John Iannarelli pointed out, "It's safe to say that anybody who is going to conduct a terrorism investigation is probably going to use them at some point. . . . It's a way to expedite information."[44]

As to the frequency with which the Justice Department has used NSLs, the best indication came in some heavily redacted documents acquired through an ACLU Freedom of Information Act (FOIA) request. The documents included five pages of logs for NSL usage between October 2001 and January 2003. All specific information about the NSL activity was, of course, blacked out, but the size of the logs and the commentary indicated that NSLs are a preferred surveillance tool to "compel the production of a substantial amount of relevant information."[45]

ACLU attorney Jameel Jaffer explained that NSLs have always been a powerful legal authority for government surveillance because they do not require judicial review, but under the Patriot Act "the letters have become a far more invasive and nefarious tool." Before the act, according to Jaffer, the letters could be issued only against people who were reasonably suspected of espionage, but now they can be issued against individuals who are not suspected of either criminal activity or acting on behalf of a foreign power.[46]

Beryl Howell, former general counsel to Senator Leahy, described NSLs as "an unchecked, secret power that makes it invisible to public scrutiny and difficult even for congressional oversight."[47]

As indicated above, the Justice Department has said that NSLs are the most appropriate legal order under which electronic transactional records in libraries and bookstores may be acquired. It is therefore reasonable to assume that some, perhaps many, of the NSLs logged in the lengthy lists acquired by the ACLU were used in libraries and bookstores. The Justice Department continues to withhold such information from the public, claiming that it is classified. In addition, despite the fact that the enabling provisions of the Patriot Act have transformed NSLs into a preferred legal tool for library surveillance, the department can still claim that, technically, the Patriot Act is not involved in their use. In any case, librarians are now familiar with the dangers posed by both the Patriot Act and NSLs, and they support political action to prevent their use in libraries.

At the June 2003 ALA conference held in Toronto, a number of librarians expressed the belief that Senator Barbara Boxer's Library and Bookseller Protection Act (S. 1158), the Senate companion to Bernie Sanders' Freedom to

Read Protection Act (H.R. 1157), is actually the stronger of the two bills because it addresses both Section 215 of the Patriot Act and NSLs. Both bills would exempt libraries and bookstores from Section 215, but Boxer's bill would also exempt libraries from being considered "wire or electronic communication service providers," thus putting them outside the reach of NSLs.

Another newly emphasized surveillance tool is the "emergency foreign intelligence warrant." As we have seen, the government has the power to obtain secret FISA warrants for telephone wiretaps, electronic monitoring, and physical searches in counterterrorism and espionage cases, but the use of such warrants has been heavily expanded into criminal cases since a recent FISA court ruling that it had the authority to do so under the Patriot Act. Less well known is a provision allowing the attorney general to authorize these secret warrants on his own during "emergency" situations. The Justice Department then has seventy-two hours from the time a search or wiretap is launched to obtain approval from the secret FISA court. Attorney General Ashcroft has testified that he personally signed more than 170 of these emergency warrants during 2002, almost four times as many as were issued in the previous twenty-three years!

Sunsetted Provisions

Section 224 of the Patriot Act specifies that several of the surveillance provisions of the act will expire or "sunset" on December 31, 2005, unless renewed by Congress. As we shall see, the secrecy surrounding the implementation of the Patriot Act will make it difficult for Congress to assess the sunsetted provisions, resulting, in all likelihood, in their renewal. Nonetheless, the library profession, booksellers, and civil rights organizations are doing their best to inform the public of the dangers inherent in the Patriot Act and encourage members of Congress to sunset the more egregious provisions.

The following provisions will expire on December 31, 2005:

- Section 201: Authority to Intercept Wire, Oral, and Electronic Communications Relating to Terrorism.

- Section 202: Authority to Intercept Wire, Oral, and Electronic Communications Relating to Computer Fraud and Abuse Offenses.

- Section 203: (b), (d): Authority to Share Criminal Investigative Information.

- Section 206: Roving Surveillance Authority under the Foreign Intelligence Surveillance Act of 1978.

- Section 207: Duration of FISA Surveillance of Non-United States Persons Who Are Agents of a Foreign Power.

- Section 209: Seizure of Voice-Mail Messages Pursuant to Warrants.

- Section 212: Emergency Disclosure of Electronic Communications to Protect Life and Limb.

- Section 214: Pen Register and Trap and Trace Authority under the FISA.

- Section 215: Access to Records and other Items under the FISA.

- Section 217: Interception of Computer Trespasser Communications.

- Section 218: Foreign Intelligence Information.

- Section 220: Nationwide Service of Search Warrants for Electronic Evidence.

- Section 223: Civil Liability for Certain Unauthorized Disclosures.

The provision sunsetting the sections above was inserted into the Patriot Act at the insistence of former Representative Dick Armey, a conservative Republican from Texas. As described in Chapter 4, the Patriot II bill would remove the sunsetting provision of the original Patriot Act, but there have been more direct attempts to accomplish the same thing. In April 2003, Senator Hatch, the influential chairman of the Senate Judiciary Committee, sought to introduce an amendment to repeal the sunset provision, making the entire Patriot Act permanent.

The amendment was attached to a bill sponsored by Senators Charles Schumer (D-NY) and Kyl that would further expand government authority under the FISA. The Kyl-Schumer bill would allow a secret FISA warrant to be issued against a person who is *not* an agent of a foreign power or a member of any terrorist group, a change that its supporters claimed would fix the problems that arose in the case of Zacharias Moussaoui, who was jailed on immigration charges in the summer of 2001 and only after 9/11 was linked to al Qaeda. Legal experts have challenged the Justice Department claim that the powers granted in the Kyl-Schumer bill might have uncovered evidence on Moussaoui *before* 9/11, saying the FBI had the ability to obtain a warrant against Moussaoui, but botched it.

Both the Kyl-Schumer bill and the Hatch amendment were openly supported by the White House, but few members of Congress, Republican or Democrat, were anxious to scrap the sunset provisions of the Patriot Act. Jeff Lungren, spokesman for Rep. Sensenbrenner, chairman of the House Judiciary Committee, said removing the sunset provisions of the Patriot Act "will happen over his dead body."[48]

Democratic Senator Leahy was less dramatic but equally decisive in opposing the Hatch amendment. "Any move to repeal the sunset provisions will be highly controversial and is not justified by the Justice Department's own record," said Leahy. "We know the government has used some of these laws incorrectly, and we know that this has been the least cooperative Justice Department in anyone's memory. Oversight is how we know how well or poorly these and other laws work in practice, and the sunset conditions give Congress and the American people at least a little leverage in getting answers. . . . This amendment would give up the ghost of any meaningful oversight about how the government is using these sweeping powers."[49]

Because the Hatch amendment was attached to a Justice Department–supported anti-terrorism bill, there were rumors that Hatch was willing to remove his amendment if Senate Democrats would withdraw any of their amendments that might weaken the Kyl-Schumer bill. Indeed, an agreement was reached in May 2003, clearing the way for a 90 to 4 Senate approval of the bill.

A Republican Senate aide said, "The Democrats weren't going to give us a vote on the thing unless there were no Hatch amendments, period. A lot of the Democrats hated the Patriot Act even though they voted for it, and they certainly didn't want to see it made permanent."[50]

A spokesperson for Senator Hatch admitted that a compromise had been worked out, but she said that the removal of the amendment did not change his position. "He continues to be opposed to the sunset provisions of the Patriot Act," she said, and would continue working to remove them.[51]

The battle over the Hatch amendment may have obscured the significance of the Kyl-Schumer bill, the so-called lone wolf anti-terrorism measure. Though the bill has yet to pass the House, the Justice Department is lobbying strongly to add this powerful new tool to its arsenal. Meanwhile, civil liberties organizations are taking the view that defeating the Hatch amendment was the more important battle. "This is a major victory," said Timothy Edgar, legislative counsel for the ACLU. "Hatch wanted to intimidate the Democrats into not offering their amendments, and that didn't work because there is widespread concern that the government has already gone too far with the Patriot Act."[52]

Indeed, not only were Democrats able to protect the sunset provision of the Patriot Act, but during committee consideration of the Kyl-Schumer bill, Senator Leahy succeeded in attaching his own amendment, which sunsets that bill on the same schedule as the Patriot Act.

Blurring the Distinction between Criminal Justice and Counterintelligence

The Patriot Act has had a more disastrous effect on personal privacy than any other statute in American history. Through its amendments to the Foreign Intelligence Surveillance Act, it has facilitated searches, seizures, electronic surveillance, data mining, and general snooping into the private lives of American citizens, all in the name of fighting terrorism. The most dangerous provisions of the Patriot Act are those that merge foreign intelligence procedures with criminal law enforcement, bringing the CIA into domestic surveillance and allowing the FBI to conduct criminal investigations under the lower legal standards originally intended only for foreign intelligence activities. Indeed, the smoke screen of anti-terrorism has obscured the fact that the Patriot Act altered the rules of criminal law enforcement more than it assisted the war on terrorism.

The Patriot Act's amendments to the FISA have brought about unprecedented changes to American law enforcement. Enacted in 1978, the FISA established procedures governing foreign intelligence investigations that were explicitly designed to protect against domestic spying. All that has been set aside by the Patriot Act.

The FISA's secret court was originally manned by seven judges, but the Patriot Act has increased the number to eleven. They come from different federal circuits, meet twice a month in Washington, D.C., and always have three judges available in Washington. If the court denies an application for surveillance, the government may appeal to the FISA Court of Review, a panel of three federal judges appointed by Chief Justice William Renquist. Because the FISA court decides its cases in secret, the public remains ignorant of the number of FISA search warrants issued against U.S. citizens, who are themselves *never* informed of the surveillance and are not represented before the court. The FISA court is not required to reveal its legal opinions, resulting in a secret body of case law without parallel in American jurisprudence.

Only in August 2002, when the Patriot Act's amendments to the FISA generated an open conflict between the secret court and the Justice Department, did the public have a fleeting glimpse behind the veil of secrecy. Prior to the Patriot Act, FISA surveillance orders were limited to investigations whose "primary purpose" was to gather foreign intelligence, and FISA originally imposed strict limits on the sharing of information between criminal prosecutors and foreign intelligence investigators, whose surveillance does not require the same constitutional safeguards. Otherwise, the FISA would be an end run around the probable cause requirement of the criminal statutes. But the Patriot Act replaced the "primary purpose" test, allowing wiretaps and physical searches without probable cause so long as "a significant purpose" of the intrusion was to collect foreign intelligence.

In its May 2002 opinion, the FISA court rejected the Justice Department's argument that the Patriot Act allows the government to obtain a surveillance order whose primary purpose was a criminal investigation, not foreign intelligence. The government appealed the court's decision, and in September 2002 the FISA Court of Review (FISCR) met for first time in its history and reversed the FISA court's decision. It accepted the government's claim that the Patriot Act enables it to obtain a surveillance order from the FISA court even where the primary purpose is a criminal investigation, so long as gathering foreign intelligence was another "significant" purpose. The FISCR concluded that if "the government entertains a realistic option of dealing with the [foreign] agent other than through criminal prosecution, it satisfies the significant purpose test."[53] Thus, the Patriot Act has relegated foreign intelligence to a secondary concern of the Foreign Intelligence Surveillance Court.

The hearing before the FISCR was extraordinary not only because the court had never met before, but also because it was an ex parte proceeding at which only the Justice Department representatives and the panel of three judges were allowed. "This is a strange proceeding because it is not adversarial," observed FISCR presiding judge Ralph B. Guy, Jr. "If one were to just read the transcript of this hearing today, one might think that the adversary, if there was one, is the lower body in this matter."[54]

Indeed, the record of the hearing is unique because of the absence of an opposing view. Other than some brief debate on technical issues, the judges generally assumed a servile posture toward the Executive branch, even consulting the Justice Department on how to handle statements from civil liberties groups.

"Do you have a view what we should do with amicus briefs?" asked Judge Laurence H. Silberman, referring to the unsolicited pleadings submitted by civil liberties groups in support of the lower court decision.

"Our position is we have no objection to the Court receiving amicus briefs," replied Solicitor General Ted Olson, who surely had never been treated so deferentially in any court.[55] Under these circumstances, how could the FISCR be expected to do other than endorse the Justice Department's desire for broader surveillance authority?

Kate Martin, director of the Center for National Security Studies, says the Patriot Act turned the premise of FISA upside down by eliminating the constitutionally mandated requirement that these extraordinary powers be used only for foreign intelligence purposes, not in criminal cases. "[T]he Act requires the DOJ to give the CIA *all* information relating to any foreigner or to any American's contacts or activities involving any foreign government or organization, without setting any standards or safeguards for using the information."[56]

Martin explains that, within days of the Patriot Act's enactment, the administration took actions suggesting the abandonment of the law enforcement paradigm in investigating individuals within the United States and the substitution of an intelligence paradigm that gathers any information that might be useful. She concludes, "These changes have been made with no public discussion of whether this fundamental shift to an intelligence model rather than law enforcement model will in fact be effective in the fight against terrorism. . . . Intelligence is no longer seen as an important means of protecting liberty and the rule of law, but rather protection of intelligence methods has come to be the justification for limiting liberty and the rule of law."[57]

James X. Dempsey, deputy director of the Center for Democracy and Technology, explains, "The implications of this change are enormous. Previously the FBI could get the credit records of anyone suspected of being an international terrorist. [Under the Patriot Act], the FBI can . . . go into a public library and ask for the records of everybody who ever used the library, or who used it on a certain day, or who checked out certain kinds of books."[58] Indeed, it can do the same at any bank, telephone company, hotel or motel, hospital, or university by simply claiming that the information is sought for an investigation to protect against international terrorism or clandestine intelligence activities.

Thus, the claim that the Patriot Act is directed against international terrorism is seen to be false. A second misrepresentation of the Patriot Act, however, is even more outrageous. That is the claim that the Bill of Rights is a luxury we cannot afford during the war on terrorism. James Dempsey explains that Americans are guaranteed the right to confront our accusers not just as an element of human dignity, but because cross examination exposes lies and forces the government to continue looking until the truly guilty party is found. Similarly, we subject government decisions to public and judicial scrutiny not only to empower individual citizens, but because openness and accountability can produce a fuller factual record, expose faulty assumptions, and check the rash behavior of elected officials acting under political pressure. We protect freedom of speech not only to ensure personal self-expression, but because it brings political stability to our society through the availability of dissent and peaceful change.

Dempsey concludes, "For these and other reasons, surrender of freedom in the name of fighting terror is not only a constitutional tragedy, it is also likely to be ineffective and worse, counterproductive."[59]

Notes

1. COINTELPRO is an acronym for the FBI's illegal domestic "counterintelligence programs" employed from 1956 to 1971. The targets of COINTELPRO were American political dissidents, not foreign spies.

2. The Senate Select Committee to Study Government Operations with respect to Intelligence Activities, chaired by Sen. Frank Church (D-ID), came to be known as the Church Committee. Its 1976 report on the CIA was the only thorough congressional investigation of U.S. intelligence and its activities ever made public.

3. Jean Patman, "First Amendment Advocates Fear Erosion of Rights in Aftermath of Attack," freedomforum.org, September 14, 2001, p. 1.

4. Robert O'Harrow, Jr., "Six Weeks in Autumn," *Washington Post Magazine*, October 27, 2002, p. 9.

5. Ibid., p. 17.

6. "Insatiable Appetite: The Government's Demand for New and Unnecessary Powers after September 11," American Civil Liberties Union, Washington, D.C., April 2002, p. 3.

7. Ibid., p. 10.

8. Patman, "First Amendment Advocates Fear Erosion of Rights in Aftermath of Attack," p. 1.

9. O'Harrow, "Six Weeks in Autumn," p. 18.

10. Ibid.

11. Ibid., p. 20.

12. *Congressional Record—Senate*, October 11, 2001, p. S10552.

13. Ibid., p. S10556, S10559.

14. Ibid., p. S10604.

15. Matthew Rothschild, "Russ Feingold," *The Progressive*, May 2002, p. 32.

16. *Congressional Record—Senate*, October 11, 2001, p. S10570.

17. Ibid., p. S10575.

18. Ibid.

19. Ibid., p. S10578–10579.

20. Robert Novak, "Congress in Crisis," September 20, 2001, TownHall.com Columnists, www.townhall.com/columnists/robertnovak/rn20010920.shtml.

21. "Provide Appropriate Tools Required to Intercept and Obstruct Terrorism (PATRIOT) Act of 2001," Report of the Committee on the Judiciary, House of Representatives, to Accompany H.R. 2975. 107th Cong., 1st Sess., October 11, 2001, p. 430.

22. Ibid., p. 291.

23. Ibid., pp. 289–91.

24. *Marc Steiner Show*, WYPR, Baltimore, MD, August 21, 2002.

25. Ibid.

26. William Raspberry, "Homeland Security Sales Pitch," *Washington Post*, July 21, 2003, p. A21.

27. *Marc Steiner Show*, WYPR, Baltimore, MD, August 21, 2002.

28. Raspberry, "Homeland Security Sales Pitch."

29. Kelly Patricia O'Meara, "Police State," *Insight on the News*, November 9, 2001, p 3. www.insightmag.com/main.cfm?include=detail&storyid=143236.

30. Ibid., pp. 1–2.

31. Ibid., p. 6.

32. "Provide Appropriate Tools Required to Intercept and Obstruct Terrorism (PATRIOT) Act of 2001," Report of the Committee on the Judiciary, p. 433.

33. "The Patriot Act and the First Amendment," A Statement from the Freedom to Read Committee of the Association of American Publishers, June 10, 2002, www.abffe.org.

34. Ibid.

35. Ibid.

36. Ibid., p. S10585.

37. *Congressional Record—Senate*, October 11, 2001, pp. S10583–10584.

38. Ibid., pp. S10570–10571.

39. Ibid.

40. Ibid., p. S10576.

41. Letter from Daniel J. Bryant, Assistant Attorney General, to F. James Sensenbrenner, Jr., Chairman, Committee on the Judiciary, U.S. House of Representatives, July 26, 2002, p. 4.

42. "National Security Letters: USA PATRIOT Act," Analysis and summary prepared by Daniel Mach and Theresa Chmara, Jenner & Block, LLC, April 2003.

43. Ibid.

44. Dan Eggen, "Justice Department's Data-Gathering Raises Rights Questions," *Washington Post*, March 24, 2003. www.bayarea.com/mld/cctimes//news/world/5470206.html.

45. "Documents Show Ashcroft Is Bypassing Courts with New Spy Powers, ACLU Says," American Civil Liberties Union, News, March 24, 2003, p. 1. www.aclu.org/SafeandFree/ SafeandFree. cfm?ID=12166&c=206.

46. Ibid.

47. "Secrecy and Surveillance," *Newsletter on Intellectual Freedom*, May 2003, p. 117.

48. Eric Lichtblau, "Senate Deal Kills Effort to Extend Antiterror Act," *New York Times*, May 9, 2003, p. 1. http://foi.missouri.edu/usapatriotact/senate.html.

49. "Leahy Threatens Floor Fight on Move to Repeal Sunset Provisions of the USA Patriot Act," Office of U.S. Senator Patrick Leahy, April 9, 2003. www.senate.gov/~Leahy/press/ 200304/040903a.html.

50. Lichtblau, "Senate Deal Kills Effort to Extend Antiterror Act," p. 2.

51. Ibid.

52. Ibid.

53. "The USA PATRIOT Act and Beyond," *Homefront Confidential*, Reporters Committee for a Free Press, 2003, pp. 4–5. www.rcfp.org/home/homefrontconfidential/usapatriot.html.

54. "Transcript Shines Light on FISA Review Court," *Secrecy News*, FAS Project on Government Secrecy, Vol. 2003, Issue No. 10, February 6, 2003, p. 1.

55. Ibid.

56. Kate Martin, "Intelligence, Terrorism, and Civil Liberties," *Human Rights*, Winter 2002, pp. 6–7.

57. Ibid., p. 7.

58. James X. Dempsey, "Civil Liberties in a Time of Crisis," *Civil Rights*, Summer 2002, p. 10.

59. Ibid., p. 8.

Chapter 3

The Patriot Act in Libraries and Bookstores

Fearing the Worst

During 2002, a series of patriotic public service television announcements were produced for the Fourth of July by the Ad Council. Each presented a disturbing Big Brother scenario followed by the admonition, "What if America Weren't America? Freedom: Appreciate It, Cherish It, Protect It." One of the public service ads showed a man approaching a librarian to ask for help in locating a book. "These books are no longer available," responds the librarian in an eerie voice. "May I have your name please?" At that point a couple of suited officials forcefully take the library patron away.[1]

The ad may be fiction, but countless real-life tales of frustrated researchers have surfaced since the passage of the USA PATRIOT Act in October 2001, just a month after the terrorist attacks on the World Trade Center. One example should suffice. In August 2003, Dr. Susan Whalen, a widely published researcher and professor at the Loyola University School of Law, visited the U.S. National Archives where she was told by the clerk that she could not see the Saudi Arabian documents stored there. This was a surprise, since all of the Archive's documents have already been reviewed, then declassified or removed. "It's part of the Patriot Act," the clerk declared. "The U.S. State Department records you requested are indeed declassified and theoretically available. But they also may contain information that terrorists can use, like names and addresses and information of U.S. citizens."

Dr. Whalen explained that the documents she sought were more than thirty-years old, and any person the records refer to will be quite elderly or already deceased. The clerk was unmoved.

"I'm sorry," she said. "You can't look at the Saudi records even if they are a hundred years old."

When Dr. Whalen tried to explain that no one was likely to try to steal the identity of King Faisel, Dwight Eisenhower, or Henry Kissinger, the clerk warned her, "Ask again and I will call security to remove you from the building and have you banned as a security risk."

After Dr. Whalen asked to see a supervisor, a man arrived and asked her in a whisper, "Why are you looking at Saudi Arabia, anyway?" Whalen explained that she was researching a history of the State Department's positions on Wahhabism, but the supervisor persisted, asking whether Whalen was working on a book or a paper and who was the publisher? In seven years of researching at the Archives, Whalen had never been asked such questions.

"Why do you want to know?" Whalen asked in return. "Am I on some kind of list?"

At this point, an eavesdropping researcher at a nearby desk laughed and said, "All of us researchers are on some kind of list now."

The supervisor smiled and said, "I'm sorry you were threatened with arrest, but a lot of people become angry or hysterical when they're told they can not see the documents. We sometimes have to remove them from the building."

Dr. Whalen left the building on her own, but she reflected, "I pass through the Archive's security gates uneasily, knowing that my country has lost something important. We're hardly any safer for keeping Saudi history a secret. The 9/11 terrorists committed a horrendous crime, but they did not take away our national security. We have done this to ourselves."[2]

In the wake of 9/11, libraries and bookstores around the nation prepared for the increased surveillance powers authorized by the Patriot Act and a host of new FBI guidelines. Meanwhile, with Rooseveltian gravity, Attorney General Ashcroft told the Senate Judiciary Committee in December 2002 that the only thing we had to fear was fear of the Patriot Act:

> [T]o those who scare peace-loving people with phantoms of lost liberty; my message is this: your tactics only aid terrorists—for they erode our national unity and diminish our resolve. They give ammunition to America's enemies and pause to America's friends.[3]

Recognizing that their hard-won state library confidentiality statutes were rendered powerless by the Patriot Act, some librarians and bookstore owners felt the need to warn their patrons and customers that records of books borrowed or sold could now be seized by the government without a subpoena, without probable cause, and under a gag order imposed on all those involved in the process. For example, both houses of the New Mexico legislature proposed resolutions encouraging libraries to post prominent signs warning patrons that their library records are subject to federal scrutiny without their permission or knowledge.

In Skokie, Illinois, the library board voted to post warning signs in their public libraries. A standard warning sign was agreed upon and soon it was posted throughout the Skokie Public Library System. In each library, the signs were posted next to every public computer, every online catalog terminal, the reference desk, the circulation desk, everywhere a patron might go. The sign read:

NOTICE

The Skokie Public Library
makes every effort to guard
your privacy in the use of Library
materials and computers.
However, due to the terms of
the USA PATRIOT Act (Public
Law 107-56), Federal officials
may require the Library to
provide information about your
use of library resources without
informing you that we have
done so. The USA PATRIOT Act
was initiated by Attorney
General John Ashcroft.

Carolyn Anthony, director of the Skokie Public Library System, explained, "It's all up to the Justice Department and what their definition is of anything related to terrorism. So, in effect, instead of having to prove there's a criminal involvement, if they just say it's related to terrorism they can come in and request this information from us and we can't tell anyone they've been here asking for it."[4]

Similar action has been taken in California, where several libraries led the way in sharing their fears with their patrons. In Santa Cruz, the following sign was posted in their ten public libraries beginning in March 2003:

> Warning: Although the Santa Cruz library makes every effort to protect your privacy, under the federal USA Patriot Act (Public Law 107-56), records of the books and other materials you borrow from this library may be obtained by federal agents. That federal law prohibits library workers from informing you if federal agents have obtained records about you.[5]

Anne Turner, director of libraries in Santa Cruz, said the response to the warning was community outrage, with most of the anger directed against the Patriot Act, not the library.

"It's only recently that people have become aware just how pernicious it is," she said. "Our board decided to take a public stand" and post warnings at its branches.[6]

In 2002, the Santa Monica city libraries posted signs: "Attention library patrons: The FBI has the right to obtain a court order to access any records we have of your transactions in the library, a right given to them by Section 215 of the USA Patriot Act."[7]

Other states have adopted similar measures. In Guilford, Vermont, librarian Cathrine Wilken greets library visitors with a warning: "You may have noticed the sign on the door," she says, pointing to a posted warning that the library is not allowed, under the Patriot Act, to tell them if their borrower records have been seized by the FBI. Inside the library, another sign asks, "Q. How can you tell when the FBI has been to your library? A. You can't."[8]

"I've been posting things since last fall about various aspects of the Act," said Wilken. "What bothers me so much is that that person who might be investigated has no defense. They're not allowed to know they're being investigated. I'm not allowed to tell them."[9]

Wilken said her real interest was to motivate people to take action after they leave the library. She pointed out a pile of bookmarks with local legislators' phone numbers and said, "I want people to take these and call Bernie (Sanders), Jim Jeffords and Pat Leahy."[10]

Meanwhile, the American Library Association's (ALA's) Intellectual Freedom Discussion List was swamped with recommendations for signs warning patrons about their fragile confidentiality. The following suggestions, received during one week in June 2002, are typical:

1. "NOTICE TO PATRONS—The Patriot Act gives the Federal Bureau of Investigation the authority to demand to see your library record with no probable cause. . . . Further, by law, if the FBI demands a patron record from us, we are not permitted to notify that patron of that fact."

2. "To our patrons: Federal law requires that all patron information regarding library use, including, but not limited to, Internet use and book borrowing, be supplied to federal authorities upon their request. This information may be used as part of a criminal prosecution pursuant to the Patriot Act of 2001."[11]

Even the American Civil Liberties Union (ACLU) has offered its own warning signs to library patrons. The New Mexico and Florida chapters of the ACLU are distributing 10-by-12 inch posters to libraries with a photo of the Statue of Liberty and text that reads, "Records of the books and other materials that you borrow from this library may be obtained by federal agents. That federal law prohibits librarians from informing you if records about you have been obtained by federal agents."[12] The posters urge patrons to direct their questions about the policy to Attorney General Ashcroft.

The five signs shown below, created half in jest by the online publication librarian.net, demonstrate the imaginative ways that libraries might come clean with their patrons.[13]

**The FBI
has not
been here**

*[Watch very closely for the
removal of this sign]*

**Q. How can you tell when
the FBI has been
in your library?
A. You can't.**

The Patriot Act makes it illegal
for us to tell you if our computers
are monitored; be aware!

We're Sorry!

Due to National Security concerns,
we are unable to tell you if your
Internet surfing habits, passwords
and email content are being monitored by federal agents;
please act appropriately.

We have been visited by the FBI.

They requested your reading lists.

Now do you feel much more secure?

Organizations Who Have
Not Stopped By
This Week

1. **Red Cross**
2. **Boy Scouts**
3. **United Way**
4. ~~**FBI**~~
5. **Rotary Club**

The decision of some libraries to share doubts about their ability to protect library confidentiality was a controversial step. Many other libraries felt this would only erode the patrons' trust, further chilling their willingness to read freely and inquire openly. Judith Krug, director of the Freedom to Read Foundation, says she opposes posting warning signs in libraries. "My concern with posting signs is that you terminate the user's expectation that what they read in libraries is protected by statute. I think there are more effective ways [than signs] to raise awareness about the need to change this particular section of the PATRIOT Act."[14] Maurice J. Freedman, president of the ALA, was also wary of placing signs in public libraries. "There are people, especially older people who lived through the McCarthy era, who might be intimidated by this," said Freedman. "As of right now, the odds are very great that there will be no search made of a person's records at public libraries, so I don't want to scare people away."[15]

Many librarians and organizations like the ACLU, however, have defended the use of warning signs. "This is a unique way for us to demonstrate to the public how the Patriot Act can infringe on their private lives," said Peter Simonson of the New Mexico ACLU, which is distributing warning posters. "We're concerned that as we get further and further away from the passage of the Patriot Act, the public becomes more apathetic and forgets about what we lost under that legislation. We're not trying in any way to scare the public into not using libraries. We want them to know about the radical and dramatic change that has affected their rights, and we hope to motivate them to demand a repeal from Congress."[16]

What Are You Going to Do When They Come for You?

With the passage of the Patriot Act, the government acquired a new array of surveillance tools to use on libraries and bookstores, including secret search warrants (with gag orders attached), Internet "trap and trace" orders, and increased availability of National Security Letters (NSLs), the administrative subpoena that the Justice Department claims is the most likely tool to be used in acquiring library records. But the government still has all the old surveillance tools, including traditional grand jury subpoenas and search warrants, not to mention FBI visits with no court order of any kind, an approach made famous during the Library Awareness Program.

With all of these surveillance weapons threatening libraries, how can the profession prepare its staff for the inevitable knock on the door? In Woodland, California, librarian Marie Bryan had been tearing up library records by hand until they acquired a shredder. "For me, it has been like waiting for the other shoe to drop," she said. "When is someone going to be knocking on the door with search warrants?"[17]

Karen Schneider, who oversaw a 2003 California Library Association survey on library responses to the Patriot Act, says librarians in California have been quick to take action. "They've really been in a hurry to implement any of the necessary procedures before the knock on the door comes," she said. "It's a tremendously proactive response on the part of the profession. Nationwide, it's typical of what's going on."[18]

The ALA has issued formal guidance in its statement "Confidentiality and Coping with Law Enforcement Inquiries: Guidelines for the Library and the Staff,"[19] which attempts to inform and instruct librarians on their rights and obligations in the face of government surveillance. The statement begins, "Increased visits to libraries by law enforcement agents, including FBI agents and officers of state, country, and municipal police departments, are raising considerable concern among the public and the library community."

The ALA advises all libraries to avoid creating unnecessary patron records, avoid retaining records beyond what is necessary for the operation of the library, and avoid placing patron information in public view. It then documents guidelines for library procedure before, during, and after law enforcement visits.

Before any law enforcement visits occur, libraries should (1) designate the person or persons who will be responsible for handling law enforcement requests, (2) train all library staff, including volunteers, on the library's procedures for handling such requests, (3) review the library's confidentiality policy and state confidentiality laws with library counsel , and (4) have plans in place to address service interruptions resulting from possible government seizure of library computers or storage devices.

Once a law enforcement visit has commenced, (1) library staff should immediately ask the agent or officer for identification and then refer that person to the library director or designee; (2) the director or designee should meet with the agent or officer, with library counsel or another colleague present; (3) if the agent or officer does not have a court order compelling the production of records or other items, the director or designee should explain the library's confidentiality policy and the state's confidentiality law and make it clear that patron records are not available except when a proper court order in good form has been presented to the library; and (4) without a court order, law enforcement has no authority to compel cooperation with an investigation or require answers to questions, other than the name and address of the person speaking to the agent or officer. If the agent or officer presents a court order, the library should respond as follows.

If the court order is in the form of a subpoena:

1. Counsel should examine the subpoena for any legal defect, including the manner in which it was served on the library, the breadth of its request, its form, or an insufficient showing of good cause. If a defect exists, counsel will advise on the best method to resist the subpoena. Usually, the library can file a motion to quash the subpoena or a motion for a protective order. A hearing would then be held where the court decides if good cause exists and if the library must comply with the subpoena.

2. Through legal counsel, the library should insist that any defect be cured before records are released and that the subpoena is limited to specifically identified records or documents.

3. Require that the agent or officer requesting the information submit a new subpoena in good form and without defects.

4. Review the requested information before releasing it. Follow the subpoena strictly and do not provide any information not specifically requested in it.

5. If disclosure is required, ask the court to enter a protective order (drafted by the library's counsel) keeping the information confidential and limiting its use to the particular case and only by those persons working directly on the case.

If the court order is in the form of a search warrant:

1. A search warrant is executable immediately. The agent or officer may begin a search of library records as soon as the library director or designee is served with the warrant.

2. Ask to have library counsel present before the search begins in order to examine the warrant and ensure that the search conforms to it.

3. Cooperate with the search to ensure that only the records identified in the warrant are provided.

If the court order is a search warrant under the Foreign Intelligence Surveillance Act (FISA) as amended by the Patriot Act:

1. The recommendations for a regular search warrant also apply to a FISA warrant, but a warrant issued by a FISA court contains a "gag order" prohibiting the person or institution served from disclosing the existence of the warrant, its target, or that records have been produced.

2. The library and its staff must comply with the FISA warrant, but, despite the gag order, the library may still seek legal advice and request that the library's counsel be present during the search.

3. If the library does not have legal counsel, it may obtain legal advice and assistance from Jenner & Block, the Freedom to Read Foundation's legal counsel. (Note: If law enforcement presents an NSL, the same conditions apply as with a FISA warrant, including the gag order. See Chapter 2 for details.)

After *any* law enforcement visit has been completed: (1) review the court order with library counsel to ensure that the library complies with any remaining requirements, (2) review library policies and make any appropriate revisions, (3) be prepared to communicate with the press. Develop a public information statement describing the need for library confidentiality and warning of the chilling effect caused by revealing personally identifiable information.

In addition to the ALA guidelines, library directors around the country have sent their own advisory memos to their staffs, informing them of the implications of the Patriot Act, but reassuring them that fundamental library policies with respect to patron confidentiality would remain unchanged. Typical of such memos is one from Valerie J. Gross, director of the Howard County (Maryland) Library System. Issued shortly after the passage of the Patriot Act, Gross's memo to her staff reads, in part:

Because the USA PATRIOT Act has been featured in the news lately and you may be asked what our Library's position is, I am providing a summary of how the Act affects us, as well as an outline of our policy and procedures relating to any request for information about our customers.

As always, Maryland law protects customer confidentiality, requiring police to obtain a court order to obtain sensitive information such as which materials someone may have borrowed or someone's use of a library or its resources. The recent USA PATRIOT Act increases the power of federal agencies to gather information *by relaxing the requirement for subpoenas and court orders.* In fact, however, the USA PATRIOT Act has not affected any change in our policies and procedures. Following the presentation of a court order, I must be notified, and the Board President and Library counsel must also be involved in each case. Due to these privacy measures in place, *although the USA PATRIOT Act presents a potential increase in requests, the scrutiny we apply remains the same.*

So, as always, please refer any police officer, FBI agent, etc., requesting information to me, even if the agent insists on immediate disclosure (know that even under the USA PATRIOT Act, we have rights to legal representation). Be courteous, conveying that we are willing to work with them.

It is also important to point out that it is only certain court orders under the USA PATRIOT Act—ones that are issued under the Foreign Intelligence Surveillance Act—that prohibit us from notifying a customer of the order. In addition, should customers express concerns, please note the following:

- Records are not maintained of what a customer has borrowed in the past unless materials are still checked out or overdue. Essentially, once materials are returned, the data are purged from customers' records.

- Since work cannot be saved on computer hard drives, there are no traces of customer work or research there.

- E-mails composed or read on a Library computer is through an account maintained with an offsite provider, so again, there are no remaining records of communications.

- When we occasionally ask customers to sign up to use the Internet, we do not retain sign-up records beyond the day they were collected.[20]

Destroying Patron Records Before They Can Be Seized

The ALA's guidelines, augmented by local library protocols, may make the government's warrants and subpoenas less disruptive to library operations, but the only way to protect library records from federal seizure is to destroy them before the FBI arrives. Mark Corallo, a spokesman for the Justice Department, says libraries are not breaking the law by destroying their patron records, even if they have accelerated the process since the passage of the Patriot Act. Corallo said, "it would only be illegal if a library destroyed records that had already been subpoenaed."[21]

During Attorney General Ashcroft's appearance before the House Judiciary Committee on June 5, 2003, he was asked by a sympathetic fellow Republican, Rep. Jeff Flake of Arizona, "A lot of the libraries have made a practice of destroying computer records and other records in defiance of the Patriot Act. They are saying, we don't agree with it and therefore we'll make it more difficult for the Justice Department to come in and actually search those records. To your knowledge, has any investigation been stymied, has the Justice Department sought information that was then destroyed by any of the libraries?"

Ashcroft's answer could have been enlightening, but instead he lapsed into an irrelevant discourse, followed by a lame joke: "I was going to give that as an answer to the library question, but I think I'm in the wrong card catalog here."[22] After receiving scattered giggling, Ashcroft moved on to another question.

Karen Rollin Duffy, city librarian in Santa Clara, California, says, "We've discussed the Patriot Act in detail. Our stance has always been that we want to protect patron privacy. But we are reviewing our practices. What records do we keep, and are we keeping them too long?"[23]

Brian Reynolds, director of the San Luis Obispo County (California) libraries, says librarians track the books people read and the Internet sites they visit, but they do not save that information with the patrons' names attached. "We strive to not know what people are reading on an individual basis," he said. "That's not our business."[24]

In Santa Cruz, California, librarians have led the way in destroying patron records before the FBI can get to them. In the past, the Santa Cruz Public Library System would destroy old paperwork as time allowed, typically once a week. But library officials recently decided that such records should be shredded daily. "It used to be, a librarian would be pictured with a book," said library branch manager Barbara Gail Snider. "Now it is a librarian with a shredder." Anne Turner, director of the library system, explained, "The basic strategy now is to keep as little historical information as possible."[25]

Even Internet sign-up sheets are being removed in many libraries. For example, in Paterson, New Jersey, public library director Cindy Czesac says that FBI agents visited her library seeking information on patron use of library computers. When the agents discovered that the library did not maintain a computer sign-in sheet they exclaimed, "We know who borrows the books, so why don't we know who uses the computers?"[26]

Some bookstores are also limiting customer records, despite that fact that this may deprive them of valuable marketing tools. Unfortunately, the larger bookstore chains tend to keep extraordinarily detailed customer records. For example, Amazon.com, the Internet bookseller, allows an individual's past purchases to be displayed on a computer screen with the click of a mouse. Borders Group, a national bookstore chain, maintains extensive historical records on patron purchases, but says it has a "long-standing commitment to protect the privacy of its customers, and we do not generally disclose to third parties information about their purchases." Spokeswoman Jenie Carlen says law enforcement agencies have requested information in the past and Borders reviewed them on a case-by-case basis. She says that Borders would not begin destroying records simply to avoid turning them over to law enforcement authorities.[27]

Other bookstores have been forced to make a painful commitment to customer confidentiality. Philip Bevis, founder and chief executive officer of Arundel Books, which sells used and rare books online and off line, says that his customers' concerns about the Patriot Act have forced him to cease retaining customer data, something that is particularly difficult for online sales. Off-line customers can avoid creating an audit trail by paying cash for their purchases, but consumer anonymity is almost impossible online, where transactions usually involve credit cards and shipping addresses.

"This has certainly had a chilling effect on us, and our customers," said Bevis.[28]

Even before the Patriot Act, Bevis had been served with an FBI subpoena seeking more than six years of customer data in connection with an investigation of Democratic Senator Robert Torricelli. Bevis fought the subpoena until the

FBI dropped its demand, but the legal battle and the subsequent passage of the Patriot Act convinced him to stop collecting customer data. "Unfortunately, that restricts our ability to serve our customers," he said. "We've had to stop customer follow-on contact, we've disabled the software that tracks customer purchases—all the things that turn a transaction into a continuing customer relationship."

The Arundel Books web site pledges to "NEVER sell, trade, or otherwise disclose ANY information regarding our customers to any person, organization, or government entity, unless fraud is involved."[29]

Christopher Kelley, an analyst with a technology consulting firm, believes that concerns about the Patriot Act will spread throughout the retail market. "Depending on how far the government goes, the issue will be so much broader than books and movies," he said. "Think about hardware stores and other places where terrorists might buy things. This has the potential to explode into an issue that would impact a lot of retailers and consumers."[30]

FBI Advice and Reassurance

On June 21, 2003, Chuck Rosenberg, counsel to FBI Director Robert Mueller, met with a small group of librarians at the ALA's annual conference, held in Toronto, as a joint conference of the ALA and the Canadian Library Association. Rosenberg was cordial and responsive to questions from the assembled librarians, although his defense of the Patriot Act and law enforcement visits to libraries seemed like boilerplate pronouncements. One area in which he did provide useful insight was the issue of what librarians should expect from agents who visit their libraries.

Rosenberg acknowledged "the apprehension about what we are and what we are doing," but he pointed out that the FBI represents a relatively small proportion of the 750,000 law enforcement officers in the United States. "Not everybody who walks into your library and flashes a badge is necessarily FBI," he said.[31]

Several librarians expressed confusion and concern over the ambiguity surrounding law enforcement visits to libraries. How can we be sure what agency is represented and what authority is being exercised? How can we recognize whether it is the Patriot Act, FISA, or some other legal authority? How do we know if there is a gag order accompanying the visit?

Rosenberg began by describing the proliferation of fake FBI badges available on the Internet:

Ebay has thrown them off, because they're illegal to sell, but other auction sites have popped up, and you can very easily buy something that looks like my credentials. Sometimes they're pretty good. So any legitimate agent, FBI, state or local, absolutely should afford you the time and courtesy to check them out and give you a number at which to do it.

It's hard to tell what a real badge looks like without comparing it to a fake one. When an agent comes to your library, they should be dressed as I am dressed [coat and tie], they should identify themselves, they should show you their badge and their credentials, hopefully privately and discreetly. And you have every right to ask them for proof that they are who they say they are.

If they have a search warrant, they should hand you a piece of paper that should look official and is signed by a clerk of the federal district court out of which it was issued. It may not be something that you have ever seen before, so perhaps it's something that Emily [Sheketoff] and her office [ALA Washington Office] could circulate. A state search warrant could look very different. A grand jury subpoena would look yet again different.[32]

When I told Mr. Rosenberg that many agents who visits libraries are vague in describing the court order or authority, if any, under which they request records, he responded,

I cannot tell you why a particular agent may not know the parameters of the order that he is handing you. They may not be sure themselves. Many of our agents are lawyers, but most are not. They all receive training, excellent training, but this is a very confusing area of the law. Even as a federal prosecutor, I'm always opening the Code book, even to re-read provisions I've read many times before. So it's probably best to seek guidance from counsel, or if you're a county librarian, from your county attorney, or if in a university, from the university general counsel. Let them make that call. We shouldn't be doing it. The FBI should not be providing legal advice to people to whom we are issuing subpoenas. I hope we're not doing that. It's entirely possible that the agent is not all that sure himself.[33]

A number of librarians asked Mr. Rosenberg about "consent searches," searches and seizures of library records without a court order. One librarian noted that an FBI "request" for library compliance can often seem like a demand, especially to a teenage student manning a circulation desk late at night. Rosenberg explained that most law enforcement agents, including FBI, use consent searches every day.

You're driving on the New Jersey Turnpike and an officer stops your car, asks if he may search the trunk of your car, and you say yes. When they search the trunk, that's a consent search. So the fact that someone came to your library and said, "We'd like to have access to your records," is not illegal or even improper. And the fact that you may have said, "I'd feel more comfortable if you got a subpoena or court order," is your right.[34]

When the questioner repeated the claim that library staff, particularly student assistants, may interpret an FBI request as a demand, Rosenberg answered,

> I hope they're not demanding consent searches, which strikes me as a bit of an oxymoron. I'm in the FBI, and I can tell you that if two guys showed up at my door and flashed a badge and credentials at me, that would be intimidating. So I can imagine what it must be for some kid working at a circulation desk at nine o'clock at night. . . . I hope if there's a problem like that, you would notify the local FBI office. One thing we try very hard to do is to be responsive, because part of our job is community outreach.[35]

Another librarian wondered if law enforcement could help out library staff by "reading them their rights," something comparable to Miranda rights but with respect to a librarian's right to deny a request for records and to insist on a court order. Rosenberg responded,

> What triggers your Miranda rights are 1) custody, and 2) interrogation. It is that custodial interrogation that triggers the requirement that a subject be given Miranda rights. So, as a matter of law, an FBI agent walking into a library and confronting an 18-year-old at the desk, it's not custody, so there's absolutely no legal requirement that he be Mirandized. It may not be completely satisfactory, but as law, there's no requirement for our agents to do that.[36]

When the librarian asked whether the FBI was complying with the "spirit of the law," Rosenberg answered, "You can inform your employees that if there's a contact with law enforcement authorities, they should politely tell them that they need to speak with a manager or director. I don't think anybody in law enforcement would quarrel with that."[37]

On a related topic, one librarian asked whether an FBI agent requesting library records in a state with a library confidentiality law was soliciting an illegal act. Rosenberg responded, "That's an interesting question. I don't know what the privacy laws are in each of the 50 states, but in terms of what your employee does when someone comes and asks for records at nine o'clock at night, the best thing for you to do is talk to your county attorney or university counsel about what your obligations are and what your state privacy law permits you to do."[38]

The librarian persisted, asking, "Doesn't the FBI have some responsibility here not to be asking library employees to perform illegal acts?"

Rosenberg seemed unsure of himself:

I've never thought of the problem quite in that way. What my sense of it is, from my FBI agent's perspective, is that they are merely asking for consent. They have an obligation to enforce federal law, but they must also comply with the laws of the state that they are in. As I have said earlier, you have the right to tell the agent that under state law you cannot provide the records without a subpoena. And if the agents are rude or obstreperous, we need to know that. We need to have well-informed agents and well-informed employees.[39]

Documenting Those Elusive Federal Visits to Libraries

Given the gag orders associated with the Patriot Act, the only way for the library profession to document law enforcement visits to libraries was through impersonal surveys, which identified neither the library nor the librarian involved. Leading the way in such research was Leigh Estabrook, director of the Library Research Center at the University of Illinois, Urbana-Champaign. In December 2001, Estabrook sent questionnaires titled "Public Libraries' Response to the Events of September 11th" to 1,503 public libraries in the United States. The questionnaire covered a broad range of service and security issues and included several questions related to the Patriot Act and library surveillance.

To the question "Have authorities (e.g., FBI, police) requested any information about your patrons pursuant to the events of September 11th?," 4.1% of all respondents answered yes, while 11.2% of the larger libraries answered yes. A clear majority of respondents said they had heard or read about the Patriot Act, and 72.2% of the larger libraries said they had.[40]

Estabrook's second library survey, conducted in October 2002 under the title "Public Libraries' Response to the Events of 9/11/2001: One Year Later," inquired much more extensively into government surveillance of libraries and the profession's response to it. (See Appendix A for full survey.) The responses to the questionnaire made it immediately clear that libraries felt forced to accommodate the new realities of the Patriot Act. Of the 1,505 directors of public libraries to whom the questionnaires were sent, 8.7% said they were more likely to monitor the kinds of materials people are checking out, and 18.9% said there were circumstances in which it would be necessary to compromise the privacy of patron records.[41]

To the question "Has your library adopted or changed any policies in response to the passage of the USA Patriot Act?," 7.2% answered yes, 78.3% said no, and 14.5% said they were in the process of developing policies. Sixty percent of respondents said they had instructed their staff on the provisions of the Patriot Act and how to respond to a search warrant or subpoena, and 7.1% said they had received expressions of concern from patrons about the Patriot Act.[42]

The most startling aspect of Estabrook's new survey was the ease with which it succeeded in providing statistical data on government visits to libraries, even when those visits were cloaked in gag orders. To the question, "In the year preceding September 11, 2001, about how many requests about your patrons did you receive from authorities such as the FBI, INS, or police officers?," 10.3% answered 1; 3.4% said 2–5; and 0.1% said 6–10.[43]

To the question "Have authorities (e.g., FBI, INS, police officers) requested information about any of your patrons since Sept. 11, 2001?," 10.7% said yes. Over 80% of those who had been visited by authorities said they had received only one request for information; 18.1% said there had been 2–5 requests; and 0.6% said there had been 6–10 requests. Respondents said 32.6% of such requests were by the FBI; 68.2% by the police; 0.6% by the INS; 0.6% by the Secret Service; and 7.6% by other.[44]

As to the kinds of information requested by authorities, respondents said 5.6% of requested information was about specific library materials (e.g., a list of patrons who borrowed a specific book); 76% was about a specific patron (e.g., a list of books borrowed or Web sites visited by a particular person); and 22.3% was about other information.[45]

Respondents described the form of the government's requests as the following: verbal request for voluntary cooperation (83.1%); written request for voluntary cooperation (8.9%); subpoena (22.3%); and court order (17.4%). About half of the respondents said they had cooperated with the requests. Of the 17.4% who were presented with court orders, 3.1% had a gag order imposed. In particular, 10.3% of the respondents said court orders issued to them referenced Section 215 of the Patriot Act or Title 50, Section 1862 of the U.S. Code. Two-thirds of the libraries served with such orders said they received 2–5 of them, while the other one-third said they received only one such order.[46]

When asked if they had declined to answer fully those portions of the questionnaire dealing with the Patriot Act "because you believe you are legally prohibited from doing so," 2.6% said yes. When asked if their library staff had ever voluntarily reported patron records and/or behavior to outside authorities like the FBI or police on matters related to terrorism, 4.1% said yes; 8.3% said patrons had reported other patrons to the library or outside authorities. When asked if they thought the gag rule imposed by the Patriot Act was an abridgement of First Amendment rights, 59.9% of respondents said yes.[47]

The questionnaire concluded by asking, "If law enforcement officials asked you for information about one of your patrons and ordered you not to disclose that they had asked for information, would you challenge their order by disclosing the request to anyone . . . other than your library's attorney?" Respondents answered as follows[48]:

Definitely would...5.5%
Probably would 16.1%
Probably would not 53.7%
Definitely would not 21.4%
Depends, no clear answer..1.0%
Refused to answer question.....................................1.0%
Don't know...1.3%

Despite the ground-breaking revelations in Estabrook's surveys, there remained significant gaps in the public's knowledge of library surveillance. For one thing, Estabrook had sent her questionnaires only to *public* libraries, leaving all colleges and universities unexamined. Also, because the success of the surveys depended upon the anonymity of the respondents, no light was shed on what libraries the FBI had visited and what librarians had cooperated.

A more recent survey conducted by the California Library Association in September 2003 covered fewer libraries (344) than the University of Illinois study, but included public, academic, school and special libraries, as well as library schools.[49] Among the survey's seventeen questions were:

Has your library instituted any new policies as a result of the USA PATRIOT Act?

Yes...140 (41%)
No...201 (59%)

What privacy related procedures does your library perform on a routine basis? Check all that apply.

Shredding paper documents, such as
   computer sign-in sheets.....................................223 (78%)
Deleting computer files, such as logs,
   proxy caches..208 (73%)

But the most interesting questions concerned FBI visits to libraries:

Has your library had any informal contact from the FBI since September 11, 2001?

Yes...16 (5%)
No...304 (95%)

If your library had informal contact from the FBI, did your library comply with its requests?

Yes...6 (3%)
No..31 (13%)
Not Applicable 198 (84%)
                                               235 (100%)

Has your library had any formal contact from the FBI since September 11, 2001?

Yes...14 (4%)
No...298 (96%)

If your library had formal contact from the FBI since September 11, 2001, did you comply with their requests?

Yes...11 (5%)
No..15 (6%)
Not Applicable 217 (89%)
243 (100%)

Though it was not made explicit in the CLA survey, "formal" contacts were presumably those accompanied by court orders, and "informal" contacts presumably were not. Karen Schneider, chair of the CLA Intellectual Freedom Committee, oversaw the survey and said she set up the survey so respondents didn't provide personal information, thus shielding librarians from federal prosecution under Section 215 of the Patriot Act.

Schneider said she found it "highly unlikely" that the FBI had not requested information under Section 215 of the Patriot Act.[50] She explained: "On the formal visits we left it intentionally vague. We set up the survey so we would not receive personal information. This not only protects the respondents but protects us as well. The government is not going to be able to come after us and get personal information because we haven't gathered it. We also steered clear of FISA or Section 215 questions. To some extent, that was to build the confidence of respondents, but I would not be surprised if some of those authorities were used within the formal visits documented. I didn't expect so many libraries to actually reveal that they had experienced formal government visits."[51]

If the Justice Department were more forthcoming with Congress and the public on the use of its surveillance tools in libraries, there would be no need to rely on anonymous surveys. The closest the Justice Department has come to a public accounting of its post-9/11 visits to libraries came in a May 20, 2003, report to Congress and a subsequent briefing by assistant attorney general Viet Dinh, John Ashcroft's point man on the Patriot Act. As described in a front-page *New York Times* article, the sixty-page report showed that federal agents had conducted hundreds of bugging and surveillance operations and had visited numerous libraries and mosques using the new powers of the Patriot Act.[52]

In his briefing to the House Judiciary Committee, Viet Dinh revealed that federal agents had contacted about fifty libraries nationwide, but he claimed that this was often at the invitation of librarians who saw something suspicious. Justice Department officials said the relatively small numbers showed that agents were using their new powers sparingly, but librarians later said they believe libraries have been contacted much more frequently than Dinh's figures suggested.

About two weeks after Dinh's briefing to Congress, Barbara Comstock, the Justice Department's director of public affairs, issued a press release challenging the *Times* report that federal agents had contacted about fifty libraries "in the course of terrorism investigations." The press release quoted portions of Dinh's testimony which said most of the library contacts were related to criminal, rather than national, security cases. Figures on the latter are classified.

> *Rep. Chabot*: Can you tell us how many times, if at all, library records have been accessed under the new FISA standards in the USA PATRIOT Act? And if they have been so accessed, have the requests been confined to the records of a specified person?

> *AAG Dinh*: Chairman, Section 215 of the USA PATRIOT Act, requires the Department of Justice to submit semi-annual reports to this committee and also to the House Intelligence Committee and the Senate counterparts on the number of times and the manner in which that section was used in total. We have made those reports. Unfortunately, because they occur in the context of national security investigation, that information is classified.
>
> We have made, in light of the recent public information concerning visits to the library, we have conducted an informal survey of the field offices, relating to visits to libraries. And I think the results from this informal survey is that libraries have been contacted approximately 50 times, based on articulable suspicion or voluntary calls from libraries regarding suspicious activities. Most, if not all, of these contacts that we have identified were made in the context of a criminal investigation and pursuant to voluntary disclosure or a grand jury subpoena, in that context.[53]

The fact that Dinh used the phrase "most, if not all" left open the question of how many of the fifty library visits were conducted under the Patriot Act.

Whereas Patriot Act warrants served on libraries are cloaked in gag orders, FBI visits to libraries under traditional court orders, or no court order at all, can still be discussed and documented openly. Some of the public accounts of such visits in the post-9/11 climate suggest that librarians may be adjusting to a "new reality," as was indicated in the Estabrook survey. The most controversial example of library accommodation to these new realities came in Delray Beach, Florida, shortly after 9/11 when a public librarian called local police to report that several men using the library's computers resembled the publicized photos of the suspected World Trade Center terrorists. The police promptly notified the FBI, who obtained a court order and seized two computers thought to have been used by the suspects.

Kathleen Hensman, the librarian at the Delray Beach Public Library, said she was aware of the Florida law that protects the privacy of library patrons, but said "people have a right to know that terrorists were here in our library using our public facilities."

Hensman's decision to call the police sparked considerable debate within the library profession. Most librarians seemed to support Hensman's decision to cooperate fully with law enforcement in their investigation of the suspects, but felt that she should not have initiated the investigation by reporting on patrons.

Still, even Judith Krug, director of the ALA's Office for Intellectual Freedom, admitted, "I would have felt better if she had followed Florida law . . . [but] I suspect most people faced with the same situation would have done what she did."[54]

A similar situation in the Howard County, Maryland, public libraries shortly after 9/11 produced a more reasoned and appropriate response. Law enforcement agents came to library director Valerie J. Gross, stating that they were conducting a terrorism investigation. They showed her photos of a particular individual and asked if he had been seen in the library. At this point, the director and her staff, along with the Library's attorney, debated the requirements of state law and library ethics.

"We went back and forth on this issue, trying to decide whether the information was protected by our code," said Gross. "They were not asking about what a customer was reading or requesting customer information in our records. We thought it was more analogous to a situation where a crime is committed, someone runs through our library, and we're asked if he had been there. We decided that these were different times, and we must make every effort to cooperate. So, under these circumstances, we thought it was all right to answer, 'Yes.' "[55]

Some time later, Gross's response to another law enforcement inquiry about a customer showed that she was offering them no blank check. When an agent asked Gross to check the library's records for a customer's address, she politely refused. "We told them, if you want this information you will need to obtain a court order," recalled Gross. "They were incredulous, asking why they would need a court order for something like this, asserting that what they were requesting is not protected information. I respectfully told them that it was an issue of privacy and intellectual freedom, that we were following our board policy as well as state law. As it turned out, they never sought a court order, because they were able to find the requested address from a simple Internet search."[56]

But how would Gross handle a Patriot Act visit with its dreaded gag order? "It may be entirely appropriate to talk about the fact that information was requested of us, but not to disclose who was the subject of the inquiry, what the requested information was, or even which library branch was involved," said Gross. "In my opinion, the simple fact that a visit occurred should not be prohibited by a gag order."

Gross concluded, "Until we've received a search warrant under the Foreign Intelligence Surveillance Act, it's a non-issue for us. Should we be served with such a warrant, I will follow our attorney's advice concerning the gag order."[57]

Since the passage of the Patriot Act, uncertainty has grown among librarians about gag orders, how to recognize them, and how to respond to them. Many librarians are beginning to assume that all FBI visits to libraries are conducted under the Patriot Act, requiring immediate compliance with requests for patron records and silence under a gag order. Judith Krug, director of the ALA's Office for Intellectual Freedom, says, "People are scared, and they think that by giving up their rights, especially their right to privacy, they will be safe. But it wasn't the right to privacy that let terrorists into our nation. It had nothing to do with libraries or library records."[58]

But despite gag orders, real and imagined, the occurrence of law enforcement visits to libraries under the Patriot Act can often be *inferred* from the negative responses of particular librarians. For example, in Florida, Broward County library director Sam Morrison acknowledged that the FBI had contacted his office, but he declined to elaborate on their request or how many branches were involved. "We've heard from them and that's all I can tell you," stated Morrison, who said the FBI specifically instructed him not to reveal any information about the request. In an earlier visit, the FBI had subpoenaed Morrison to provide information on the use of computer terminals by suspected terrorists.

Jean Purnell, dean of the library at Stockton, California's University of the Pacific, said she was uneasy when asked if any law enforcement agencies had requested records from her library. In response to the inquiry she said only, "That I cannot answer."[59]

Recognizing the effectiveness of using a negative to prove a positive, some librarians are doing an end run around Patriot Act gag orders by documenting the *absence* of FBI visits. Anne Turner, chief librarian in Santa Cruz, California, public libraries, describes the roundabout way in which she informs her library board of such visits. "At each board meeting I tell them we have not been served by any (Patriot Act search warrants). In any months that I don't tell them that, they'll know."[60]

During their June 19, 2003, board of trustees meeting, the Freedom to Read Foundation (FTRF) discussed the problem of intimidation and uncertainty among librarians visited by the FBI. When the FBI visits libraries, they have been, let us say, ambiguous in identifying the legal authority under which they request information. As a result, librarians often *assume* a Patriot Act visit with its accompanying gag order, even when that may not be the case.

Judith Krug told me, "We know there have been some law enforcement visits to libraries under the authority of the Patriot Act, but I don't think librarians are asking the right questions to identify which visits really are conducted under that authority. The agents who visit libraries are after information, and if a librarian assumes that the visit is under the Patriot Act, the agents are not going to dispel that notion. Knowing these agents and how they operate, they are not going to correct any inaccurate assumption about who they are, what they are doing, and how they are doing it. In addition, we in the library profession have not done a good job of getting out to librarians information about the various kinds of court orders that they may receive and sample copies of each of these orders."[61]

Krug then promised to provide such copies to me for inclusion in this book, and they appear as Appendices C–F.

A good example of the legal ambiguity surrounding FBI visits to libraries can be seen in the Hartford, Connecticut, public libraries. In November 2002, Bill Olds, a reporter for the prestigious *Hartford Courant*, the oldest continuing newspaper in the country, asked local librarians if they had been presented with warrants or other court orders for FBI surveillance. He received predictably evasive answers.

"I can't disclose that we were presented with anything," responded Louise Blalock, Hartford's head librarian. "I cannot answer that question," responded Nancy Billings, the library's technical services manager. Billings did, nevertheless, confirm that in recent months the FBI had made two visits to the Hartford library during which there were discussions about "computer-related information." Billings concluded, "The library is now working on a public notice that it can't guarantee that there isn't third-party monitoring" of library computers.[62]

Olds then proceeded to report on a new FBI surveillance technique that uses special software to allow the FBI to copy a library patron's Internet use and e-mail messages. He concluded the article with a warning to library users concerning ongoing surveillance. "There's no way you're going to be able to find out," he said. "The librarians can't tell you, and you're not going to spot the special software in the computers. Even if the software hasn't been installed, there's a back door for the FBI to tap in through. The Internet service providers . . . are required to cooperate with the authorities, and spy software can be installed at that end."[63]

On November 7, 2002, the *Hartford Courant* issued a retraction on Bill Olds' story after Michael Wolf, the state's most senior FBI agent, publicly declared that the Bureau had used a traditional search warrant, not a FISA order, to seize evidence from a specific computer in the Hartford system that had been used to "hack" into a business computer system in California. Wolf said that no bugging software had been installed on any computer in the library. Hartford Public Library Director Louise Blalock said that she had been requested by the FBI not to discuss the inquiry, but had not been served with a formal gag order. Still, she said, "I don't think I could have said that this has nothing to do with the Patriot Act."[64]

Chris Finan, president of the American Booksellers Foundation for Free Expression, says bookstores are also uncertain about Patriot Act visits. "To date, no bookseller has contacted us to request legal assistance in connection with a court order issued under the Patriot Act. However, because of the gag provision, we cannot be sure there have not been any."[65]

Gag Orders

The confusion surrounding FBI visits to libraries under the Patriot Act derives from the uncertainty about whether there is a legal gag order associated with the visits or whether the agents have simply "requested" that libraries avoid discussing the matter with others. Often the confusion is exacerbated by ambiguity in the law and in the way in which visiting agents represent the law. The gag order associated with Section 215 of the Patriot Act states that once librarians or bookstore owners turn over requested information, they are prohibited from disclosing "to any other person (other than those persons necessary to produce the tangible things under this section) that the Federal Bureau of Investigation has sought or obtained tangible things under this section."[66]

First Amendment author Nat Hentoff points out that gag orders are imposed by judges on prosecution and defense attorneys, as well as the press, in certain cases where, for example, classified information must be protected or a witness might be in danger. "But, whenever that happens," says Hentoff, "the press can expose that the gag order has been imposed and can contest it in open court. However, under this particular provision of the U.S.A. Patriot Act, there has never before, to my knowledge, been so rigid a gag order in First Amendment history."[67]

The problem is not just the Patriot Act gag order. It is the ambiguity surrounding the imposition of that order. When Chuck Rosenberg, counsel to FBI Director Robert Mueller, met with librarians at the 2003 ALA conference in Toronto, I asked him if law enforcement agents who visit libraries could be more explicit in describing their legal authority and the librarians' obligations, particularly with respect to gag orders. Rosenberg answered, "I want to point out that the gag order provisions that you refer to were not created by the Patriot Act and are not unique to National Security Letters (NSLs). There are [gag order] provisions in the Federal Code that predate the Patriot Act. . . . In the banking part of the Code, certain subpoenas or court orders issued to banks may not be disclosed to the customer of the bank whose information is being sought. Similarly, in Title 18 of the Criminal Code, orders for wire taps cannot be disclosed. So by no means is it exclusive to the Patriot Act or the NSLs."[68]

At this point, another librarian asked whether a librarian under a gag order was allowed to discuss the visit with "someone like your employer or your member of Congress." Rosenberg responded, "Well, I don't see how you could or should disclose it to your member of Congress. The idea behind it is to protect the confidentiality of an ongoing investigation. We've learned in law enforcement that when you tell the target of an investigation that you're subpoenaing his bank or his pen register information, the investigations don't tend to go so well. So the gag order is not so much an attempt to gag the phone company or the bank or the librarian or the recipient of the order, as it is to protect the integrity of the investigation. Secrecy is, at times, not just important, but imperative."[69]

I pointed out to Rosenberg that gag orders on librarians seemed to extend far beyond the length of an investigation. If the gag order is not an attempt to silence the librarian, but only to "protect the integrity of the investigation," as Rosenberg had claimed, why were librarians being silenced in perpetuity? This produced a brief interaction between Rosenberg and myself.

> *Rosenberg*: Herb, it may be slightly apples and oranges. I'm convinced the gag order was not aimed at libraries. It was intended in the same way that prohibitions on disclosure are used in other places in the Federal Code, as I mentioned. So I don't think it's in any way aimed at libraries.

Foerstel: But when do they end?

Rosenberg: They don't necessarily end, because the purpose behind them is to protect the integrity of an ongoing investigation.

Foerstel: So when the investigation ends, librarians should be able to speak freely of the visit?

Rosenberg: I don't think that's the case.

Foerstel: I don't either.

Rosenberg: Nor do I think it should be, and I'll tell you why. In the grand jury context, for instance, grand jury proceedings are secret, and the intent is that they remain secret in perpetuity.

Foerstel: That's what I was afraid of.

Rosenberg: Let's agree to disagree on this answer.[70]

At this point, Rosenberg explained that the real reason for imposing a gag order in perpetuity was to protect the privacy of the target of an investigation. I asked, "So the gag order is not intended to protect the agency, just the privacy of individuals under investigation?" Rosenberg answered, "Yes."

"And you expect us to believe that?" I asked, at which point Rosenberg said he would eat a good meal and have a good night's sleep whether I believed him or not.[71]

Given the gag orders imposed on federal visits to libraries under the new authority of the Patriot Act, how can the library profession document the extent of FBI intrusions on library confidentiality? "That's what I find particularly frightening about the whole thing," said Dale Thompson, director of the Providence, Rhode Island, Public Library. "We can't let them know."[72]

Bookstore owners feel the same concern. "It's one of the scariest things to come down the pike," said Sarah Zack, owner of Books on the Square in Providence. "If the FBI wants information we have, they can have it. And we can't complain about it. We can't inform the people about it. We have no legal recourse. . . . It's beyond me that we are living in a country in which something major happens to you and you can't say a thing. I don't think of the United States like that."[73]

Chris Morrow, general manager of a Vermont bookstore, said the Patriot Act's gag order was of particular concern. "As it reads, we're not supposed to call a lawyer, which is completely unconstitutional," he said. "We couldn't talk about it with our staff, customers or the press."[74]

Other librarians express confidence in the grapevine, saying even a gag order cannot prevent word of an FBI visit from getting out. In March 2003, Deborah Barchi, director of the Barrington, Rhode Island, Public Library, said that in tiny Rhode Island it would be difficult to keep a lid on news of an FBI search under the Patriot Act. "I don't think it's happened [here]," she said. "I think I would be aware. I don't know many people who meet as much as librarians. . . . Somehow, the rest of us would have known."[75]

A small cadre of dedicated librarians advocates going beyond the furtive grapevine by openly challenging the legality of the gag order. Recall that the Estabrook survey revealed that 21.6% of the public library directors who received questionnaires said that if the FBI visited their library and requested patron records under the Patriot Act, they "definitely" or "probably" would challenge the gag order "by disclosing the request" to "the patron, the press, and/or a public interest organization such as the ACLU."

Where are these bold librarians who would risk a lengthy prison sentence in order to assert their First Amendment rights? On October 28, 2002, *Newsweek* magazine ran a story under the headline "Librarians Keep Quiet," in which it described the library profession's silent and sullen acceptance of the Patriot Act's gag rule:

> [T]he ACLU has been searching for a librarian who doesn't want to co-operate and is willing to serve as a test case in the courts. . . . Yet despite widespread outrage among librarians, so far no one has come forward, and the statute remains untested in the courts. The search for Conan the Librarian continues. There's little chance that the role will be filled by the nation's most famous librarian: Laura Bush.[76]

Notes

1. Alisa Solomon, "Things We Lost in the Fire," *Village Voice.com*, September 11–17, 2002, p. 5.

2. Sarah Whalen, "Secret Saudi History," *Portside*, August 12, 2003. www.portside.org.

3. Becca MacLaren, "Sanders Introduces 'Freedom to Read Protection Act,' " *The Advocate*, March 14, 2002, p. 3. http://bernie.house.gov/documents/articles/20030319102732.asp.

4. *Flashpoints USA*, Public Television series premiere, July 15, 2003, WETA, Washington, D.C.

5. "Calif. Libraries Warn Patrons about Government Monitoring," *Washington Post*, March 12, 2003, p. A22.

6. Ibid.

7. Sam Stanton, "Librarians Step Up," *Sacramento Bee*, September 22, 2003, p. 1. www.sacbee.com/content/politics/v-print/story/7463141p-8405751c.html

8. Michael Neary, "Guilford Librarian Supports Free Thought, Study—Despite USAPA," *Brattleboro Reformer*, February 27, 2003, p. 1. www.reformer.com/Stories/0,1413,102~8862~1207927,00.html.

9. Ibid.

10. Ibid.

11. "Grass Roots Protest Ideas," *ALA Intellectual Freedom Discussion List*, June 24–25, 2002. www.mjfreedman.org/currentissues/Grassrootsprotestideas.pdf.

12. "ACLU State Chapters Launch Campaign to Warn Patrons about Patriot Act," American Libraries Online, August 4, 2003. www.ala.org/alonline

13. "Five *Technically* Legal Signs for Your Library," June 23, 2003. www.cocoscomer.com/archives/000088.html or www.librarian.net/technicality.html.

14. "Libraries Warn of FBI Spying," *Newsletter on Intellectual Freedom*, May 2003, p. 94.

15. Dean E. Murphy, "Librarians Use Shredder to Show Opposition to New F.B.I. Powers," *New York Times*, April 7, 2003, p. A12.

16. "ACLU State Chapters Launch Campaign to Warn Patrons about Patriot Act," American Libraries Online, August 4, 2003. www.ala.org/alonline

17. Sam Stanton, "Librarians Step Up," *Sacramento Bee*, September 22, 2003, p. 1.

18. Ibid.

19. American Library Association, January 23, 2003. www.ala.org/alaorg/oif/guidelineslibrary.html.

20. Memorandum from Valerie J. Gross, director, Howard County Libraries, to the library staff, 2002.

21. Murphy, "Librarians Use Shredder to Show Opposition to New FBI Powers," p. A12.

22. Question by Rep. Jeff Flake (R-AZ) and answer by Attorney General John Ashcroft at hearing on the USA PATRIOT Act, U.S. House of Representatives, Committee on the Judiciary, June 5, 2003. Transcribed from live cable TV broadcast on C-SPAN, June 5, 2003.

23. "Is It Legal," *Newsletter on Intellectual Freedom*, January 2003, p. 25.

24. Jeff Ballinger, "Opening the Book on Libraries," *San Luis Obispo Tribune*, January 11, 2003, p. 1.

25. Ibid.

26. "FBI Begins Visiting Libraries," *Newsletter on Intellectual Freedom*, September 2002, p. 239.

27. Brian C. Jones, "Under Siege," *Phoenix.com Features*, March 28, 2003, p. 6. www.providencephoenix.com/archive/features/03/03/20/LIBRARY.html.

28. Bob Tedeschi, "Patriot Act Curbing Data Retention," *New York Times.com*, October 13, 2003. www.nytimes.com/2003/10/13/technology/13ecom.html?ex=1067053712&ei=1&en=340628b407904a69.

29. Ibid.

30. Ibid.

31. Chuck Rosenberg, counsel to FBI Director Robert Mueller, Remarks at the American Library Association Annual Conference, Washington Office Update, June 21, 2003, Toronto, Canada.

32. Ibid.

33. Ibid.

34. Ibid.

35. Ibid.

36. Ibid.

37. Ibid.

38. Ibid.

39. Ibid.

40. "Public Libraries' Response to the Events of September 11th," Library Research Center, University of Illinois at Urbana-Champaign, December 4, 2001, p. 6. www.lis.uiuc.edu/gslis/research/national.pdf.

41. "Public Libraries' Response to the Events of 9/11/2001: One Year Later," Library Research Center, University of Illinois at Urbana-Champaign, October 2002, p. 1. www.lis.uiuc.edu/gslis/research/finalresults.pdf.

42. Ibid., pp. 1–2.

43. Ibid., p. 2.

44. Ibid., pp. 2–3.

45. Ibid., p. 3.

46. Ibid., p. 3.

47. Ibid., p. 4.

48. Ibid., p. 6.

49. A text copy of the CLA survey can be found in Appendix B of this book.

50. Sam Stanton and Emily Bazar, "Librarians Step Up," *Sacramento Bee*, September 22, 2003, p. 1.

51. Author interview with Karen Schneider, California Library Association, October 20, 2003.

52. Eric Lichtblau, "Justice Dept. Lists Use of New Power to Fight Terror," *New York Times*, May 21, 2003, p. A1.

53. "Statement of Barbara Comstock, Director of Public Affairs, on DOJ Testimony Regarding Libraries," Department of Justice, June 2, 2003. www.usdoj.gov/opa/pr/2003/June/03_opa_323.html.

54. "Delray Beach Florida," *Newsletter on Intellectual Freedom*, January 2002, p. 35.

55. Author interview with Valerie J. Gross, director, Howard County Libraries, August 21, 2003.

56. Ibid.

57. Ibid.

58. Ibid.

59. "Librarians Grapple with Civil Liberties," *The Record*, March 19, 2003, p. 2. www.recordnet.com/daily/news/articles/031903-gn-2.php.

60. Bob Egelko and Maria Gaura, "Librarians Try to Alter Patriot Act," *San Francisco Chronicle*, March 10, 2003, p. 3. www.sfgate.com/cgi-bin/article.cgi?file=/c/a/2003/3/10/LIBRARIES.TMP.

61. Author interview with Judith Krug, executive director, Freedom to Read Foundation, July 31, 2003.

62. Ibid.

63. Bill Olds, "The FBI Has Bugged Our Public Libraries," *Hartford Courant*, November 3, 2002, p. 2.

64. "Did FBI Bug Hartford Library? Nope," *Library Journal*, November 11, 2002. http://libraryjournal.reviewsnews.com/index.asp?layout=article&articleid=CA258072.

65. Ibid., p. 3.

66. USA PATRIOT Act, Public Law 107-56. www.politechbot.com/docs/usa.act.final.102401.html.

67. Nat Hentoff, "The FBI Among the Bookshelves," *Jewish World Review*, February 25, 2002, pp. 2–3. www.jewishworldreview.com/cols/hentoff022502.asp.

68. Chuck Rosenberg, counsel to FBI Director Robert Mueller, remarks at the American Library Association Annual Conference, Washington Office Update, June 21, 2003, Toronto, Canada.

69. Ibid.

70. Ibid.

71. Ibid.

72. Jones, "Under Siege," p. 2.

73. Ibid., p. 5.

74. MacLaren, "Sanders Introduces 'Freedom to Read Protection Act,' " p. 2.

75. Jones, "Under Siege," p. 5.

76. Adam Piore, "Librarians Keep Quiet," *Newsweek*, October 28, 2002, p. 12.

Chapter 4

Making Things Worse:
Government Actions Beyond the Patriot Act

Executive Orders, Regulations,
and Administrative Guidelines

As the criticism of the Patriot Act grows from liberals and conservatives alike, the question arises: How could Congress have voted so overwhelmingly for such flawed legislation? Democratic Rep. John Conyers explained in Chapter 2 that most of those who voted for the Patriot Act had never read it. But conservative Bob Barr, former Republican congressman from Georgia, explains his vote and those of his colleagues somewhat differently. "Something that neither I nor the others knew at the time was the extent to which the government would use the Patriot Act for non-terrorism investigations. Second, we really didn't have any inkling at the time of exactly how far the government would go with other programs that when added on top of the Patriot Act present a very oppressive, privacy-invasive move on the part of the government. So now, after two years, if you look back at what the Patriot Act has done in conjunction with all of these other powers, . . . it becomes much more problematic than it appeared to us two years ago."[1]

Indeed, the total package of invasive federal power that was assembled during 2002 and 2003 is what makes the Patriot Act so fearsome. And we should have known it was coming. Shortly after the passage of the Patriot Act, Justice Department spokesperson Mindy Tucker warned, "This is just the first step. There will be additional items to come."[2] Since then, numerous legislative and non-legislative extensions of executive power have been inspired by the Patriot Act, most of them related to government secrecy and surveillance and many of them affecting libraries.

In the wake of the terrorist attacks on New York City and the Pentagon, Attorney General John Ashcroft reversed previous Justice Department guidelines on compliance with the Freedom of Information Act (FOIA) by notifying executive agencies that they should resist FOIA requests whenever possible, regardless of whether disclosure of the information might prove harmful or not. The Justice Department assured all agencies that it would litigate to support agency decisions to deny *any* information.

On October 31, 2001, the Justice Department published a new regulation authorizing prison officials to monitor communications between detainees and their lawyers. This new authority, which could be exercised without the need for a court order, went beyond what was granted by Congress just days before in the Patriot Act.

On November 13, 2001, President George Bush issued an executive order investing the government with the unprecedented power to try any noncitizen suspected of being a terrorist, or of aiding or harboring a terrorist, in a military tribunal rather than in a criminal court. The order was issued without congressional authorization or consultation, and it excluded any court review of the military proceedings. The Bush administration promptly declared that no U.S. court had jurisdiction to challenge the massive detentions at the U.S. military base in Guantanamo, Cuba, and claimed that those detainees could be held indefinitely and their names withheld from the public.

Another executive order issued in November 2001 limited the release of presidential documents from previous administrations, despite the fact that public availability of those documents appeared to be mandated by statute. Librarians and historians protested that the Bush order will deny researchers the information necessary to document presidential history.

A succession of executive agency guidelines beginning in late 2001 restricted the amount of information available to the public on agency web sites, even though the majority of this information had little or nothing to do with terrorism. As American libraries rely increasingly on electronic information, they find essential government information denied to their patrons.

In 2002 Attorney General Ashcroft created an interagency task force to consider legal and administrative penalties for those who leak classified information to the media. Media organizations warned that such actions would discourage whistle-blowers and undermine government accountability.

Of all the non-legislative federal initiatives put into effect since 9/11, the new *Attorney General Guidelines on the FBI* have most directly threatened library privacy and confidentiality. The revisions, issued on May 30, 2002, by Attorney General Ashcroft, removed a host of restraints from FBI agents, all justified in the name of fighting terrorism. In remarks that raised more than a few eyebrows, Ashcroft characterized the FBI as "the tireless protector of civil rights and civil liberties for all Americans," and he declared that, in response to September 11, "we in the FBI and the Department of Justice began a concerted effort to free the field agents . . . from the bureaucratic, organizational and operational restrictions and structures that hindered them from doing their jobs effectively."[3]

Unfortunately, many of the restrictions that Ashcroft removed from FBI agents were the ones that had been imposed in the wake of such shocking excesses as the COINTELPRO program and other domestic spying scandals. Many of the new guidelines suggested that the FBI would resume the practice of keeping dossiers on anyone expressing political dissent. The revisions also seem to be preparing the way for a new and improved Library Awareness Program.

The deceptively simple statement that FBI agents will now have clear authority to visit public places that are open to all Americans will open a Pandora's box of new surveillance since this new authority specifically includes visits to libraries and places of worship. As we saw in Chapter 1, the Bureau has always reserved the right to pursue their investigations wherever they may lead, including libraries. Indeed, proactive programs like the ill-fated Library Awareness Program have employed "fishing expeditions" in libraries where no investigative lead existed, but Ashcroft's new guidelines allow the Bureau to go beyond the intrusive inquiries of the Library Awareness Program by routinely posting undercover agents in libraries to observe and record the behavior of patrons.

Why did FBI guidelines in the past discourage agents from secretly frequenting libraries, churches, mosques, and temples? Shouldn't FBI agents have the same freedom to read and worship that is granted to all American citizens? The problem, of course, is one of intent, of purpose. The FBI is not entering libraries out of a love for books. The only reason an undercover agent will "hang out" in libraries is to spy secretly on other patrons, and a library inhabited by plain-clothed snoops quickly becomes a chilling place.

Let's take a closer look at the full package of new FBI guidelines. In his May 30 press conference, Ashcroft explained that shortly after 9/11 he authorized the FBI to waive existing guidelines in extraordinary cases to prevent and investigate terrorism, and he directed a top-to-bottom review of the old guidelines. The result of that review, he said, were the May 30 revisions, which reflect four overriding principles:

1. The war against terrorism is the central mission and highest priority of the FBI.

2. Terrorism prevention is the key objective under the revised guidelines.

3. Unnecessary procedural red tape must not interfere with the effective detection, investigation, and prevention of terrorist activities.

4. The FBI must draw proactively on all lawful sources of information to identify terrorist threats and activities.[4]

Ashcroft complained that the old guidelines frequently barred FBI field agents from taking the initiative to detect and prevent future terrorist acts unless the FBI was aware of possible criminal activity. "Under the current guidelines,

FBI investigators cannot surf the web the way you or I can," said Ashcroft as he announced the changes. "Nor can they simply walk into a public event or a public place to observe ongoing activities. They have no clear authority to use commercial data services that any business in America can use." The new guidelines, said Ashcroft, expand the scope of FBI investigations "to the full range of terrorist activities under the USA Patriot Act."[5]

Ashcroft concluded by reading from the new guidelines: "For the purpose of detecting or preventing terrorist activities, the FBI is authorized to visit any place and attend any event that is open to the public, on the same terms and conditions as members of the public generally."[6]

But, of course, the general public does not go to libraries in order to spy on their neighbors. Those are not the "terms and conditions" under which we attend libraries. Were ordinary citizens found to be surreptitiously to be monitoring the conversations and reading habits of fellow library patrons, they would likely be asked to leave the library, and I hope that undercover FBI agents will be similarly regarded as unwelcome intruders on library confidentiality.

The Fact Sheet provided by Ashcroft to accompany his May 30, 2002, comments explained, "The new guidelines clarify that FBI field agents may enter any public place that is open to other citizens, unless they are prohibited from doing so by the Constitution or federal statute, for the specific purpose of detecting or preventing terrorist activities."[7]

It was no oversight that state statutes were not included among the prohibitions on such FBI surveillance. Otherwise, every state in the nation would quickly pass local laws against FBI surveillance in libraries, just as forty-eight of our fifty states passed library confidentiality statutes in the wake of the Library Awareness Program. (Note: The only two states without such statutes, Kentucky and Hawaii, have state attorney general guidelines that protect library confidentiality in the same way. Currently, all such state protections are overridden by the Patriot Act and Ashcroft's FBI guidelines.)

Under the heading, "Enhancing Information Gathering," the guidelines expressly state that FBI agents may engage in online research on individuals and may use commercial "data-mining" services, such as those companies that track commercial transactions, including book purchases. The FBI has never been prohibited from surfing the Internet or using commercial data-mining services, but in the past, such activities had to be related to an investigation. Now, this high-tech snooping into the personal behavior of American citizens has become the basis for generating the suspicion of criminal conduct in the first place.

The Center for Democracy and Technology (CDT) warns, "The FBI will now be conducting fishing expeditions using the services of people who decide what catalogues to send you or what spam e-mail you will be interested in. The problem is, the direct marketers can only . . . mail you another credit card offer based on that information—the FBI can arrest you."[8]

Another of the disturbing changes in the FBI guidelines allows the surveillance of groups before evidence has been uncovered to justify an investigation.

The revised guidelines authorize a special agent in charge to initiate such "preliminary inquiries" for up to a year without the evidence required for an investigation. The new guidelines also remove previous restraints on investigations of religious or political groups.

Under the heading, "Protecting Constitutional Rights," the new guidelines offer what is intended to be a reassurance to the civil liberties community: "It is important that . . . investigations not be based solely on activities protected by the First Amendment or on the lawful exercise of any other rights secured by the Constitution or laws of the United States."[9]

Note the prominent inclusion of the word "solely" in describing constitutional rights. Thus, the new guidelines would allow FBI surveillance directed "partly," "primarily," or "overwhelmingly" against activities protected by the Constitution. This is hollow assurance indeed. It is no coincidence that this feeble excuse for constitutional protection is almost identical to what is offered in the Patriot Act.

Several civil liberties organizations have issued detailed critical analyses of the new FBI guidelines, and they have shown particular concern over the Bureau's expanded electronic surveillance powers. The CDT has published the most comprehensive of these analyses in which it states that Ashcroft's revisions are "predicated on misleading claims and unexamined justifications."[10]

Ashcroft's invocation of anti-terrorism as the justification for expanded domestic investigative authority is misleading because the Bureau traditionally investigates terrorist organizations like al Qaeda under separate foreign intelligence guidelines that are largely classified, and Ashcroft has *not* revised those guidelines. All of Ashcroft's revisions relate to the FBI's domestic law enforcement, not the international terrorism guidelines under which Osama bin Laden and al Qaeda were being investigated before September 11.

Three aspects of Ashcroft's revisions most concerned the CDT:

1. Expanded authority for the FBI to attend public meetings and events of domestic groups, without even a suspicion of criminal or terrorist activity, with little guidance on what can be recorded, and with no time limits on the retention of data

2. Indiscriminate data-mining of vast commercial databases containing personal information about citizens and organizations, with no criminal nexus, no guidelines on inferences to be drawn, no limits on the action that may be taken, no limits on the sharing of acquired information, and no time limits on retention

3. Decreased internal supervision and coordination during investigations, expanding the scope and duration of preliminary inquiries, encouraging the use of more intrusive techniques, and allowing such investigations to continue without internal review or independent scrutiny.[11]

The CDT notes that the most identifiable cause of the September 11 intelligence failure was the inability of the FBI and other intelligence agencies to interpret and use the vast information they already had. Therefore, concludes the CDT, the indiscriminate vacuuming of personal information authorized by the new guidelines "can only compound that defect."[12]

Indeed, the CDT maintains that the net result of Ashcroft's new program of surveillance will actually decrease homeland security: "An agent at every meeting sows distrust and suspicion and dries up sources of information. An agent behind every web page wastes resources on fishing expeditions. Moreover, the risk of chilling effects and infringement on civil liberties outweighs any ostensible gains in law enforcement."[13]

The CDT made a series of recommendations for congressional oversight of the new guidelines that are briefly summarized below.

1. Require prior FBI notice and congressional consultation before future changes to guidelines.

2. Require congressional consultation in producing guidelines for collection, use, disclosure, and retention of public event information and data-mining.

3. Require the General Accounting Office and the Justice Department's inspector general to analyze Attorney General Ashcroft's guidelines and submit to Congress public and classified reports on their (a) impact on free speech and privacy, (b) costs to the private sector, and (c) benefits and costs to national security.

4. Require public reporting of statistical information on issues such as

    a) Number and length of anti-terrorism inquiries under the guidelines

    b) Number of undercover visits to places of worship and public meetings

    c) Description of data-mining contracts and arrangements

    d) Number of individuals listed as suspected terrorists

    e) Use of intrusive techniques

    f) Number and duration of pen registers and trap-and-trace devices

    g) Number of subpoenas, requests, or orders for stored records, including number of disclosures under Section 215 of the Patriot Act

    h) Number of instances of consensual electronic surveillance

    i) Number, duration, cost, and effectiveness of undercover operations.[14]

Another advocacy group, the Electronic Privacy Information Center (EPIC), has also attacked the new FBI guidelines, warning that they "pose serious threats to the right of individuals to speak and assemble freely without the specter of government monitoring."[15]

EPIC concluded, "Ashcroft's changes will allow for mining of commercial databases where there is no suspicion of criminal conduct and infiltration of groups that have not demonstrated any evidence of criminal activity. . . . The guidelines also allow FBI to engage in searches and monitoring of chat rooms, bulletin boards, and websites without evidence of criminal wrongdoing. Additionally, agents are permitted to visit public places and events to monitor individuals' activities with no predicate of criminal suspicion. These powers are not limited to terrorism investigations—they can be used for any violation of federal law."[16]

Homeland Security Act

On November 25, 2002, President Bush signed the Homeland Security Act of 2002 (H.R. 5005) into law. Not since 1947, when President Harry Truman restructured and unified the entire U.S. armed forces and created the Department of Defense, has there been such a massive realignment of the federal bureaucracy. The Coast Guard and the Transportation Security Administration have been taken from the Department of Transportation, the Customs Service and the Secret Service from the Treasury Department, and the Immigration and Naturalization Service from the Justice Department, and all of them must be made to work together with the seventeen other federal agencies that make up the new Department of Homeland Security.

"The statute is elephantine," asserted Allen Weinstein, president of the Center for Democracy and Technology. "It means we're probably going to have to deal with a law of unintended consequences."[17]

Intended or unintended, it is the unprecedented imposition on American privacy, not the bureaucratic awkwardness, that worries people most about this new department. Seen in the context of already broadened federal surveillance powers acquired through the Patriot Act and other legislation, it represents another step toward a surveillance society, one that could give the appearance of library complicity in such snooping. Among the many provisions that concern privacy advocates is the one that allows libraries, Internet service providers, and other organizations "voluntarily" to hand over Internet users' e-mail and other personal data to the government, without a warrant or probable cause.

An entire computer secrecy bill, formerly known as the Cyber Security Enhancement Act (CSEA), was rolled into the Homeland Security Act as Section 225. This monstrous new provision expands the "emergency exception" to judicial review requirements for obtaining voice mail and e-mail. An emergency is no longer required to be "imminent" for disclosure to be made. Also, by relaxing the standard from "a reasonable belief" to "a good faith belief," Section 225 uses scare tactics rather than evidence to uncover information. Under this section, an Internet provider has no obligation to report inquiries and no incentive to protect a customer's privacy.

Section 225 allows disclosure of information to "a Federal, State, or local government entity," not just to law enforcement agents. This would allow public library directors, high school principals, and tax collectors to request information from Internet service providers and make it available to federal agents.

Like its predecessor, the Patriot Act, the Homeland Security Act is a monstrous document hastily passed and poorly understood by those who voted for it in Congress. Its 484 pages are divided into seventeen titles, as follows:

Title I: Department of Homeland Security

Title II: Information Analysis and Infrastructure Protection

Title III: Science and Technology in Support of Homeland Security

Title IV: Directorate of Border and Transportation Security

Title V: Emergency Preparedness and Response

Title VI: Treatment of Charitable Trusts for Members of the Armed Forces of the United States and Other Governmental Organizations

Title VII: Management

Title VIII: Coordination with Non-Federal Entities; Inspector General; United States Secret Service; Coast Guard; General Provisions

Title IX: National Homeland Security Council

Title X: Information Security

Title XI: Department of Justice Divisions

Title XII: Airline War Risk Insurance Regulations

Title XIII: Federal Workforce Improvement

Title XIV: Arming Pilots Against Terrorism

Title XV: Transition

Title XVI: Corrections to Existing Law Relating to Airline Transportation Security

Title XVII: Conforming and Technical Amendments

Under the Homeland Security Act, the new department may enlist government agencies and private companies to provide data on individuals and groups, American citizens and noncitizens alike, and to troll that data for patterns suggesting terrorist plots. Agencies will now "mine" data that combine personal, governmental, and corporate records, including e-mail and Web sites. Jerry Berman, executive director of the CDT, stated that the new department "is going to data-mine hundreds of millions of records of Americans to figure out who may or may not be a terrorist threat."[18]

David Holtzman, a former naval intelligence analyst and author of a book on privacy, declared, "We're institutionalizing a loss of privacy."[19]

The Homeland Security Act also imposes a new reign of secrecy, placing limits on the information citizens may request under the FOIA. Among the new and very broad exemptions to the FOIA is one allowing businesses to evade liability for safety violations, hazards to consumers, and other abuses. By simply claiming that such information is related to homeland security, a corporation can have it designated "Critical Infrastructure Information" under the Homeland Security Act, and therefore exempted from the FOIA. If a government whistle-blower were to reveal such information, he would be jailed. Software and computer hardware companies can now hide critical security flaws or other bugs by invoking the exemptions of the Homeland Security Act.

In another extension of official secrecy, the Homeland Security Act instructs the president to "identify and safeguard homeland security information that is sensitive but unclassified." Because no definition of "sensitive" is provided, this provision could be used to justify broad new restrictions on the disclosure of unclassified information. It may be recalled that the phrase "sensitive but unclassified" was introduced by John Poindexter during the 1980s to justify the FBI's Library Awareness Program and its restrictions on access to unclassified scientific information in libraries.

One of the more ludicrous effects of the Homeland Security Act has been the appearance of signs on America's highways urging citizens to "Report Suspicious Activity" to the new department. Courtland Milloy wrote a column for the *Washington Post* in March 2003 describing his attempt to comply with this aspect of the Homeland Security Act. While driving into our nation's capital he noticed a sign above the highway advising motorists to "Report Suspicious Activity" to the Office of Homeland Security. An 800 number was provided. "As a reporter, I figured this was right up my alley and set out . . . to report on things that struck me as suspicious," wrote Milloy.

Near the Jefferson Memorial he noticed a five-foot-tall metal box hooked up to an electrical outlet and fitted with an antenna dome receptor. He asked a couple of National Park Service workers and some Cherry Blossom Festival organizers what the contraption was. Soon he was approached by two U.S. Park Police officers carrying semiautomatic pistols.

"We hear you've been asking curious questions," said the officer. "Why are you doing that?"

Milloy said he felt bold enough to respond, "Why are you asking me that?"

"Let me see your ID," the officer said.

"Why?" Milloy asked.

"Call for backup," the officer firmly told his cohort as he seized Milloy's notebook and pen and began to search him. Eight more officers responded to the call for backup. One of them told Milloy that he was not under arrest, just under "investigative detention."

Another officer told Milloy, "There have been reports of suspicious activity regarding you." When Milloy asked what kind of activity was suspicious, he was told, "Apparently you have been showing interest in equipment on the grounds, making notes, that sort of thing."

When Milloy said he simply wanted to know what kind of machine was next to the Jefferson Memorial, an officer asked him, "Are you aware of the current threat level?"

Milloy said he was, and the officer explained that under this heightened state of alert, "if anyone shows a particular interest in something, we get suspicious."

Milloy, an African American, then pointedly asked whether his dark skin might make him particularly suspicious. The officer just smiled. After about an hour and a half, when the word got around that Milloy was a writer for the *Washington Post*, things lightened up considerably. He was told that the contraption he had asked about was an air-quality testing device. Finally, as Milloy was about to leave, the officer paid him the ultimate compliment by asking, "Have you noticed any suspicious activity in the area?"[20]

Total Information Awareness

Total Information Awareness (TIA) is a Pentagon-funded project intended to produce the most expansive electronic surveillance network in human history. Functioning as America's "Big Brother," it would monitor every American's reading habits, Internet surfing, financial transactions, mental health histories, and a vast range of personal information to create individual profiles designed to predict future behavior.

The program was created by the Pentagon's Defense Advanced Research Projects Agency (DARPA) through its Information Awareness Office (IAO), headed by Admiral John Poindexter, the discredited former national security adviser to President Ronald Reagan. Poindexter was convicted in 1990 on five felony counts of making false statements and misleading Congress about his illicit sale of missiles to Iran to support the contras in Nicaragua. An appeals court overturned the verdict on a technicality, saying Congress had given him immunity for his testimony. Now, in January 2002, Poindexter was quietly returning to government to develop new surveillance technologies in the wake of the 9/11 terrorist attacks.

Senator Charles Schumer (D-NY) commented, "If we need a 'Big Brother,' John Poindexter is the last guy on the list I would choose."[21]

Conservative columnist William Safire warned, "Poindexter is now realizing his 20-year dream: getting the 'data-mining' power to snoop on every public and private act of every American. . . . Every purchase you make with a credit card, every magazine subscription you buy and medical prescription you fill, every Web site you visit and e-mail you send or receive, every academic grade you receive, every bank deposit you make, every trip you book and every event you attend—all these transactions and communications will go into what the Defense Department describes as 'a virtual, centralized grand database.' "[22]

Poindexter himself said, "We must become much more efficient and much more clever in the ways we find new sources of data, mine information from the new and old, generate information, make it available for analysis, convert it to knowledge, and create actionable options."[23]

On January 14, 2003, a nonpartisan coalition of organizations, including such disparate groups as the American Civil Liberties Union (ACLU) and the American Conservative Union, sent a letter to the House and Senate Armed Services Committees, Judiciary Committees, Defense Appropriations Committees, and Government Reform and Affairs Committees, urging them to stop further development of the TIA program. The letter concluded, "At a time when Americans are calling for more privacy of personal information, this program would provide a backdoor to databases of private information. At a minimum, Congress should put such programs on hold and ask the tough policy questions up front, long before domestic surveillance systems scoop up Americans' personal information."[24]

As dangerous as Poindexter's new domestic spying techniques were, they could not be loosed upon the American public without enabling legislation. As it turned out, the Homeland Security Act provided the statutory authority necessary to deploy the TIA program. Marc Rotenberg, director of EPIC, described the birth of TIA: "The vehicle is the Homeland Security Act, the technology is DARPA and the agency is the F.B.I. The outcome is a system of national surveillance of the American public."[25]

In March 2003, DARPA's Web page provided the following description:

> The Total Information Awareness (TIA) program is a FY03 new-start program. The goal of the . . . new program is to revolutionize the ability of the United States to detect, classify and identify foreign terrorists. . . . [T]he TIA program is focusing on the development of: 1) architectures for a large-scale counter-terrorism database, for system elements associated with database population, and for integrating algorithms and mixed-initiative analytical tools; 2) . . . new algorithms for mining, combining and refining information for subsequent inclusion into the database; and, 3) revolutionary new models, algorithms, methods, tools, and techniques for analyzing and correlating information in the database to derive actionable intelligence.[26]

There is no doubt that TIA research is proceeding apace, but there remains some ambiguity about its deployment under the Homeland Security Act. In November 2002, House Majority Leader Dick Armey (R-TX) claimed that the Homeland Security Bill "does not authorize, fund or move into the department anything like it [TIA]." He said that the bill's authorization of "data-mining" tools was "intended solely to authorize the use of advanced techniques to sift through existing intelligence data, not to open a new method of intruding [on] lawful, everyday transactions of American citizens."[27]

In the Senate, Joseph Lieberman (D-CT) inserted an explanatory paragraph into the Congressional Record after the passage of the Homeland Security Act: "Nothing in this legislation should be construed as requiring or encouraging HSARPA (Homeland Security Advanced Research Projects Agency) to adopt or replicate any specific programs within DARPA, such as the Total Information Awareness Program, or as conferring HSARPA with any additional authority to overcome privacy laws when developing technologies for information-collection."[28]

Both the Armey and Lieberman comments were personal interpretations of the Homeland Security Act, carrying no legal authority. Only on February 20, 2003, when President Bush signed Public Law 108-7 was some clarification brought to the matter. The new law, which had been inserted as an amendment to a Senate omnibus spending bill, would place certain restrictions on the use of TIA against "United States persons" and would require a joint report from the secretary of defense, attorney general, and director of central intelligence to Congress describing the intended use of funds for each TIA project and the schedule for proposed research and development. The report would also assess the likely impact of the TIA program on privacy and civil liberties.

Senator Ron Wyden (D-OR), who had sponsored the amendment against TIA, said, "It looks like Congress is getting the message from the American people loud and clear and that is: Stop trifling with the civil liberties of law-abiding Americans."[29]

Though the restraints of Public Law 108-7 were reassuring, the law allowed the president to ignore most of them if "the cessation of research and development on the Total Information Awareness program would endanger the national security of the United States." In addition, most of the restraints would not apply if TIA were deployed in support of:

(a) Lawful military operations of the United States conducted outside the United States

(b) Lawful foreign intelligence activities conducted wholly overseas, or wholly against non-United States persons.[30]

Thus, the restraints did not apply to military or foreign intelligence activities overseas, even if used against American citizens, and, of course, no restraints applied in the case of non-U.S. citizens within the United States. As for the joint report, delivered to Congress on May 20, 2003, it showed the Pentagon's continued support for the program, but under a new name, the Terrorist Information Awareness (TIA) program. So TIA was still alive and well, but, like virtually every other current government initiative, it was packaged more explicitly as anti-terrorism.

The Pentagon's DARPA explained, "The program's previous name, 'Total Information Awareness' program, created in some minds the impression that TIA was a system to be used for developing dossiers on U.S. citizens. DoD's purpose in pursuing these efforts is to protect U.S. citizens by detecting and defeating foreign terrorist threats before an attack." In a further attempt at public relations, DARPA's spokeswoman, Jan Walker, expressed the agency's "full commitment to planning, executing and overseeing the TIA program in a way that protects privacy and civil liberties."[31]

Many in Congress are not impressed by the new and improved TIA, and they say they intend to keep an eye on the program. In 2003 Senator Chuck Grassley (R-IA) promised, "Congressional oversight of this program will be a must. . . . Congress won't sit on its hands as the TIA program moves forward."[32]

Another covert attempt to resuscitate TIA was revealed in February 2003 when the draft of a secret bill, the Domestic Security Enhancement Act (DSEA), was leaked from the Justice Department. Dubbed "Patriot II" by the press, this bill would authorize police surveillance powers to the government that go well beyond the original Patriot Act. Journalist Anita Ramasastry wrote, "Patriot II, as drafted by the Attorney General and his staff, would begin to make TIA the law."[33]

Ramasastry notes that Patriot II "would open the wedge for TIA to be implemented" by authorizing a huge government database of personal information on American citizens, including credit reports, all acquired without the need for a subpoena or court order.[34] Federal agents would only have to certify that they would use the information in connection with their duties to enforce federal law. They would not have to certify that persons whose information was collected were suspected of terrorism or any other crime, and those persons would not be notified that their data had been accessed.

On July 29, 2003, new controversy swirled around DARPA and its head, John Poindexter, after revelations of a DARPA proposal to create a "futures" stock market plan allowing investors to bet on the likelihood of terrorist attacks. Publicized examples included betting on the assassination of Palestinian leader Yasser Arafat or the overthrow of Jordan's monarchy. Though the proposal had no connection to TIA, it reflected badly on DARPA and Poindexter. Even Deputy Defense Secretary Paul Wolfowitz officially rejected the idea. "I share your shock at this kind of program," he told Congress. "We'll find out about it, but it is being terminated."

"There is something very sick about it," said Senator Barbara Boxer (D-CA), and she demanded that Congress "end the careers of whoever it was who thought that up."[35]

Two days later, a senior Pentagon official announced that Poindexter would be leaving his job as head of DARPA within a few weeks. "He realizes that it's become difficult for projects that he's involved in to get a dispassionate hearing," said the official.[36] Indeed, on August 12, 2003, Poindexter submitted his resignation, stating, "I regret we have not been able to make our case clear and reassure the public that we do not intend to spy on them."[37]

What about Poindexter's pet project, TIA? Let us hope it goes the way of the futures market on terrorism.

TIPS Program

On May 29, 2002, a Justice Department Web site proudly announced Operation TIPS (Terrorist Information and Prevention System), which it called "a national reporting system for reporting suspicious and potentially terrorist-related activity." The site said the government would now use the eyes and ears of "millions of American workers who, in the daily course of their work, are in a unique position to see potentially unusual or suspicious activity." Such workers could include truckers, letter carriers, train conductors, ship captains, utility employees and, in all likelihood, librarians.[38]

Rep. Dennis Kucinich (D-OH) was outraged at the new program of surveillance. "It appears we are being transformed from an information society to an informant society," he said. "Do the math. One tip a day per person and within a year the whole country will be turned in."[39]

The citizenscorps.gov Web site instructs citizens how to report suspicious activity under Operation TIPS:

> Everywhere in America, a concerned worker can call a toll-free number and be connected directly to a hotline routing calls to the proper law enforcement agency or other responder organizations. . . . Every participant in this new program will be given an Operation TIPS information sticker to be affixed to the cab of their vehicle or placed in some other public location so that the toll-free number is readily available.[40]

By July 16, the government Web site had ceased listing specific kinds of employees as designated informants and instead provided general advice to all workers to "use their common sense and knowledge of their work environment to identify suspicious or unusual activity."[41] It was left to these workers/informants to figure out what "suspicious" or "unusual" meant. Not only would innocent citizens be placed under scrutiny, but the names of these innocent suspects would be transferred by the Justice Department to FBI, CIA, and other government databases that are permitted to exchange "intelligence" information under the Homeland Security Act.

On July 17, the *Boston Globe* ran an editorial titled "Ashcroft vs. Americans" which began,"Operation TIPS—The Terrorist Information and Protection System—is a scheme that Joseph Stalin would have appreciated. Plans for its pilot phase, to start in August, have Operation TIPS recruiting a million letter carriers, meter readers, cable technicians, and other workers with access to private homes, as informants to report to the Justice Department any activities they think suspicious." The *Globe* article concluded, "Ashcroft's informant corps is a vile idea not merely because it violates civil liberties . . . or because it will sabotage general efforts to prevent terrorism by overloading law enforcement officials with irrelevant reports about Americans who have nothing to do with terrorists. Operation TIPS should be stopped because it is utterly anti-American."[42]

On August 6, 2002, the online magazine *Salon.com* revealed that the Justice Department was forwarding incoming TIPS phone calls to FOX Television Network's show *America's Most Wanted*. Characterizing this development as "surreal," the ACLU's legislative counsel, Rachel King said, "It's a completely inappropriate and frightening intermingling of government power and the private sector. What's next—the government hires *Candid Camera* to do its video surveillance?"

The author of the *Salon* article had signed up for the TIPS program, but when he called the Justice Department he was referred to another number, which he was told was set up by the FBI. When he dialed that number, he was greeted by a receptionist from *America's Most Wanted*, who told him, "We've been asked to take the FBI's TIPS calls for them."

The ACLU warns that by coupling the TIPS program with the sensationalism and profit incentives of television, TIPS could become America's Big Brother. "Why stop with *America's Most Wanted*?" asks King. "If a sensational story is what it was looking for, the Department of Justice should just have hired Jerry Springer as its public information officer."[43]

In October, in response to congressional criticism and public outrage, the Bush administration announced a revised version of the program that would not seek to recruit postal and utility workers, but would allow *anyone* to volunteer of their own accord to be a snitch. TIPS would still actively recruit individuals who work in industries such as transportation, trucking, shipping, maritime, and mass transit, but it would reach out to all workers.

There were other obstacles in the path of Ashcroft's national surveillance program. First, the postal service, considered by the Justice Department to be perfectly suited for an informant program, refused to participate in TIPS. Then, House Majority Leader Armey, a prominent conservative, took advantage of his role in the markup procedure on the Homeland Security Department bill to scrap Ashcroft's domestic surveillance scheme. Armey's markup on the bill reads, "*Citizens Will Not Become Informants*. To ensure that no operation of the Department can be construed to promote citizens spying on one another, this draft will contain language to prohibit programs such as 'Operation TIPS.' "[44]

The House passed the Homeland Security bill with Armey's provision against TIPS. Still, the Justice Department insisted that the program would continue until Armey's provision became law. Fortunately, the Senate eventually passed the House version of the bill, including the following section: "Section 880. Prohibition of the Terrorism Information and Prevention System—Any and all activities of the Federal Government to implement the proposed component program of the Citizen Corps known as Operation TIPS (Terrorism Information and Prevention System) are hereby prohibited."[45]

This statutory prohibition on TIPS seems clear and unambiguous, but the rash of signs that appeared on America's highways after the invasion of Iraq in March 2003, raised suspicions that TIPS may be functioning as a loose cannon. The signs that I saw on Interstate 95 South leading toward Washington, D.C., said,

Report Suspicious Activity. Heightened Homeland Security Alert.

The signs concluded with an 800 phone number to the Homeland Security Office, and, interestingly, the last four digits were letters rather than numbers: "TIPS."

There are other indications suggesting that the government has not yet given up on Operation TIPS. When the secret draft bill titled the Domestic Security Enhancement Act, dubbed Patriot II by the press, surfaced in February 2003, analysts immediately saw the imprint of TIPS. Patriot II would not only provide immunity from liability to law enforcement agents engaged in spying operations against American citizens, but it would eliminate civil liability for businesses and employees that report "suspected terrorists," no matter how malicious or unfounded the tip may be. Reporter Anita Ramasastry wrote, "[T]his is TIPS all over again. If they like, your package courier or cable guy can report you to the feds with impunity."[46]

CAPPS II

The current version of the Enhanced Computer Assisted Passenger Pre-Screening System (CAPPS II) is a data-mining program that seeks to profile every American for his or her flight worthiness. The CAPPS II system will rely heavily on commercial databases of names, telephone numbers, former addresses, financial data, and other personal information to profile airline passengers and provide "no-fly" lists to the Transportation Safety Administration (TSA). Without their knowledge and without recourse, passengers are assigned a risk assessment "score" based on computer models created by the TSA, allowing innocent people to be branded security risks on the basis of potentially flawed data. The government's determination of risk will in large part determine whether a passenger will be allowed to board a flight and may not be challenged in any meaningful way.

The "no-fly" watch list was actually created back in 1990, at which time it contained the names of individuals who had been "determined to pose a direct threat to civil aviation." This list was administered by the FBI, but since the TSA assumed full responsibility for the list in November 2001, one month after passage of the Patriot Act, the watch list "has expanded almost daily as Intelligence Community agencies and the Office of Homeland Security continue to request the addition of individuals to the . . . lists."[47]

With no clear rules and no appeals system, CAPPS II would brand some Americans as a "risk to transportation," a label that could circulate throughout government databases and haunt the individual for life. Such a person has no way to confirm that he or she has been so labeled and has no right to see the information that the label was based on. The TSA has also indicated its intention to use the CAPPS II system to screen truckers, railroad conductors, subway workers, and other transportation employees.

On March 13, 2003, the Senate Commerce Committee made an attempt to assuage critics of CAPPS II by endorsing a plan to require the TSA to disclose details on how the system would be applied to American citizens and how it would affect their personal privacy. The TSA would also be required to explain how it would avoid errors in its personal profiling and how it would enable appeals from passengers who may have been incorrectly labeled as a risk to transportation. Senator Wyden, who introduced the amendment requiring TSA reporting on CAPPS II, said, "This is really the beginning of a debate of how our country can fight [terrorism] ferociously, without gutting civil liberties."[48]

Shortly after the Commerce Committee action, EPIC acquired information on CAPPS II through an FOIA request. The FOIA documents showed that the TSA actually administered two watch lists: a "no-fly" list and a "selectee" list, the former preventing an individual from boarding an airliner, and the latter requiring a passenger to go through a special set of security measures. Names are provided to air carriers through security directives and are stored in their computers so that a listed individual can be flagged when getting a boarding pass. A no-fly listing immediately brings in a law enforcement officer to detain and question the passenger. A selectee listing causes an "S" to be printed on the boarding pass, resulting in additional security screening for that individual at security.

The FOIA documents revealed numerous complaints from airline passengers who had no idea why their names were on the list or how to get off the list. There appeared to be no formal approval process to verify that names are appropriately listed and that the information is accurate and up to date. Nor is there any process by which individuals may request that their names be removed from the list.

In July 2003, Public Television's series *Flashpoints USA* premiered with a show about the loss of privacy since 9/11. One portion of the show was introduced with an amusing popular song, "The Ballad of David Nelson," which describes the trials and tribulations of airline passengers named David Nelson. The host, Bryant Gumbel, noted that the song was not very amusing to those whose names really were David Nelson. Gumbel had assembled three such David Nelsons, a business consultant from Florida, a graduate student from New York, and a coach for the Milwaukee Brewers baseball team. All of these men, who share a name with someone who is on the federal no-fly list, have experienced constant hassles when they try to board a plane. The David Nelson from New York described his scenario: "It tends to vary according to where you are in the country, but typically it will show up [on the computer] and the person working behind the desk will look at you quizzically for a few minutes after they see something on their computer screen, but they're not really allowed to tell you what they see. Then they'll rush around and grab a telephone and make some very mysterious phone calls and tell you to wait a while. Since we've been through this so many times, I know that they're doing a background check where they're calling the police and the FBI."[49]

The New York David Nelson said this had been going on for almost two years. The David Nelson from the Milwaukee Brewers said he was actually pulled off a flight in Denver because of his name. "I was through security . . . and was on the plane and all of a sudden the flight attendant said, 'We need you to get off the plane . . . and talk to security people for a while.' "

Coach David Nelson, who is an African American, eventually discovered that the David Nelson on the no-fly list was white and Irish. "That eliminates me right away, because there's no common characteristics," he said, "so I don't understand why it takes so long on every trip."[50]

Even the David Nelson from the old *Ozzie and Harriet* TV show suffers similar indignities when he flies. Perhaps most absurd, a nine-year-old David Nelson from Alaska was stopped for security reasons when he traveled with his family. The airline held him until they could obtain a release from a law enforcement officer. Even then, his family had to undergo additional security checks before being allowed to board the plane.

As for the real David Nelson, whom the government wants to keep off airliners, no one is sure who he is. Host Bryant Gumbel pointed out, "The folks at the Transportation Security Administration say that information is classified."[51]

Patriot Act II and the Victory Act

Even as libraries and bookstores prepared for the intrusive new surveillance powers authorized in the Patriot Act, the Justice Department was secretly preparing a new bill to expand those powers. On February 7, 2003, Bill Moyers' Public Television series *NOW* aired a scoop, an exclusive story about a highly confidential Justice Department draft bill, the DSEA, which moved beyond even the Patriot Act in authorizing oppressive new government surveillance powers. The bill, drafted by Attorney General Ashcroft, was to be maintained in secrecy until delivered to Congress, where the Justice Department hoped to rush it through to passage, just as had been done with the Patriot Act. Someone in the Justice Department, however, leaked the draft bill to Charles Lewis, the executive director of the nonpartisan Center for Public Integrity, who promptly made it public.

Lewis initially received a phone call asking if he was interested in legislation involving national security, surveillance, and secrecy. He said, "Yes."

"When I got it, I was incredulous," admitted Lewis. "I realized this was a historic piece of legislation. . . . The reason the Justice Department wants to keep it under wraps is they know it's a hot potato. They know it's controversial and they want to keep it quiet for as long as possible."[52]

The Justice Department declined Moyers' request for an interview but confirmed in a statement that additional anti-terrorism measures were under active review. The cover sheet to the draft bill indicated that it had been shared only with House Speaker Dennis Hastert (R-IL) and Vice President Dick Cheney. Moyers asked Lewis why the bill had not been sent to the appropriate congressional committees.

"It's a way to say you've consulted Congress without really consulting Congress," answered Lewis. "It appears that virtually no one on Capitol Hill has seen this legislation."[53]

Indeed, in response to rumors about Ashcroft's legislative intentions, senior members of the Senate Judiciary Committee had inquired about Patriot II for months and were told repeatedly that no such legislation was being planned. Similarly, House Judiciary Committee spokesman Jeff Lungren told the Center for Public Integrity, "We haven't heard anything from the Justice Department on updating the Patriot Act. They haven't shared their thoughts on that. Obviously, we'd be interested, but we haven't heard anything at this point."[54]

Even Mark Corallo, deputy director of the Justice Department's own Office of Public Affairs, told the Center for Public Integrity that his office was unaware of the draft bill. "This is all news to me," said Corallo. "I have never heard of this."[55] Eventually, Justice Department spokesperson Barbara Comstock acknowledged the existence of Patriot II, but she said the leaked copy was no longer "the operational draft." Comstock insisted, "We don't make any apologies for continuing to assess whether there's a need for improved information sharing or tools to help protect the American people against terrorism."[56]

Reporter Alex Jones shed some light on the mysterious ignorance, or feigned ignorance, of Patriot II on Capitol Hill when he wrote, "I discovered that not only was there a House version that had been covertly brought to Hastert, but that many provisions of the now public Patriot Act II had already been introduced as pork barrel riders on Senate Bill S. 22. Dozens of subsections and even the titles of the subsections are identical to those in the House version."[57]

Thus, the Justice Department claim that Patriot II was brought to Hastert only for study was a lie. Whether the copy leaked to Charles Lewis remains the "operational draft" or not, it clearly forms the basis for the Justice Department's legislative efforts that have now spread to both houses of Congress.

The draft received by Lewis was stamped, "Confidential—Not for Distribution," but it was not a classified document and the person who made it available did not betray an official secret. Indeed, Lewis said he considered his informant to be a genuine patriot. "I think it takes incredible guts," said Lewis. "They know they're going to be polygraphed and questioned. There's going to be a clamp-down and a witch hunt after this. . . . I have an enormous amount of respect for anyone who does that."[58]

Moyers noted that many of the powers granted to the government in Patriot II were powers taken away from the intelligence community years ago because they were abused. He asked if there were any protections against potential abuse built into Patriot II. Lewis said, "The safeguards seem to be pretty minimal. . . . It does appear that everything that people were concerned about with the Patriot Act, this is times 5 or times 10." Lewis warned, "I see a lot of opportunism here around the fear and paranoia of September 11th, and that is incredibly offensive to me. . . . They can get your credit card data, your library records, your Internet searching, and they'll decide whether you're a suspect. . . . There are 40 sections in this thing [Patriot II]. The public needs to have a sense of exactly what we are getting here."[59]

A quick look at a few of the forty sections of the DSEA reveals why so many people are concerned.

Sections 101, 102, and 107 would make it easier for the government to initiate surveillance and wiretapping of U.S. citizens under the secret Foreign Intelligence Surveillance Act (FISA) court. They would expand FISA's definition of foreign power "to include all persons, regardless of whether they are affiliated with an international terrorist group, who engage in international terrorism." Section 102 states that any information gathering, whether or not the activity is illegal, can be considered clandestine intelligence gathering for a foreign power.

Sections 103 and 104 would eliminate judicial oversight of a range of surveillance actions and authorize the U.S. attorney general to conduct wiretaps for fifteen days without court oversight whenever Congress authorizes the use of force or the White House declares an emergency. The federal government could now use wartime martial law powers domestically and internationally without a declaration of war.

Section 106 would immunize federal agents engaged in illegal surveillance, searches, and seizures without a court order if they are determined to be acting on the orders of higher Executive Branch officials.

Section 109 allows secret courts to issue contempt charges against individuals who refuse to incriminate themselves or others, thus removing Fifth Amendment rights.

Section 110 removes the "sunset" clauses from all provisions of the first Patriot Act.

Section 111 further expands the definition of "enemy combatant," allowing uncontrolled detention of individuals outside the criminal justice system.

Section 122 formally declares the government's power of "surveillance without a court order."

Section 123 states that the government no longer needs search warrants, and "thus the focus of domestic surveillance may be less precise than that directed against more conventional types of crime."

Section 126 grants the government the power to mine the entire range of public and private information, from bank records to educational and medical records. This would effectively enact the TIA program.

Section 127 allows the government to take over medical examiners' operations.

Sections 128 and 206 impose gag orders on any person who receives a subpoena in regard to a terrorist investigation and prevents anyone from trying to quash a federal subpoena.

Section 129 removes all whistle-blower protection for federal agents.

Section 201 would make it a criminal act for any citizen to release any information concerning the incarceration of detainees. It would empower the Justice Department to conduct secret arrests when investigating international terrorism, keeping those arrests secret until criminal charges are filed, if ever. Litigation seeking information about detainees would be prohibited, and FOIA requests would routinely be denied.

Section 202 would threaten public health by severely restricting access to information about environmental health risks posed by facilities that use dangerous chemicals. It would also discourage Freedom of Information Act (FOIA) requests for EPA reports, removing an established level of transparency within private industry.

Section 204 allows the government to make secret presentations of evidence to the court which neither the defendant nor his attorney may see.

Section 205 allows top federal officials to keep their financial dealings secret.

Sections 301 to 306 authorize the collection of DNA samples and DNA records from innocent American citizens, without a court order and without consent. The DNA would be used to create an identification database of "suspected terrorists," expansively defined to include association with suspected terrorist groups. It would also establish a national DNA database for anyone who has been on probation for any crime, and it orders state and local governments to collect the DNA for the federal government.

Section 311 would permit the federal government to share sensitive personal information about U.S. citizens with local and state law enforcement, even if that information has no connection to terrorism. It would also open sensitive visa files to local police for the enforcement of immigration laws.

Section 312 would immediately terminate any "consent decrees" restricting illegal police spying on citizens that were initiated before September 11, 2001. This gives immunity to law enforcement engaged in spying against the American people. The original court-approved limits were put in place to prevent McCarthy-era persecution based on political or religious affiliation.

Section 313 provides liability protection for businesses that spy on their customers for the Homeland Security Office. By providing an incentive for neighbor to spy on neighbor, it establishes the access hub for the TIA program and Operation TIPS.

Section 321 authorizes foreign governments to spy on American people and share that information with other governments.

Section 322 allows the Homeland Security Office secretly to extradite American citizens from anywhere in the world.

Section 402 criminalizes association with any organization labeled as terrorist by our government, even if there is no intent to commit acts of terrorism.

Section 403 expands the definition of weapons of mass destruction to include anything that affects interstate or foreign commerce.

Section 404 makes it a crime for terrorists or "other criminals" to use encryption.

Section 405 allows suspected terrorists to be held without bail before their trial.

Section 408 creates "lifetime parole," a form of slavery, for a host of crimes.

Section 410 removes the statute of limitations for terrorist acts or support of terrorism.

Section 411 would apply the death penalty to offenses that, because of the definition of "domestic terrorism" in the Patriot Act, could include civil disobedience and protests.

Section 421 states that any type of financial activity connected to terrorism will result in prison time and heavy fines.

Section 427 establishes asset forfeiture for anyone engaging in terrorist activities.

Section 501 expands the Bush administration's "enemy combatant" designation to any American citizen who "may" have violated Section 802 of the first Patriot Act. That section introduced a definition of "domestic terrorism" that could cover protest groups like Operation Rescue, Greenpeace, or People for the Ethical Treatment of Animals. Patriot II would allow the government to strip the citizenship of an American citizen if that person provided "material support" to a group designated by the government as a "terrorist organization," even if the support is given to completely lawful activities. For example, giving money to an overseas religious charity that was *later* classified as a front group for a terrorist organization could cause an American citizen to lose his citizenship.

Section 502 imposes extended jail terms on undocumented workers for common immigration offenses.

Section 503 gives the U.S. attorney general unchecked authority to deport any person, including lawful, permanent residents, if he determines that their presence is inconsistent with our national security. Such deportation requires no crime or criminal intent and is not reviewable by the courts.

Section 504 provides an "expedited removal" procedure for lawful, permanent residents convicted of criminal offenses and explicitly exempts these cases from habeas corpus, an unconstitutional act not seen since the Civil War. Fair hearings and court inquiry into this procedure are prohibited.

Now that legal scholars have had a chance to examine the Patriot II draft, they are unanimous in regarding it as an unprecedented extension of federal police powers. Law reporter Anita Ramasastry concluded, "In sum, Patriot II puts in jeopardy the First Amendment right to speak freely, statutory and common law rights to privacy, the right to go to court to challenge government illegality, and the Fourth Amendment right against unreasonable searches and seizures."[60]

Patriot II also puts in jeopardy the right we all presume, the right to walk the streets without being "disappeared" by the government, an act once common in such nations as Chile and Guatemala. Section 501 of Patriot II calls this "denationalization." If a U.S. citizen is suspected of terrorist activity, he may be expatriated "if, with the intent to relinquish his nationality, he becomes a member of or provides material support to, a group that the United States has designated as a 'terrorist organization.' " The trick here is the "intent to relinquish his national-ity" is *inferred* from his conduct. Thus, any association with even the legal activi-ties of a designated terrorist group or any act that can be interpreted as disloyal is sufficient for the government to infer intent. Your citizenship is revoked, and you are summarily deported.

Now that the whistle has been blown on Patriot II and its threat to our Con-stitution, is there a chance that Congress will have the backbone to reject the bill when it comes to a vote? The fact that many conservative Republicans have ex-pressed reluctance to go beyond the original Patriot Act suggests that a coalition against Patriot II may be building. Russ Feingold (D-WI), the only member of the Senate to vote against the Patriot Act, has said, "There's not a big difference between the intensity of conservatives and liberals on this issue. I think I'm go-ing to have allies this time. I don't think I'm going to be alone."[61]

But even as Congress prepared for Patriot II, Senate Republicans circulated the draft of another acronym-laden anti-terrorism bill called the Vital Interdiction of Criminal Terrorist Organizations Act, or the VICTORY Act. The draft bill, which carries the names of Senator Orrin Hatch (R-UT) and four other Republican senators, would dramatically expand the government's power to seize records and conduct wiretaps in connection with "narcoterrorism" investigations.

Title V of the VICTORY Act has the most effect on privacy and civil liber-ties, with Section 503 giving the attorney general the power to issue administra-tive subpoenas in investigations related to the Patriot Act's very broad definition of domestic terrorism. Section 504 mentions subpoena power to acquire con-sumer records from telecommunications companies, Internet service providers, and financial service institutions such as banks. Both sections would grant im-munity from civil liability for cooperating with the subpoena without challeng-ing it, even if the subpoena is later found to be unconstitutional.

Democratic presidential candidate Howard Dean warned in a news release that the Victory Act was "a dangerous piece of legislation." Tim Edgar, legisla-tive counsel for the ACLU, declared, "The Victory Act represents a major ex-pansion of federal surveillance, asset forfeiture and other powers under the guise of linking the war on drugs to the war on terrorism." Attorney General Ashcroft, however, was quick to endorse the Victory Act, saying, "We'll probably need to add some more tools in our tool kit against terror."[62]

In the fall of 2003, four new bills were introduced in Congress in an at-tempt to give Ashcroft more tools for his tool kit. On September 9, 2003, Rep. Tom Feeney (R-FL) introduced the Antiterrorism Tools Enhancement Act (H.R. 3037), which would give the attorney general the authority to issue "ad-ministrative subpoenas" in terrorism cases. These subpoenas, which require the approval of neither a judge nor a grand jury, allow the attorney general to "compel the attendance and testimony of witnesses, and require the production of any records (including books, papers, documents, electronic data, and other tangible things that constitute or contain evidence) that he finds relevant or ma-terial to the investigation."[63]

The Feeney bill also specifies that a "nondisclosure agreement" accompany the subpoena if the attorney general believes disclosure would represent a danger to national security. The bill's use of administrative subpoenas to seize any "tangible thing" and its imposition of a gag order gives it an eerie resemblance to both Section 215 of the Patriot Act and national security letters. Award-winning journalist Charles Levendosky warns, "This power to search and seize records does not have to meet a probable cause standard—as constitutionally required by a valid search warrant. An impartial judge, the traditional check on police power to search and seize, is eliminated from the equation. The Fourth Amendment's protection against unreasonable searches and seizures would be lost if the Feeney bill becomes law."[64]

On the same day that the Feeney bill appeared, Rep. Bob Goodlatte (R-VA) introduced the Pretrial Detention and Lifetime Supervision of Terrorists Act (H.R. 3040), which would deny bail to anyone accused of domestic or international terrorism. Given the broad definition of domestic terrorism in the Patriot Act, Goodlatte's bill threatens the right to bail granted in the Eighth Amendment.

On September 10, 2003, Senator Arlen Specter (R-PA) introduced the Terrorist Penalties Enhancement Act (S. 1604), which would authorize the death penalty for any act of domestic or international terrorism that results in the death of a person.

The most significant of the recent anti-terrorism bills was the Anti-Terrorism Intelligence Tools Improvement Act (H.R. 3197), introduced on September 25, 2003 by Rep. James Sensenbrenner (R-WI), chair of the House Judiciary Committee, and Rep. Porter Goss (R-FL), chair of the House Intelligence Committee. The bill would: 1) provide new penalties (between one and five years in prison) for violating the non-disclosure provision of national security letters; 2) provide for judicial enforcement of requests for information under national security letters; and 3) facilitate the use of information collected under the FISA in immigration proceedings.

Among the new bills, the Sensenbrenner-Goss bill may represent the greatest danger to libraries because the powerful positions of the two sponsors make eventual passage more likely, and because the bill increases the power of a heavily used surveillance tool already acknowledged by the Justice Department as the most appropriate tool for seizing library records.

Ashcroft's National Tour

Even as draft legislation to expand the Patriot Act was circulating through Congress, Attorney General Ashcroft announced an aggressive publicity campaign and national tour to shore up support for the original act. That tour, represented as a defense of the Patriot Act as a vital tool in the war against terrorism, began with a policy speech in Washington on August 19, 2003, and proceeded to cities like Philadelphia, Detroit, Milwaukee and Salt Lake City. A Justice Department official explained, "The decision has been made that it's time that we get out there and talk about the successes. There have been a host of mischaracterizations of certain authorities that Congress gave the Justice Department, and we need to set the record straight."[65]

The campaign seemed to be spurred by the passage of a House amendment in July 2003 repealing the "sneak and peak" provision of Section 213 of the Patriot Act (see Chapter 5), but the fact that more than 150 cities and towns had passed anti–Patriot Act resolutions also moved the Justice Department to action. As part of the initiative, the Justice Department sent a memo to all U.S. attorneys describing the "16-state 18-city Patriot Act tour" and encouraging federal prosecutors "to call personally or meet with . . . congressional representatives" to discuss "the potentially deleterious effects" of the "sneak and peek" amendment. The July 14 memo lists names and phone numbers of House members, with an asterisk placed next to the names of those who voted for the amendment.

On August 19, 2003, Ashcroft issued a veiled warning against any attempts to scale back the powers of the Patriot Act: "To abandon these tools would disconnect the dots; risk American lives; sacrifice liberty; and reject September 11th's lessons." Senator Patrick Leahy (D-VT), ranking Democrat on the Judiciary Committee, maintained that the Bush administration "has been arrogant in the use of many of the new powers Congress has given the government, and now they are having to deal with the backlash."[66]

The first stop on Ashcroft's Patriot Act tour was the National Constitution Center in Philadelphia, two blocks from the Liberty Bell and three from Independence Hall. The Center has a tradition of placing "post-its" in various places around the museum to solicit answers from visitors to constitutionally significant questions. One of those questions was, "Does the Patriot Act strike the right balance between security and freedom?" Despite Ashcroft's hard sell, almost all of the citizens who jotted answers said no. A typical answer was, "No, the terrorists win if we do this." Another answer said, "This Act is the beginning of our freedoms being watched and limited. I believe security is important, but it should not take away our rights."[67]

Ashcroft's tour used carefully scripted media events with audiences limited to prosecutors and law enforcement, causing concern among critics that the public was being excluded. Rep. Bernie Sanders (I-VT) said, "Attorney General Ashcroft is clearly on the defensive and said he would hold public hearings on the Patriot Act nationwide. Now we find out that's not true. Instead of holding real public meetings, he's holding closed meetings with selected audiences where he gives scripted remarks for the television cameras. . . . It is a bit ironic that Attorney General Ashcroft is using closed meetings to try to build public support for a law that expands secret court proceedings. That's the way the Ashcroft Department of Justice likes to operate—without any public scrutiny or accountability. That's just wrong. If he supports the sweeping new powers for federal agents in the Patriot Act then he should be prepared to defend that position in the court of public opinion."[68]

State Anti-Terrorism Legislation in the Wake of 9/11

Time magazine reported in January 2002 that forty-six state legislatures were scheduled to debate anti-terrorism legislation during 2002, and many of the bills would expand local law enforcement powers in ways similar to the Patriot Act. The U.S. Congress is encouraging such state mimicry, and the Patriot Act has already relaxed privacy safeguards by enabling state and local police to obtain sensitive intelligence information gathered by federal agents. Massive law enforcement databases containing personal information about suspects and nonsuspects alike are shared among law enforcement agencies. The Patriot Act's authorization of domestic spying by the CIA makes it particularly dangerous for state and local law enforcement agencies to share CIA data without normal constitutional restrictions.

By the time of the September 11, 2001, terrorist attacks, most state legislatures had either adjourned or neared the end of their 2001 sessions, so their first opportunity to address new anti-terrorism legislation came in 2002. For those legislatures that meet biennially, the first chance to pass new laws came in 2003.

Some of the new state laws were clearly designed to mimic the Patriot Act. For example, shortly after 9/11, Idaho Attorney General Al Lance recommended broader state authority to wiretap private communications and keep government information secret. Lance's recommendations came from a report requested by Governor Dirk Kempthorne that suggested thirty-four changes to Idaho laws. Many Idaho lawmakers were uneasy about the changes, and an ACLU attorney said they were "frightening." Among the recommendations were the following:

1. Authorization to exempt records or documents from public disclosure "when necessary for the security or safety of the state."

2. Authorization to conduct wiretaps forty-eight hours before obtaining a court order if there is "a danger of death or serious physical injury, threat to national security or conspiracy . . . of organized crime."

3. Authorization for public employees to question those who request public documents.

4. Exemption of blueprints of state buildings, evacuation plans, and travel plans of state officials from public disclosure.

5. Increased response time for public records requests from three to five days, with extensions of up to fifteen days.

Marty Durand, legislative counsel for the Idaho ACLU, said she was particularly concerned about wiretaps authorized by prosecutors, the routine grilling of people who request public documents, and the closing of records by executive order.[69]

On March 22, 2002, the Idaho legislature added further wiretapping provisions to state law, allowing law enforcement to intercept computer and cell phone communications.

In Illinois, on October 16, 2001, just days after passage of the Patriot Act, Attorney General Jim Ryan unveiled state anti-terrorism legislation that borrowed heavily from the federal act. Ryan said the legislation was necessary to allow state and local law enforcement to assist in the nationwide hunt for terrorists. "We must use every tool available to prevent the mass murders of thousands of Illinois citizens," said Ryan, playing to the climate of fear following 9/11. "We should put aside any partisan differences and try to enact these measures as quickly as possible."[70]

The Illinois anti-terrorism bill contains both criminal and civil provisions that would

1. Authorize the state, for the first time, to acquire intelligence via wiretaps for suspected acts of terrorism.

2. Amend wiretap authority to apply to an individual rather than a phone, allowing the tap to "rove" from phone to phone.

3. Allow the attorney general to seek an immediate order freezing the assets of suspected terrorists, require financial institutions to freeze funds they believe are used for terrorism, and make it a civil and criminal violation to assist terrorists financially.

4. Allow for swifter search warrants in terrorism cases by relying on telephone or oral court approval, rather than the usual written approval.

5. Allow the attorney general to use the Statewide Grand Jury to prosecute terrorism.

6. Require those convicted of terrorism-related acts to submit blood to the statewide DNA database.

7. Limit the ability of nonresident aliens to acquire a state Firearms Owners ID card.

8. Create the new Class X offense of terrorism with penalties of twenty years to life and mandatory life when death is caused. Make terrorism a qualifying factor for the death penalty.

9. Create new Class X offenses of Solicitation of Material Support for Terrorism and Making a Terrorist Threat.

On May 31, 2002, the Illinois anti-terrorism bill, as amended by the Senate, was passed and sent to the governor for his signature. The final version of the bill incorporated changes suggested by the governor. For example, it provides a "sunset" date of January 1, 2005, for the surveillance provisions, just as was done with the Patriot Act.

Attorney General Ryan, who regarded the bill as a personal and political victory, said, "President Bush, Vice President Cheney, Attorney General Ashcroft and other high-ranking officials in Washington welcome and urge just this kind of state support in the war on terrorism."[71]

In Florida, during a special legislative session held on December 10, 2001, Gov. Jeb Bush signed eleven bills designed to increase state security. The bills close public records, create seven regional domestic security task forces and a state counterterrorism center and database, increase punishment for terrorists, and impose penalties for using biological poisons on food and water supplies. A new wiretap law allows police to maintain surveillance of suspected terrorists without having to go to another judge when suspects change jurisdictions. Governor Bush explained, "We have a delicate balance here . . . to protect the civil liberties of Americans as well as to deal with the fact that we're in a new realm now where people in our midst who hate our way of life have attacked our basic freedoms."[72]

On April 22, 2002, the Florida legislature passed another bill expanding the use of wiretapping against terrorism, and the following month it passed several so-called shell bills, which contain no specific language but address subjects like seaport and transportation security.

In Georgia, a bill, titled "Georgia's Support of the War on Terrorism Act of 2002" and signed on May 16, 2002, expands police wiretapping powers and requires electronic communications service providers to divulge any communications that are in their possession or are reasonably accessible.

In Maryland, the Maryland Security Protection Act of 2002, enacted on April 25, 2002, provides for expanded authority for pen registers and other wiretapping procedures. Another bill establishing the Maryland Security Council was signed on April 9, 2002, and state agencies were required to cooperate with the Council.

In South Carolina, the Omnibus Terrorism Protection and Homeland Defense Act of 2002, signed on July 2, 2002, criminalizes aid to a terrorist or terrorist organization, increases penalties for terrorist activity, and increases the government's power to conduct roving wiretaps.

The District of Columbia passed the Omnibus Anti-Terrorism Act of 2002 in April 2002, which defines the crime of terrorism and sets up a response plan for threats of bioterrorism. The law also exempts all plans and assessments intended to prevent terrorist attacks from the city's freedom of information act.

Nevada, South Dakota, and Tennessee passed laws in 2002 defining the crime of terrorism and establishing tough penalties for such crimes. Utah passed a law in 2002 enacting new penalties for terrorism through weapons of mass destruction and hoaxes threatening their use.

The most common provisions in the new state anti-terrorism laws are secrecy measures designed to override state "open records" and "open meetings" laws. In the name of security, states have made the dubious assumption that they could protect themselves against terrorism by wrapping themselves in secrecy. For example, Ohio may never reveal its new anti-terrorism plans, because it first passed a law preventing officials from disclosing any information from a meeting dealing with security issues.

The federal government has, of course, already succeeded in reducing access to federal records through Justice Department guidelines advising federal agencies to withhold information requested through the FOIA and through executive decisions to classify all statistical data relating to the implementation of the Patriot Act. As the selected list below indicates, most states have chosen to impose their post-9/11 secrecy through legislation.

Alabama passed a law in June 2002 to exempt state infrastructure and security plans from disclosure.

California passed a law in July 2002 allowing meetings to be held in secret if they are in response to terrorist threats. The state passed three more secrecy laws in September 2002, the first limiting access to meetings discussing matters posing a threat to the security of public buildings, services, or facilities; the second making it a crime for public officials to divulge information discussed in a closed meeting; and the third allowing the state to hold closed sessions when it believes there may be a threat of criminal activity against state personnel or property.

In Colorado, a law signed on June 3, 2002, created the Office of Preparedness, Security and Fire Safety, allowing the state to deny public access to any records containing details of security arrangements or any other records given voluntarily to the state for security purposes.

Connecticut created a law on June 3, 2002, which exempts information on sabotage prevention and response from the FOIA. Another law, signed on June 13, 2002, prohibits disclosure of security manuals and architectural drawings of government buildings.

On July 3, 2002, Delaware exempted from the Delaware freedom of information act any records that could jeopardize the safety of state residents. Florida signed a law on April 22, 2002, closing any meetings that would reveal security system plans. Idaho signed a law on March 4, 2002, exempting from disclosure any evacuation or emergency response plans when disclosure of such documents would jeopardize public safety. In Illinois, a bill exempting geographic system data from the state's freedom of information act became law on July 11, 2002.

A major controversy erupted in 2002 when the Indiana legislature passed a bill exempting itself entirely from the state public records act. After the governor vetoed the bill, the legislature threatened to override the veto. In Iowa, a bill was signed on April 1, 2002, prohibiting disclosure of information about school security procedures and emergency preparedness. Another Iowa bill, signed on April 8, 2002, allows state agencies to close meetings that discuss information about airports, utilities, and water districts. Such information is also exempted from disclosure under the Iowa public records laws.

On May 29, 2002, a law was passed in Kansas exempting from disclosure any records pertaining to utilities, sewer treatment, and water and communication systems. In Kentucky, a bill in 2003 created a Task Force on Homeland Security to study ways to increase the security of records related to the war on terrorism. In Louisiana, a law signed on April 23, 2002, exempts from disclosure any information relating to security procedures, vulnerability assessments, or criminal intelligence information pertaining to terrorist activity. In Maine, a law signed on April 11, 2002, exempts information regarding security plans or procedures from freedom of access laws.

A Maryland law passed on April 9, 2002, denies access to any record if it would endanger the public. Another law signed May 6, 2002, created a Biological Agents Registry program and exempts the registry information from the open records act. In Massachusetts, a law signed on September 5, 2002, exempts building blueprints, security measures, preparedness plans, and vulnerability assessments whose disclosure could jeopardize public safety.

A Michigan bill signed into law on April 9, 2002, exempts from disclosure any information relating to the state's critical infrastructure or that could have a debilitating effect on the security and welfare of the state. A Missouri law, signed on July 1, 2002, expands the emergency powers of the governor when there is a major disaster, an act of biological terrorism, or an imminent threat of a disaster. A New Hampshire law signed in 2002 exempts matters pertaining to terrorism or emergency functions from the state's open meetings laws.

On July 9, 2002, one day after New Jersey's revised Open Public Records Act went into effect, Governor James McGreevey signed an executive order allowing government agencies to exempt from disclosure 483 categories of public records. After public protests against the action, the governor amended the order, reducing the closures to 80 categories. Another executive order proposed by the governor would allow agencies to withhold records if their release would hamper the state's ability to fight terrorism.

In North Dakota, a law signed on May 7, 2002, exempts from the definition of public record all records relating to security or infrastructure and allows agencies to hold closed sessions when dealing with emergency response procedures. In South Dakota, a law signed on February 25, 2002, defines terrorist acts and increases related penalties.

Tennessee's Terrorism Prevention and Response Act of 2002, enacted on July 9, 2002, expands the crime of terrorism and increases the penalties for such crimes. In Utah, a law signed in March 2002 classifies all records containing information about explosives. Another law signed in 2002 exempts from release records concerning security matters and enacts new penalties for criminal offenses, including terrorism through weapons of mass destruction and hoaxes threatening their use.

A new Virginia law exempts from disclosure plans to respond to or prevent terrorist activity and any engineering or architectural drawing or manual whose disclosure might harm the security of government buildings or people. A provision also requires individuals who request public records to provide their names and addresses. Three other bills in Virginia exempting records from disclosure were passed by both the House and Senate in 2003. In Washington, a bill signed into law on April 3, 2002, exempts any architectural or infrastructure designs or other records that show the location or layout of telecommunications or network facilities.

Countless other state anti-terrorism bills have been introduced and await passage or rejection by the local legislatures. All are driven by the fear that followed 9/11 and the political stampede that followed the Patriot Act.

Notes

1. *NOW, with Bill Moyers*, PBS television show, November 16, 2003.

2. "Insatiable Appetite: The Government's Demand for New and Unnecessary Powers after September 11," ACLU Report, April 2002, p. 3.

3. "Remarks of Attorney General John Ashcroft: Attorney General's Guidelines," May 30, 2002, p. 1. www.usdoj.gov/ag/speeches/2002/53002agpreparedremarks.html.

4. Ibid., p. 2.

5. Ibid., p. 3.

6. Ibid.

7. "Fact Sheet: Attorney General's Guidelines: Detecting and Preventing Terrorist Attacks," May 30, 2002, p. 2. www.fas.org/irp/news/2002/05/ag-guidelines-factsheet.pdf.

8. "CDT's Guide to the FBI Guidelines: Impact on Civil Liberties and Security—The Need for Congressional Oversight," Center for Democracy and Technology, June 26, 2002, p. 7. www.cdt.org/wiretap/020626guidelines.shtml.

9. "Fact Sheet: Attorney General's Guidelines: Detecting and Preventing Terrorist Attacks," p. 5.

10. "CDT's Guide to the FBI Guidelines: Impact on Civil Liberties and Security—The Need for Congressional Oversight."

11. Ibid.

12. Ibid.

13. Ibid.

14. Ibid., pp. 3–4.

15. "The Attorney General's Guidelines," Electronic Privacy Information Center, p. 1. www.epic.org/privacy/fbi/.

16. Ibid., pp. 1–3.

17. Gail Russell Chaddock, "Security Act to Pervade Daily Lives," *Christian Science Monitor*, November 21, 2002, p. 2. www.csmonitor.com/2002/1121/p01s03-usju.

18. Carrie Kirby, "Personal Privacy Takes Alarming Hit, Critics Say," *San Francisco Chronicle*, November 20, 2002, p. 1. www.sfgate.com/cgibin/article.cgi?file=chronicle/archive/2002/11/20.

19. Ibid.

20. Courtland Milloy, "Something Suspicious Is in the Air," *Washington Post*, March 24, 2003, p. B1.

21. "At What Price 'Awareness'?" *Censorship News: The National Coalition Against Censorship Newsletter*, Winter 2002–2003, number 88, p. 1.

22. William Safire, "You Are a Suspect," NYTimes.com, November 14, 2002, pp. 1–2.

23. John Markoff, "Pentagon Plans a Computer System That Would Peek at Personal Data of Americans," *New York Times*, November 9, 2002, p. A12.

24. Letter to Rep. Duncan Hunter, House Committee on Armed Services, from American Civil Liberties Union et al., January 14, 2003. www.epic.org/privacy/profiling/TIA_coalition_letter.pdf.

25. Markoff, "Pentagon Plans a Computer System That Would Peek at Personal Data of Americans," p. A12.

26. "TIA Overview (vision)," www.darpa.mil/iao/TIASystems.html, pp. 1–2.

27. "Rep. Armey: Homeland Security Bill Does Not Authorize TIA," Electronic Privacy Information Center, November 25, 2002, www.epic.org/privacy/profiling/tia/.

28. *Congressional Record—Senate*, November 19, 2002, p. S11412.

29. "Secrecy and Surveillance," *Newsletter on Intellectual Freedom*, May 2003, p. 118.

30. H.J. Res 2 (Public Law 108-7), www.epic.org/privacy/profiling/tia/pub_law_108-7.html.

31. Ariana Eunjung Cha, "Pentagon Details New Surveillance System," *Washington Post*, May 21, 2003, p. A6.

32. "Voices of Protest Sometimes Get Through," *Censorship News: National Coalition Against Censorship Newsletter*, Spring 2003, p. 1.

33. Anita Ramasastry, "Patriot II: The Sequel," *Find Law's Legal Commentary*, February 17, 2003, p. 2. http://writ.news.findlaw.com/ramasastry/20030217.html.

34. Ibid.

35. David Ignatius, "Back in the Safe Zone," *Washington Post*, August 1, 2003, p. A19.

36. Bradley Graham, "Poindexter to Leave Pentagon Research Job," *Washington Post*, August 1, 2003, p. A9.

37. Bradley Graham, "Poindexter Resigns but Defends Programs," *Washington Post*, August 13, 2003, p. A2.

38. Dan Eggen, "Ashcroft: No Database for TIPS," *Washington Post*, July 26, 2002, p. A10.

39. Bill Berkowitz, "AmeriSnitch," *The Progressive*, May 2002, p. 28.

40. www.citizencorp.gov/tips.html.

41. Ibid.

42. "Ashcroft vs. Americans," *Boston Globe*, July 17, 2002. Quoted in Nat Hentoff, "Ashcroft's Master Plan to Spy on Us," *Village Voice.com,* August 2, 2002, p. 1. www.villagevoice.com/issues/0232/hentoff.php.

43. "War on Terrorism," *Newsletter on Intellectual Freedom*, November 2002, p. 273.

44. Nat Hentoff, "Ashcroft's Master Plan to Spy upon Us," August 2, 2002, p. 2. www.villagevoice.com/issues/0232/hentoff.

45. Nat Hentoff, "The Death of Operation TIPS," December 13, 2002, p. 1. www.villagevoice.com/issues/0251/hentoff.php.

46. Anita Ramasastry, "Patriot II: The Sequel," *Find Law's Legal Commentary*, February 17, 2003, p. 4. http://writ.news.findlaw.com/ramasastry/20030217.html.

47. "Documents Show Errors in TSA's 'No-Fly' Watchlist," *EPIC Alert*, Electronic Privacy Information Center, April 9, 2003, p. 2. www.epic.org/privacy/airtravel/profiling.html.

48. Robert O'Harrow, Jr., "Aviation ID System Stirs Doubts," *Washington Post*, March 14, 2003, p. A16.

49. *Flashpoint USA*, PBS television series, WMPT, July 15, 2003.

50. Ibid.

51. Ibid.

52. *NOW, with Bill Moyers*, February 9, 2002.

53. Ibid.

54. Charles Lewis and Adam Mayle, "Justice Dept. Drafts Sweeping Expansion of Anti-Terrorism Act," Center for Public Integrity, February 7, 2003, p. 1. www.publicintegrity.org/dtaweb/report.asp?ReportID=502&L1.

55. Ibid.

56. Jill Zuckman, "Some Fear Big Brother Lurks Inside Patriot II," *Chicago Tribune*, April 23, 2003, p. 1. www.chicagotribune.com/news/access-registered.intercept.

57. Alex Jones, "Secret Patriot Act II Destroys Remaining US Liberty," *www.infowars.com*, February 11, 2003, p.1.

58. *NOW, with Bill Moyers*, February 9, 2002.

59. Ibid.

60. Ramasastry, "Patriot II: The Sequel," p. 5.

61. Ibid.

62. Dan Eggen, "GOP Bill Would Add Anti-Terror Powers," *Washington Post*, August 21, 2003, p. A3.

63. Charles Levendosky, "US Constitution under Threat in a Climate of Fear," *Taipei Times*, September 26, 2003, p. 9. www.taipeitimes.com/News/edit/archives/2003/09/26/2003069320.

64. Ibid.

65. Dan Eggen, "Ashcroft Planning Trip to Defend Patriot Act," *Washington Post*, August 13, 2003, p. A2.

66. Dan Eggen, "Ashcroft Defends Anti-Terrorism Law," *Washington Post*, August 20, 2003, p. A10.

67. Nancy Szokan, "Is This a Great Place or What?" *Washington Post*, August 24, 2003. p. B2.

68. "Sanders Challenges Ashcroft to Hold Open Public Meetings on Patriot Act," Rep. Bernie Sanders, U.S. House of Representatives, August 21, 2003. http://bernie.house.gov/documents/releases/20030821144352.asp.

69. Szokan, "Is This a Great Place or What?," p. 103.

70. "Attorney General Ryan Unveils Legislation to Fight Domestic Terrorism," *Today's News*, October 16, 2001. www.prnewswire.com/cgibin/stories.pl?ACCT=104&STORY=/www/story/10-16-2001.

71. "Anti-Terrorist Bill Wins Final Legislative Approval," *Chicagoland.com*, May 31, 2002. www.chicagolandconstruction.com/news.asp?article=2071.

72. "After September 11 Legislatures Restrict Access," *Newsletter on Intellectual Freedom*, March 2002, p. 68.

Chapter 5

Fighting Back: Responses to the Patriot Act

Congressional Oversight of the Patriot Act

Given the unprecedented secrecy built into the provisions of the Patriot Act, the Homeland Security Act, and other laws and administrative guidelines introduced since 9/11, the normal process of congressional and public oversight of the government's exercise of these new powers has been extremely difficult. How can Congress and the public hold the FBI accountable for abuses and excesses if they cannot discover and document what the FBI is doing?

Even as the Patriot Act was rushed through Congress without meaningful debate, lawmakers recognized that careful congressional oversight after passage of the act would be necessary to prevent this legislative monster from overwhelming American civil liberties. During the very restricted Senate debate, Maria Cantwell (D-WA) declared, "The administration was said yesterday to be pressing for quick passage by both houses of the Senate measure; the more careful work of the House Judiciary Committee would be set aside. That's wrong, and an acquiescent step that in the long run Congress likely would regret."[1]

As we showed earlier, Congress acquiesced to the administration's demand for an end run around the House Judiciary Committee, after which Cantwell warned her Senate colleagues that the many provisions of the Patriot Act would not stand constitutional scrutiny. "We cannot await court review," she declared. "May I ask the Chairman, do you agree that, under these circumstances, it is incumbent upon the committee, which has jurisdiction over the Department of Justice, to maintain vigilant oversight of the Department in its use of the Foreign Intelligence Surveillance Act (FISA) authorities after enactment of this legislation?"

Chairman Patrick Leahy, a fellow Democrat from Vermont, responded, "I agree with you completely, and you can rest assured that the Judiciary Committee under my chairmanship will conduct meaningful oversight."[2] Leahy's assurances soon became irrelevant when Republicans ascended to power in both houses of Congress, removing Leahy from chairmanship of the Senate Judiciary Committee.

Since October 2001, when Senator Leahy promised meaningful oversight, Congress has been able to exercise only the most superficial oversight of the implementation of the surveillance provisions of the Patriot Act. During the first ten months after the passage of the Patriot Act, the Senate Judiciary Committee sent twenty-seven unanswered letters to the Justice Department seeking information on the Patriot Act and related matters. Committee chairman Leahy commented, "Since I've been here, I have never known an administration that is more difficult to get information from that the oversight committees are entitled to."[3]

Not only has the Justice Department withheld most significant data on the implementation of the Patriot Act, but when it has released data, it has insisted that it be given to congressional intelligence committees rather than the Judiciary Committee. Professor David Rosenbloom at American University said Attorney General John Ashcroft's attempt to bypass the Judiciary Committee, which has the oversight authority for the Patriot Act, was improper. "I don't think the executive can forum shop," he said. "It doesn't have the authority to choose which committee will exercise oversight. That's for Congress to decide."[4]

Professor Harold Koh of the Yale Law School warned that as "traditional law enforcement is moved under the umbrella of foreign intelligence surveillance, the more difficult it will be to continue the traditional Congressional process of oversight of law enforcement activities."[5]

The public watchdog Center for Democracy and Technology (CDT) has urged strong congressional oversight of the Patriot Act and the dramatically revised FBI guidelines:

> Consistent Congressional oversight is vital to protect our security and our civil liberties. The FBI guidelines were changed by Attorney General Ashcroft with the stroke of a pen without prior notice or consultation with Congress. This is not only unprecedented but does not bode well for Congressional oversight over FBI activity to ensure both protection of constitutional rights and success in the fight against terrorism.[6]

The CDT urged Congress to focus on four key questions:

1. Is the Executive Branch committed to consultation with Congress in policy making? Why was Congress cut out of this process? How can Congress be included in the future?

2. As the FBI expands its surveillance capability, will the Judiciary Committees engage in parallel build up of oversight capability? Will more staff be devoted to oversight?

3. Will the Executive Branch report to the Committees the critical data which may yield patterns of Bureau activity requiring oversight and investigation?

4. What is the alternative for keeping the FBI on the criminal investigative course and our citizens safe?[7]

Despite such public advice and criticism, the Justice Department continued to ignore the Senate Judiciary Committee's requests for information on the implementation of the Patriot Act. Senator Leahy said the Department reflected an attitude of "we will tell you what we want you to know, and we won't tell you anything else."[8]

Finally, on December 23, 2002, Assistant Attorney General Daniel Bryant provided a response to a question Leahy had asked at a May 8, 2002, Judiciary Committee hearing. The three-part question concerned the use of Section 215 of the Patriot Act to obtain records from a library or bookstore. In response to part (a) of the committee's question, "Has the FBI . . . requested such records in any investigation of terrorism?," the Justice Department said only, "That classified information is being delivered to the Committee under separate cover. . . . " In response to part (b), "Can such an order be served on a public library to require the library to produce records about where a library patron has surfed on the Internet?" and "Has such an order been sought by the Department or the FBI?," the Justice Department responded, "Such an order could conceivably be served on a public library although it is unlikely that public libraries maintain those types of records."[9]

Part (c) of the question asked, "Do you think that library and bookstore patrons have a 'reasonable expectation of privacy' in the titles of the books they have purchased from a bookstore or borrowed from a library?" The Justice Department answered, "Any right of privacy possessed by library and bookstore patrons in such information is necessarily and inherently limited since, by the nature of these transactions, the patron is reposing that information in the library or bookstore and assumes the risk that the entity may disclose it to another. Whatever privacy interests a patron may have are outweighed by the Government's interest in obtaining the information in cases where the FBI can show the patron's relevance to an authorized full investigation to protect against international terrorism or clandestine intelligence activities."[10]

The Justice Department also provided Leahy with answers to several questions he had asked of Attorney General Ashcroft at a July 25, 2002, hearing before the Judiciary Committee. The first question concerned federal demands under the Patriot Act "for records of the use of library services, as well as orders to librarians to keep those requests secret." Part (a) asked, "Please clarify what the Department is doing to impose secrecy on its demands for information from libraries." The answer stated that an order under Section 215 of the Patriot Act to compel production of records "would contain language which prohibits officers, employees or agents of companies or institutions receiving such an order from disclosing to the target or to persons outside the company or institution the fact that the FBI has sought or obtained access to those defined categories of business records."[11]

Part (b) of the first question asked how many such demands for library information had been made and what legal authority was used to require secrecy, to which the Justice Department responded that such information was "classified at the SECRET level and, accordingly, is being delivered to the Committee under separate cover."

Part (c) asked, "How many libraries has the FBI visited (as opposed to presented with court orders) since the passage of the USA Patriot Act?" Note that this question addressed the kinds of FBI visits conducted under the Library Awareness Program, visits with no subpoena or other court order. The answer from Assistant Attorney General Bryant was instructive:

> Information has been sought from libraries on a voluntary basis and under traditional law enforcement authorities not related to the Foreign Intelligence Surveillance Act or the changes brought about by the USA Patriot Act. While the FBI does not maintain statistics on the number of libraries visited by FBI Agents in the course of its investigations, an informal survey conducted by the FBI indicated that field offices had sought information from libraries.[12]

In other words, whereas all information on FBI visits to libraries and bookstores under the Patriot Act is classified secret, the Bureau is free to acknowledge that the old Library Awareness–type inquiries are still being conducted.

Another question addressed by Assistant Attorney General Bryant was, "What precautions is the Attorney General taking to isolate out only those records related to a specific target? How is the Attorney General ensuring the security and confidentiality of the records of others?" Here Bryant could only cite the gag order that the Patriot Act imposes on libraries and other institutions visited by the Bureau.

The Justice Department also responded on December 23, 2002, to two questions posed in a July 24, 2002, letter from Senator Russ Feingold (D-WI), chairman of the Senate Subcommittee on the Constitution. The first question concerned the number of times the FBI had used Section 215 of the Patriot Act to acquire business records from libraries, bookstores, and so on, and it was answered with the Justice Department's usual claim: "That information is classified at the SECRET level." The response also included a repeat of the statement sent to Leahy acknowledging that the FBI had sought information from libraries "on a voluntary basis." The second question concerned the Justice Department's use of "roving surveillance" under Section 206 of the Patriot Act. Again, all specific data on such use were described by the Department as "classified at the SECRET level."[13]

At the conclusion of its uninformative answers about Section 215, the Justice Department attached a copy of an interesting October 26, 2001, FBI memo, "Policy Guidance or Directives to Law Enforcement on Section 215," which issued guidance to all FBI divisions on changes made by the Patriot Act. The memo advised all FBI agents that, whereas the old standard for seizing business records in libraries and other institutions required a showing of "specific and articulable facts" giving reason to believe that the person to whom the records related was an agent of a foreign power, "Section 215 changes this standard to simple relevance." The memo adds, "In the past, the FBI has encountered situations in which the holders of relevant records refused to produce them absent a subpoena or other compelling authority. When those records did not fit within the defined categories for National Security Letters or the four categories then defined in the FISA business records section, the FBI had no means of compelling production. With the new language the FBI can seek a FISA court order for any such materials."[14]

In other words, agents are now being told that if librarians insist on a subpoena, they can just rely on the Patriot Act, which authorizes an automatic and unchallengeable warrant from the secret FISA court.

The FBI memo also advised agents on how to exploit Section 214 of the Patriot Act, which authorizes pen/trap and trace orders under a simple relevance standard. The originator of the memo also felt it necessary to interpret the phrase that is included in Sections 214, 215, and several other sections of the Patriot Act authorizing new powers of surveillance and investigation " . . . provided that such an investigation of a United States person is not conducted *solely* [author's emphasis] on the basis of activities protected by the First Amendment of the Constitution . . . "

As I indicated in Chapter 2, this phrase not only fails to offer protection for American civil liberties, it is in fact a hollow and absurd gesture. In its memo to all divisions, the FBI also seems to interpret the phrase as meaningless: "Congress inserted this to indicate that the technique will not be used against U.S. persons who are merely exercising constitutionally protected rights. However, it is highly unlikely, if not entirely impossible, for an investigation to be authorized under the FCI AGG [Foreign Counterintelligence Attorney General Guidelines] that is 'solely' based on protected activities. In other words, all authorized investigations of U.S. persons will likely involve some allegation or possibility of illegal activity . . . which is not protected by the First Amendment."[15]

Note the FBI's assumption that "some allegation or possibility of illegal activity" is sufficient to outweigh the U.S. Constitution.

The U.S. House of Representatives fared no better than the Senate in exercising oversight over the implementation of the Patriot Act. On June 13, 2002, Rep. James Sensenbrenner (R-WI) and Rep. John Conyers (D-MI), the chairman and ranking member of the House Judiciary Committee, sent a letter to Attorney General Ashcroft describing their responsibility to conduct oversight of the implementation of the USA Patriot Act and requesting answers by July 9, 2002, to fifty questions about the use of the new authorities granted by the act.

Among the fifty questions, those most relevant to libraries and bookstores were as follows:

11. How many applications and orders, pursuant to Section 215 of the [Patriot] Act, have been made or obtained for tangible objects in any investigation . . . ? What procedures are in place to ensure that such orders are not sought solely on the basis of activities protected by the First Amendment . . . ?

12. Has Section 215 been used to obtain records from a public library, bookstore, or newspaper? If so, how many times . . . ? How many times have the records sought related to named individuals? How many times have the records sought been entire databases? Is the decision to seek orders for bookstore, library, or newspaper records subject to any special policies or procedures . . . ?

13. How many roving pen register and trap and trace orders have been issued under Section 216?

14. Since the enactment of the Act, how many FISA surveillance order applications certifying under Section 218 of the Act that a "significant purpose" of the surveillance was the collection of foreign intelligence information could not have been certified, pursuant to prior law . . . ?

15. How many U.S. citizens or lawful permanent residents have been subject to new FISA surveillance orders since enactment of the Act?

27. How many FISA applications for "roving" surveillance authority . . . and how many for "roving" search authority have been approved since enactment of the Act? How many surveillances and how many searches have been conducted pursuant to those approved applications?[16]

After more than two months had passed without a response from the Justice Department, Rep. Conyers appeared with me on a National Public Radio show to discuss the Patriot Act. When asked what he would do if he received no response from the Justice Department, Conyers answered, "I'll call up the attorney general and remonstrate with his secretary for ignoring my letters. I won't tolerate this." When asked if he had subpoena power to require a response, Conyers answered, "Absolutely not. If the attorney general continues to thumb his nose at me and everybody in the Congress, then I'm in the same place as 275 million other people."[17]

In October 2002, the House Judiciary Committee revealed that it had received three letters of response from the Justice Department. The first letter addressed the questions of most interest to librarians but provided little information. For example, Question 10, which concerned Section 214 and the use of pen registers and trap trace devices, was answered as follows: "The number of times the tools in section 214 have been used against U.S. persons . . . is classified, but will . . . be provided to the intelligence committees in an appropriate channel."

Questions 11 and 12, which asked for the number of times Section 215 had been invoked to seize information from libraries or bookstores, was greeted once more with the Department's claim that such data were classified. However, just as in its letter to the Senate Judiciary Committee, the Department did concede that an order under Section 215 "could conceivably be served on a public library, bookstore or newspaper." Questions 15 and 27, which asked for statistics on the use of new FISA surveillance orders under the Patriot Act, were answered again with a claim of secrecy and referred to the intelligence committees. Indeed, the only response worth noting in the Justice Department's first letter was its strong argument against allowing the "sunsetted" provisions of the Patriot Act to expire.[18]

The Justice Department's second letter to the House Judiciary Committee covered the remainder of the original fifty questions but shed little light on the use of surveillance under the Patriot Act. The third letter addressed follow-up questions posed by staff of the Judiciary Committee who sought clarification of some of the Department's earlier answers. The most significant clarification offered by the Justice Department concerned its assurance to the committee that it had "practices in place" to ensure that orders pursuant to sections 214 and 215 "are not sought solely on the basis of activities protected by the First Amendment." The Bureau gave an identical statement for both sections:

> A great deal of care is given to ensure that an order [pursuant to sections 214 and 215] is not sought solely on the basis of activities protected by the First Amendment. . . . The Attorney General or his designee . . . personally approves the filing of every application to the Court. A brief statement of facts in each case is then presented to the Court, along with the Government's certification, signed by the individual applicant, that the order is not being sought solely for activities protected by the First Amendment.[19]

The real "clarification" is found not in this lame statement to the committee, but in the internal FBI memo to all divisions, discussed above, in which the Bureau advised its agents that it was "entirely impossible" for an investigation to be based "solely" on activities protected by the First Amendment because any investigation "will likely involve some allegation or possibility of illegal activity."[20]

On April 1, 2002, the House Judiciary Committee submitted thirty-eight new questions to Attorney General Ashcroft attempting once more to acquire information on the implementation of the Patriot Act, including "the use of preexisting authorities and the new authorities conferred by the Act." Question 1, which concerned Section 215 and its authority to seize "tangible things" from libraries, bookstores, and so on, asked,

  a. What guidelines has the Attorney General approved . . . for the conduct of such investigations?

  b. Before such an order can be sought, do the guidelines require that the FBI have already established probable cause that a person under investigation is an agent of a foreign power?

  c. Please produce all guidelines . . . for the conduct of such an investigation.[21]

Question 2 concerned Section 215 and any other provisions that could not be used "solely on the basis of activities protected by the First Amendment," and asked,

  a. Does the government make an explicit certification that an investigation of a United States person is not being conducted solely on the basis of activities protected by the First Amendment?

  b. Does the court make an express finding that an investigation of a U.S. person is not being conducted solely on the basis of activities protected by the First Amendment?

Question 3 noted the increased use of National Security Letters (NSLs) requiring businesses, including libraries and bookstores, to turn over records and asked,

  a. Please identify the specific authority relied on for issuing these letters.

  b. Has any litigation resulted from the issuance of these letters?

Question 4 asked, "Has any administrative disciplinary proceeding or civil action been initiated under Section 223 of the Act for any unauthorized disclosure of intercepts?

Question 9 referred to Section 213 of the Patriot Act, which allows a court to "delay notice of the execution of a search warrant if it may have an adverse result," and asked,

  a. How many times has DOJ sought an order delaying notice of a warrant?

  b. How many times has a court ordered the delay?

Questions 10 and 11 continue the inquiry about delayed notices for warrants, focusing on the provisions that require the court to find reasonable and good cause.

Question 12 addressed the Patriot Act's amendment to FISA permitting a surveillance order when "a significant purpose" of the surveillance is to collect foreign intelligence, asking:

a. Prior to the amendment, did the more strict requirement that foreign intelligence be "the purpose" of a surveillance order represent a legal impediment to prosecution?

b. Identify all cases since the amendment in which information has been acquired that could not have been acquired under the earlier standard.

c. Explain why such information became available under the "significant purpose" standard.

Question 14 asked, "How many emergency FISA orders did DOJ process between FISA's enactment and September 11, 2001? How many has it processed since then?"

Question 25 concerned the new FBI administrative guidelines. Among the issues were the following:

a. Why were the guidelines for criminal and domestic security investigations revised, when the apparent threat to the United States is from foreign terrorist groups?

b. The new guidelines allow the FBI to perform routine surveillance in public libraries, churches, etc., and to use data-mining services to prevent or detect terrorism. How will it be determined that the purpose of attending the public event or institution or using data mining is to prevent or detect terrorism?

c. How many religious sites have federal authorities entered without disclosing their identities?

d. How many and what kinds of public meetings have federal authorities entered in this way?

e. Before they attend public events or perform data-mining, do FBI agents document in writing how such activities serve the purpose of detecting or preventing terrorism?

h. Who at the FBI is responsible for making or approving the decision to enter a public place?

n. What type of supervision will be required when agents use data-mining?

o. What data-mining services has the FBI used? How long will the data be retained?

r. The new guidelines permit acceptance and retention of information "voluntarily provided by private entities." How will the FBI ensure the accuracy of such information?

s. How is information obtained through data-mining stored? Is access to such data limited to those involved in a particular investigation? How is erroneous information purged?

t. Is retained information reviewed at intervals to determine its relevance to antiterrorism efforts?

Question 34 asked, "Is the government seeking membership lists from mosques? If so, why?"

Question 35 asked, "Is DOJ assisting in the implementation of the Computer Assisted Passenger Prescreening System (CAPPS I or II) to screen airline passengers?"

Question 36 concerned "Operation Liberty Shield," which involves stopping cars at airports, truckers who transport hazardous materials on the highway, and monitoring Internet and financial transactions. It asked:

a. Identify the specific authority on which "Operation Liberty Shield" was created.

b. What predication is required for an agent to monitor Internet or financial transactions?

c. What terrorism investigations or prosecutions have resulted from "Operation Liberty Shield?"

On May 20, 2003, the Justice Department responded to the Judiciary Committee's April 1 letter and questions with a sixty-page report and accompanying testimony from Assistant Attorney General Viet Dinh. Predictably, the Justice Department claimed that the specific data requested by the Committee were classified and could not be revealed to the public. As reported in the *New York Times*, the Department did, however, acknowledge the use of hundreds of secret search warrants and said that some fifty people had been detained without charges as material witnesses. It said "fewer than 10" FBI field offices had visited mosques as part of their investigations, and that in the first year after 9/11, Attorney General Ashcroft had approved 113 emergency authorizations for secret foreign intelligence warrants for electronic or physical evidence, as compared to fewer than fifty in the previous twenty-three years.

The most interesting information came in the testimony of Viet Dinh, John Ashcroft's hard-line force behind the Patriot Act, who, according to the *New York Times*, said, "[A]gents have contacted about 50 libraries nationwide in the course of terrorism investigations, often at the invitation of librarians who saw something suspicious."[22] Dinh concluded that "libraries should not be allowed to become safe havens for terrorists."[23]

About ten days after Viet Dinh's testimony, the Justice Department issued a press release with excerpts from Dinh's testimony suggesting that the library visits described by Dinh had been criminal cases, not terrorism investigations (see Chapter 3). But since the Patriot Act had blurred the lines between criminal and foreign intelligence investigations, many librarians remained unsure of the nature of the fifty visits, and, in any case, the number seemed very low compared to the data available from library surveys.

Overall, both Congress and the library community were unimpressed with the Justice Department's presentation. American Library Association (ALA) President Maurice J. Freedman remarked that the Justice Department report and testimony "raise more questions than they answer," and he suggested that the government could fight terrorism without "incursions into the civil liberties of library users and the dismantling of due process." Freedman said that the ALA "agrees with Rep. Conyers, the ranking member of the House Judiciary Committee, that the Justice Department 'could have been more forthcoming in terms of the manner in which and how freely the new powers have been used.' "[24]

On June 5, 2003, Attorney General Ashcroft himself made a long-overdue appearance before the House Judiciary Committee to answer questions about the Patriot Act. Chairman Sensenbrenner introduced Ashcroft with the following comment: "[M]y support for this legislation is neither perpetual nor unconditional. I believe the [Justice] Department and Congress must be vigilant toward short term gains which ultimately may cause long term harm to the spirit of liberty and equality which animate the American character. . . . To my mind, the purpose of the Patriot Act is to secure our liberties and not to undermine them."[25]

Sensenbrenner then chided Ashcroft for the arbitrary way in which he introduced the new FBI guidelines in August 2002. Sensenbrenner noted that the previous "Levy guidelines" had been prepared only after "extensive consultation with Congress," and he asked Ashcroft, "What justified departing from the tradition of consulting with Congress?" and "If further revisions are planned, do you intend to return to the spirit of cooperation which typified the earlier revisions?"

In response, Ashcroft admitted, "In terms of the change in the guidelines which govern the internal operation of the Justice Department, the consultation was not substantial or significant." Ashcroft then had the nerve to suggest that he had simply followed the approach used by the Justice Department to railroad the Patriot Act through Congress. "Perhaps I came to the conclusion that extending those [FBI] guidelines in the same spirit as the Patriot Act had been extended was something that would be appropriate and would meet with the approval of Congress," said Ashcroft apologetically. "But I must say that we did not have extensive consultations about this exercise of Executive responsibility."[26]

What followed were four and a half hours of testimony by Ashcroft, most of which consisted of rambling, often incomprehensible answers to questions from committee members. Frequently, Ashcroft turned to his legal staff for advice on the provisions of the Patriot Act, and occasionally he avoided direct answers by giving irrelevant discourses. When the committee member attempted to point out that the question had not been answered, Chairman Sensenbrenner struck his gavel and declared that the congressman's allotted five minutes was used up.

The closest Ashcroft came to providing specific answers occurred during questions from Rep. Tammy Baldwin (D-WI) about Section 215 of the Patriot Act:

> *Baldwin*: Prior to the enactment of the USA PATRIOT Act, a FISA order for business records related only to common carriers, accommodation and storage facilities, and vehicle rentals, is that correct?
>
> *Ashcroft*: Yes it is.
>
> *Baldwin*: And what was the evidentiary standard for obtaining that court order?
>
> *Ashcroft*: [Long pause] I don't think the evidentiary standard has changed. [Whispers from Ashcroft's legal staff cause him to turn around.] OK, maybe it has. It used to be that the target is an agent of a foreign power.
>
> *Baldwin*: Right. It was relevance and specific articulable facts giving reason to believe that a person to whom the records related was an agent of a foreign power. Is that your understanding?
>
> *Ashcroft*: I think that sounds good to me.
>
> *Baldwin*: And as evidentiary standards go, that's a pretty low standard, or maybe I should say, it's one of the lower thresholds that's possible, correct?
>
> *Ashcroft*: Well, yeah, . . . in criminal matters, certainly, they don't have high standards.
>
> *Baldwin*: It's lower than reasonable suspicion or probable cause, is it not?
>
> *Ashcroft*: I think it may be said to be lower than probable cause.
>
> *Baldwin*: Now, under Section 215 the government can obtain any relevant tangible items, is that correct?
>
> *Ashcroft*: I think they are authorized to ask for relevant tangible items.
>
> *Baldwin*: And that would include things like book purchase records?
>
> *Ashcroft*: I think it's possible that, in the narrow arena in which they are authorized to ask, yes.
>
> *Baldwin*: Library book or computer records?
>
> *Ashcroft*: I think it could include library book or computer records.

Baldwin: Medical records?

Ashcroft: I don't know. Do you guys know? [Turns around to his staff] Some of them are nodding, and some of them are nodding in the other direction.

Baldwin: Education records?

Ashcroft: I think there are some education records that would be susceptible to demand under the court's supervision of FISA, yes.

Baldwin: Genetic information?

Ashcroft: I don't know about that. It might be that DNA in the possession of someone who had committed a crime had taken a drink of water and left a little DNA on the glass. We might be able to get that.

Baldwin: Under the Patriot Act, what is the evidentiary standard for the FISA court order to obtain these sorts of records?

Ashcroft: [Long delay, looks around] Let me find where I am here and see if I can get a specific standard. [Turns around] You guys want to help me on this?. . . . [Turns around and asks] Is that a probable cause or what is it?

An aide whispers: Relevance.

Ashcroft: If the judge finds that the investigation is for these purposes, he orders the FISA.[27]

Many of Ashcroft's critics noted his somewhat addled performance before the House Judiciary Committee. Laura Murphy of the American Civil Liberties Union (ACLU) commented, "I don't think he's as knowledgeable about the policies that he has implemented as he should be. When he was before the House Judiciary Committee on June 5th he really could not articulate answers to some of the specific questions that many of the House . . . members asked him. He wasn't clear on Section 215 of the Patriot Act, that allows the government to seize library records, for example. He was not entirely accurate in his response about the use of 'sneak and peek' warrants, which allow the government to come into your home, search your belongings, remove belongings without telling you. . . . So I think he's in trouble."[28]

In response to the woeful level of congressional oversight of the Patriot Act, many voices on Capitol Hill can be heard wistfully asking, "Where is Don Edwards when we need him?" Edwards, the former FBI agent turned congressman, was given the title "the congressman from the Constitution" by Nat Hentoff. He almost single-handedly stopped the FBI's Library Awareness Program in its tracks, and since he retired from Congress eight years ago, no one has stepped forward to fill his shoes.

Edwards recently stated, "Congress is not exercising its oversight powers over the Department of Justice, including the FBI. Committees should be hauling in Justice Department officials to justify what they're doing."[29]

On July 10, 2003, I spoke briefly with Edwards and asked him to elaborate.[30]

"I'm glad you're doing some writing on this subject," he told me. "Of course it's been eight years since I left Congress, but, as you know, I was an enemy of the Library Awareness Program for many years. When my subcommittee had oversight responsibility over the FBI we constantly criticized them to their face and told them that they had to stop this meddling in libraries, that it was a bad idea and in the long run was not worth much. It was also very dangerous to the libraries and to the librarians. And now the Patriot Act, which is a monstrosity anyway, turns the librarians and the other employees of the library into federal agents, spies and snitches."

I told Edwards of the difficulty I had had in getting firsthand accounts of Patriot Act visits to libraries because of the gag order imposed on librarians.

"That's something that just has to be changed," he said, "and I'm afraid it's not going to happen very soon, given the political climate that we're in. You know, we've had three or four periods in American history where we were gripped with fear over some particular phobia of the time. We had it in 1800, when the Federalists were so frightened of the Republicans and the French Jacobins that they legislated the Alien and Sedition Acts. Then after World War I we had the Palmer Raids that locked up thousands of people. And then, of course, the McCarthy era after World War II. So this is, I hope, a kind of passing phase in American history, but there's a certain rhythm to it that's very disturbing."

Given the veil of secrecy that has been cast over Patriot Act visits to libraries, I wondered how Edwards was able to conduct his very effective public hearings on the Library Awareness Program without being told that the program was classified and could not be discussed publicly. He responded forcefully, "Well, we just paid no attention to any nonsense like that. You know, if they told us it was classified, we told them that it shouldn't be and that we were going to hold a public hearing on it anyway. It's up to Congress to say that this information belongs to the public. Congress can do anything it really wants to do, but there doesn't seem to be any will or desire there. There's more in the Senate than there is in the House. In the House it's hopeless, and you're not going to get any help from the White House or the Department of Justice. You've got to turn to Congress."

I asked Edwards whether Congress would have the will to "sunset" the library surveillance provisions of the Patriot Act in 2005. He answered, "Not if they're Republicans, but if the Democrats take over, I think they'll have the will to do it."

In the meantime, I asked, what can we do to encourage openness and move the democratic process forward? "Just what you're doing," he answered. "In this country, all you can do is stir the pot."

Public Oversight of the Patriot Act

The Justice Department's minimal cooperation with congressional oversight committees and its insistence that any significant information it does provide must be in classified form has left the public in the dark about the Patriot Act. How can the people advise their representatives in Congress on the dangers of the Patriot Act if they are denied all details on its implementation? The only hope seemed to reside in the Freedom of Information Act (FOIA), the statute that represents the "People's Right to Know."

On August 21, 2002, the ACLU, in alliance with the Freedom to Read Foundation (FTRF), the American Booksellers Foundation for Free Expression (ABFFE), and the Electronic Privacy Information Center (EPIC), submitted an FOIA request for records concerning the implementation of the Patriot Act, citing concerns that the new surveillance authority threatened constitutionally protected activities of librarians, library patrons, booksellers, and investigative journalists. Among the specific information requested was the number of times the government has directed a library, bookstore, or newspaper to produce "tangible things;" initiated surveillance of Americans under the expanded FISA; conducted "sneak and peek" searches, which allow law enforcement officers to enter and search people's homes and belongings without prior notice; authorized monitoring of telephone calls and e-mails of people who are not suspected of a crime; and investigated American citizens or permanent legal residents on the basis of activities protected by the First Amendment.

In a September 3 response, the court granted the ACLU's request for expedited review, and the Justice Department conceded that the FOIA request concerned "a matter of widespread and exceptional media interest in which there exist possible questions about the government's integrity which affect public confidence."[31] Both the Justice Department and the FBI promised a swift response to the request, but by late October neither agency had disclosed any records or indicated which records it would provide.

Some of the information requested by the ACLU had been earlier sought by the House Judiciary Committee in its "50 Questions" described above. As we saw, the scattered information released to the committee was cloaked in secrecy, and the ACLU request seemed destined for a similar fate. David Sobel, general counsel to EPIC, complained that the Justice Department was using its classified stamp too broadly and that the public was entitled to know, in general terms, what the government's policies were. "We are asking only for aggregate statistical data and other policy-level information," he said. "The release of this information would not jeopardize ongoing investigations or undermine the government's ability to respond to new threats."[32]

ACLU attorney Jameel Jaffer said, "As the Justice Department has conceded, there is widespread public concern about the scope of the new surveillance powers and the possibility that the government is abusing them. The records we have identified would enable the public to judge for itself whether these new surveillance powers are necessary and whether they are being used as they should be."[33]

ABFFE President Chris Finan said, "Revealing how many subpoenas have been issued will not threaten national security. It will tell us how often the Justice Department is using the very broad power it received in the Patriot Act to monitor First Amendment-protected activity."[34]

On October 24, 2002, the ACLU and its allies decided that they would have to file a lawsuit to compel the release of the requested material. Plaintiffs asked the U.S. District Court for the District of Columbia to order the government to disclose what relevant records it had within seven days and to release those records within twenty days. For almost three months, the Justice Department continued to delay, but finally, on January 17, 2003, it supplied a batch of mostly blacked-out pages to the ACLU.

"Although the Attorney General has supplied us with over 200 pages of material in response to our request, none of those pages addresses our concerns about the new surveillance powers," said ACLU attorney Jaffer. "Much of the material is so heavily redacted that it is meaningless. . . . Once again, the Attorney General is insisting on keeping the public in the dark about matters of pressing national concern. Over the next weeks we hope to persuade the district court to order the government to disclose any records that are being withheld arbitrarily or unnecessarily."[35]

Despite the Justice Department's heavy-handed censorship of most of the released documents, the ACLU was able to draw certain conclusions about the FBI's conduct of surveillance under the Patriot Act. For one thing, the documents contain lengthy, blacked-out lists of the use of NSLs, indicating that they are a frequently used surveillance tool. These letters need only be signed by Attorney General Ashcroft or a designee and require no judicial approval.

The FOIA documents also reveal that:

1. The FBI is conducting wiretaps and secret searches in criminal investigations without complying with the usual probable cause requirements.

2. The government is using a broad surveillance provision that could force libraries and bookstores to report on their patrons' and customers' reading habits.

3. The FBI is aggressively using pen registers and trap-and-trace devices to track phone calls and e-mails.

4. The government plans to use its new surveillance powers not only against suspected terrorists but also against ordinary Americans and permanent residents.[36]

Still, the truly crucial data concerning the government's use of the Patriot Act in libraries and bookstores were denied to the ACLU alliance. David Sobel, general counsel for EPIC, expressed hope that the court would order the government to turn over the records it had withheld. "The government is so aggressively using its power to classify records that the public is now being denied essential information about government policy and conduct," he said. "This kind of secrecy is indefensible, and it suggests a lack of basic principles of democracy."[37]

In commenting on the Justice Department's lack of responsiveness, award-winning journalist Charles Levendosky commented, "The Justice Department has erected a one-way mirror between itself and the American People— department officials can look out but Americans can't look in. The Bush administration aims to gather more and more information on American citizens, but intends to share less and less of it with them."[38]

After the Justice Department declared that it would release no more documents without further litigation, attorneys for the ACLU were forced to return to district court in an effort to compel disclosure. District Court Judge Ellen Segal Huvelle ordered the government to submit legal papers by January 24, 2003, justifying its refusal to provide the requested information. On March 28, the Justice Department responded in a ninteen-page memorandum, claiming that the withheld information was either classified, and thus protected under FOIA Exemption 1, or deliberative and predecisional, which is protected under Exemption 5.

> The information that plaintiffs seek, and that DOJ has properly withheld, relates to the frequency with which the Government has sought to use particular investigative and surveillance techniques authorized by the Foreign Intelligence Surveillance Act . . . as amended by the USA Patriot Act. . . . If released to the public, the information would provide our nation's adversaries with critical information about the Government's counterintelligence capabilities, targets and areas of relative safe harbor, and allow them to avoid and defeat our counterintelligence efforts.[39]

In rejecting the FOIA request, the Justice Department trivialized the notion of the people's right to know about the workings of their government:

> Plaintiff's entire first argument, that they seek disclosure of the withheld information because the public has an interest in it, is wholly irrelevant to this case. . . . [T]he mere fact that there may be a public interest in disclosure does not warrant disclosure if the material falls within one of the well-recognized FOIA exemptions. . . . Inherent in Congress' enactment of Exemptions 1 and 5 is a balancing of interests and a decision to elevate national security concerns and the Government's need to conduct confidential deliberations over the public's interest in certain government information.[40]

The Justice Department's memorandum asserted that the people's right to know resides in Congress, not in the people themselves: "Members of Congress are, of course, the actual elected representatives of the public. Thus, the public's interest in knowing this information is in fact accommodated by the disclosure of this information to the public's elected representatives, while at the same time the protection of national security interests (which is also in the public interest) is served by keeping this information out of the public domain and out of the hands of our enemies."[41]

The Justice Department's memo concluded that "public accountability over the Government's use of specific FISA techniques is to be achieved through Congressional oversight rather than through direct dissemination of this sensitive intelligence information to the public." Indeed, the department claimed that much of the requested information consisted of the *classified* answers made available to the House Permanent Select Committee on Intelligence, and thus had already been provided to the public's elected representatives. In particular, the department said that any statistical information on the use of the Patriot Act in libraries and bookstores would have to remain classified because

> Each technique authorized under FISA is a tool employed by the Government flexibly and covertly, as a part of a larger deployment of all the tools of FISA. . . . Each of the documents classified and withheld under Exemption 1 would, if publicly disclosed, harm our national security by enabling our adversaries to conduct their intelligence or international terrorist activities against us more securely.[42]

The Justice Department contemptuously rejected the ACLU's arguments for disclosure, saying,

> Plaintiffs are not . . . charged with possessing the relevant expertise in national security matters to opine on the effect that disclosure of this information could have on our national security, and their conclusory, unsupported opinion in this regard is entitled to little or no weight. In contrast, the Government's reasoned judgement that disclosure of the information would pose a risk to national security is entitled to substantial weight.[43]

After its lengthy defense of the use of Exemption 1 to withhold classified information from the public, the department concluded by explaining its use of Exemption 5 to withhold "deliberative" material:

> [T]he material withheld pursuant to the deliberative process privilege was generated by staff as they worked on responding to congressional inquiries about DOJ's implementation of the Patriot Act. The entire context of these discussions was deliberative and predecisional including any discussion about how many times various Patriot Act and FISA

tools had been used. The Government did attempt to segregate and release purely factual material, but any purely factual material—including statistical information—was determined itself to be deliberative.[44]

Thus, implausibly, even hard statistics on the use of the Patriot Act were characterized as "deliberative," and thus protected from public scrutiny, simply because staff had calculated the numbers in answering congressional inquiries.

On April 4, 2003, the ACLU and EPIC submitted a brief reply and rebuttal to the district court. The memo began, "The records sought by Plaintiffs in this case are critical to the public's ability to evaluate new surveillance authorities and the government's use of them. Americans cannot evaluate government conduct if they are not permitted to know what the government's policies are. . . . In arguing that the public has no right to know the extent to which the FBI has relied on new surveillance authorities, Defendant repeatedly insists that this Court should defer to the government's own determination that disclosure of the information would jeopardize national security. While Plaintiffs do not dispute that a certain degree of deference is appropriate, the question whether particular records fall within the ambit of Exemption 1 is a question ultimately to be answered by the courts, *not* by the executive branch."[45]

The ACLU/EPIC memo notes that the Justice Department regularly discloses information similar to the requested data but "does not explain why statistics relating to the FBI's use of those provisions can safely be released to the public, whereas the public must be kept in the dark concerning the FBI's use of FISA's physical search, pen register, and 'tangible things' provisions." The memo rejects the department's argument that disclosing such statistics would reveal how the FBI is using these provisions and assist terrorists in evading them:

A statistic indicating the number of times the FBI has relied on FISA's pen register provision would disclose nothing about the way in which the FBI used the provision generally or in any particular case. . . . The FBI could use the ["tangible things"] provision to obtain records pertaining to a specific individual from a particular library. It could use the provision to obtain records about an entire class of individuals from a particular hospital. It could use the provision to obtain a membership list from a political organization. A statistic indicating the number of times the FBI has relied on FISA's "tangible things" provision would disclose nothing about the way in which the FBI used the provision generally or in any particular case.[46]

The ACLU/EPIC memo requested that the department's motion for summary judgment be denied and that the plaintiff's cross-motion for summary judgment be granted. The memo concluded, "The Court indicated at the hearing held in this case on November 26, 2002, the possibility that it would conduct an *in camera* review of the records that Defendant seeks to withhold. Plaintiffs respectfully suggest that *in camera* review is particularly appropriate here because the segregability of factual and other non-exempt material is in dispute."[47]

In May 2003, the court rejected the plaintiff's request for summary judgment. Judge Huvelle held that the plaintiffs had advanced a "compelling argument that the disclosure of this information will help promote democratic values and promote government accountability," but that the FOIA did not require the Justice Department to release any further information. The court concluded that "records that indicate how DOJ has apportioned its counterespionage resources, that reveal the relative frequency with which particular surveillance tools have been deployed, and that show how often U.S. persons have been targeted may undoubtedly prove useful to those who are the actual or potential targets of such surveillance, and may thereby undermine the efficiency and effectiveness of such surveillance."[48]

After apparently failing in its attempt to bring the light of day to the implementation of the Patriot Act, the ACLU decided to initiate the first constitutional challenge to the act. On July 30, 2003, the ACLU joined several Islamic and Arab Americans in filing a legal challenge to Section 215 of the Patriot Act, the provision that allows the government to seize business, library, and bookstore records without disclosing that it has done so. Ann Beeson, the ACLU's lead attorney in the lawsuit, said, "Ordinary Americans should not have to worry that the FBI is rifling through their medical records, seizing their personal papers, or forcing charities and advocacy groups to divulge membership lists."[49]

The lawsuit argues that the Patriot Act violates free speech rights and constitutional protections against unreasonable searches and seizure, and that the act has targeted individuals on the basis of their ethnic and religious characteristics. The plaintiffs also claim that the gag rule attached to Section 215 makes it impossible to determine the degree to which Islamic groups have been illegally subjected to records searches. "Because the orders are secret, there is no way to know for sure who has been a target," said Beeson. "This is one of the constitutional arguments against the law."[50]

Just a week later, on August 5, the Center for Constitutional Rights filed another suit challenging the constitutionality of the Patriot Act, claiming it infringed on free-speech protections by outlawing "expert advice and assistance" to groups that the United States has labeled as terrorists, even if the assistance is humanitarian and has no connection to terrorism. The suit primarily involves American aid workers and activists with ties to Turkey's Kurdistan Workers' Party or the Liberation Tigers of Tamil Eelam, groups that have been declared terrorist organizations by the State Department.

Nancy Chang, one of the plaintiff's attorneys, stated, "In its rush to pass the Patriot Act just six weeks after the Sept. 11 attacks, Congress overlooked one of our most fundamental rights: the right to express our political beliefs, even if they are controversial."[51]

The Patriot Act in Art and Humor

As we saw in Chapter 1, the media's relentless ridicule of the FBI's Library Awareness Program played a major role in discouraging library surveillance. With political cartoonists and humorists leading the way, the FBI's incursions were depicted as not just a sinister conspiracy, but an absurd waste of the taxpayer's money. The former dean of Washington's political cartoonists, Herblock, published two delightful but scathing cartoons on the Library Awareness Program, one of which was reproduced in my first book, *Surveillance in the Stacks*. A comparable caricature of today's Patriot Act incursions on libraries would be Danziger's cartoon with the heading, "The FBI Now Empowered to Seize Library Records! Marianne is not cooperating." Danziger depicts a half dozen FBI agents, with guns drawn, trying to get librarian Marianne to reveal patron records. One agent, upon seeing the reference desk sign saying, "Silence," tells her, "So! Silence, eh? We have ways of making you talk!"[52]

The gag orders imposed on librarians under the Patriot Act made it impossible for them to document their responses to government requests for patron information in their libraries, leaving the public unsure about the confidentiality of their reading habits. As a result, we have seen something unheard of during the Library Awareness Program: political cartoons suggesting library complicity with FBI surveillance. For example, on October 15, 2001, the Cincinnati *Post*'s editorial cartoonist Jeff Stahler depicted a small boy patiently waiting at a library circulation counter on which rests a newspaper with the headline, "Bush: Report Anyone Suspicious." With her back turned to the young patron, a gray-haired librarian peeks back suspiciously at the boy and whispers into the phone, "He's requested '1001 Arabian Nights.' "[53]

Though the Patriot Act's surveillance of libraries and bookstores is even more aggressive than was the case under the Library Awareness Program, there is less media coverage of today's surveillance owing to the unprecedented political and social pressure to silence all criticism as unpatriotic. Even the music and film industries have changed their programming to accommodate this new chilling climate. Clear Channel Communications, one of the nation's largest radio networks, sent to its program directors throughout the country a list of songs that should not be played on the air because they were considered inappropriate in the post-9/11 environment. Over 100 songs were on the "no-play" list, including John Lennon's *Imagine*, the Bangles' *Walk Like an Egyptian*, Elvis Presley's *You're the Devil in Disguise*, and Pat Benetar's *Love Is a Battlefield*.[54]

The film industry has taken similar action, canceling or postponing the release of certain films and rewriting scripts since 9/11 in an effort to avoid any content that might be considered offensive or unpatriotic. Universal Studios deleted a trivial use of the word "terrorism" from its twentieth anniversary edition of *ET* in 2002. Several film studios have removed references to the World Trade Center, and Paramount Pictures has removed shots of the towers from *Zoolander*. A television episode of *Friends* removed scenes of a character who endured a lengthy delay at an airport. Some advertisers and local TV stations dropped the ABC show *Politically Incorrect* after host Bill Maher said suicide bombers were less cowardly than American pilots firing missiles from a distance.[55]

Despite all these restraints on the media coverage of the Patriot Act, art and comedy would not be muzzled. Of all the media critics of the new obligatory patriotism, political cartoonists seem to be the most outspoken, and they have paid the price for their candor. When political cartoonists began examining their government's foreign and domestic policies, they found their work suppressed by their editors and branded as unpatriotic by the media at large. Aaron McGruder's comic strip "The Boondocks" was removed from many newspapers after 9/11 because of its allegedly unpatriotic and antiwar content. In late 2001, a Utah newspaper, *The Spectrum,* felt obliged to issue an apology for a cartoon it published from Pulitzer Prize winner Steve Benson, which criticized the war in Afghanistan. Many subscribers threatened to cancel if the paper refused to apologize. Cartoonist Mike Marland's cartoon for the *Concord Monitor* depicted President Bush crashing into two towers, one labeled "Social" and the other labeled "Security." The editor issued a formal apology for the cartoon, and Tim McCarthy, a prize-winning journalist for the *Courier,* was fired for defending Morland's cartoon.[56]

Cartoons targeting Attorney General Ashcroft's assaults on the Constitution were punished even more frequently. In October 2001, cartoonist Todd Persche was fired after publishing two cartoons in Wisconsin's *Barbaroo News Republican*, one of which was about Big Brother's "turning our civil rights upside down" and the other about the media drumbeat for war. Persche didn't think the cartoons were controversial at all. "Kind of milquetoast, really," he said. Persche said the first indication of trouble came on October 11, when his editor told him, "You aren't going to believe this. They are going to fire you. You're done."[57]

Persche later reflected, "It's a creepy time. I watched George Bush when he was at ground zero and said, 'The people who did this hate freedom.' Well, I feel like I've lost my freedom. I'm an American. I'm being told I'm unpatriotic and I resent it. . . . When citizens of the United States stand up and question their government's policies, they are exercising a cherished constitutional right. Yet when the employees of our nation's media subsequently deny us this freedom of speech in the name of 'national unity,' which one is the threat to real democracy?"[58]

In response to the growing climate of censorship, a group of political cartoonists led by Gary Huck, Mike Konopacki, Matt Wuerker, and writer Alec Dubro put together a traveling show of political art they call "USA PATRIOT ART: Cartooning and Free Speech in War Time." The poster accompanying the show describes the art works as "Political cartoons by fired cartoonists, censored cartoonists, indignant cartoonists."[59]

Mike Konopacki, one of the organizers of the show, declared, "We had lots to work with. Under the guise of the USA PATRIOT Act . . . Bush et al. were poking holes the size of Texas in the Constitution in an all-out effort to stifle dissent and criminalize otherwise innocuous behavior. Administration puff daddy

Ari Fleischer issued the warning: 'You need to watch what you say.' The mainstream media (i.e., kept press) snapped to attention. . . . The Bush Administration is flexing its military muscle abroad and shredding the Constitution at home. Whether out of fear, apathy or ignorance, the public—'we the people'—have had no say about any of this. We hope our show will get people to think, to question, to challenge and debate, and ultimately to act. Our democracy is at risk. A full and open debate is more crucial than ever.''[60]

Among the cartoons in the show were Carol Simpson's depiction of a man in a decontamination suit stuffing the Bill of Rights into a trash can labeled "Hazardous Material"; Dennis Draughon's drawing, under the banner "Liberty vs. Security," of a free-flying American eagle next to an eagle confined to a cage papered at the bottom with Bill of Rights; Russel Hodin's cartoon of John Ashcroft peeking through holes cut in the Bill of Rights as he spies on those around him; Mike Konopacki's picture, under the heading "The Next Attack," of an airplane about to crash into a tall building labeled "Bill of Rights"; Kevin Kallaugher's cartoon, under the heading "One Nation . . . Under Guard," showing three furtive spies labeled "FBI," "Police," and "CIA"; Jimmy Margulies' caricature of a commercial ad for a store called Ascrofts, which is selling the Bill of Rights "Reduced 60%"; Signe Wilkinson's cartoon of John Ashcroft paring down a document labeled "Constitutional Protections" as he says, "This year we really give thanks for the LITTLER things in life."[61]

Also included in the PATRIOT ART show was Tom Tomorrow's cartoon strip in four frames: The first frame, headed "We can't afford to worry about constitutional protections against unreasonable search and seizure at a time like this," shows police raiding an office and demanding "to download your email, change the battery on your phone tap, and perform a full body cavity search." The second frame, headed "Nor can we allow dissenters to use freedom of speech as an excuse to undermine our unity," shows a woman being silenced for questioning the Pentagon's budget. The third frame, headed "And we certainly can't allow freedom of the press to get in the way of the war effort," shows two government agents examining footage of CNN news and concluding that "a re-education squad" must be sent to CNN immediately. The fourth frame, headed "We must dismantle our democracy in order to save it," shows a man declaring, "Gee, isn't it stirring to see the flag . . . so proudly proclaiming our right to, um. . . . " His companion suggests, " . . . to display the flag?" The man agrees, "That's it."[62]

This unique art show premiered at the Institute for Policy Studies in Washington, D.C., on June 21, 2002. It continues to travel around the country, to places like Bothell, Washington; SUNY Stoney Brook (New York); the Community Folk Art Center in Syracuse, New York; and the University of Massachusetts in Boston.

Legislative Attempts to Modify the Patriot Act

After October 26, 2001, when the USA PATRIOT Act was signed into law by President Bush, the press and the public at large began to have second thoughts (first thoughts for many) about some of the more extreme provisions of the act. Congress was understandably a bit slower in acknowledging the error of its zombie-like acquiescence to Ashcroft's Patriot Act, but even on Capitol Hill there were signs of a change of heart.

In 2003 a flurry of bills in Congress included a House bill and three Senate bills designed to repeal those sections of the Patriot Act authorizing surveillance of libraries and bookstores under the FISA; several amendments to appropriations bills restricting funding for Patriot Act surveillance; House and Senate bills requiring improved reporting to Congress on the implementation of the Patriot Act; a Senate bill removing a broad FOIA exemption created by the Homeland Security Act; and a bill establishing a national commission to determine how to maintain an open society while improving security. There was even a local statute passed in California that criminalized cooperation with Patriot Act surveillance.

On March 6, 2003, Rep. Bernie Sanders (I-VT) introduced H.R. 1157, the Freedom to Read Protection Act, which would return the standard under which the FBI could obtain library and bookstore records to that which applied prior to the passage of the Patriot Act. H.R. 1157 would also require better public reporting on the implementation of the Patriot Act. "One of the cornerstones of our democracy is the right of Americans to criticize their government and to read printed materials without fear of government monitoring," said Sanders. "This tri-partisan legislation will go a long way in protecting the privacy and First Amendment rights of all Americans."[63]

Thirty-two groups representing booksellers, librarians, book publishers, authors, and others joined several companies, including Barnes and Noble Booksellers and Borders Group Inc., in issuing a statement supporting H.R. 1157. "Protecting the confidentiality of one's use of the library is of primary concern to librarians," said Judith Krug, executive director of the ALA's Office for Intellectual Freedom. "Rep. Sanders' bill would restore this core value of librarianship."[64] Chris Finan, president of the ABFFE, echoed the ALA's position: "The book community is united in believing that Section 215 of the Patriot Act threatens First Amendment freedom by making people afraid that their purchase or borrowing records may be monitored by the government."[65]

Under the Sanders bill, the FBI would still have access to such records with a standard court-ordered search warrant or subpoena, but it would be required to provide "specific and articulable facts" giving reason to believe that the person to whom the records pertain is a foreign power or agent of a foreign power. The records must be sought for "an investigation to gather foreign intelligence information or an investigation concerning international terrorism," whereas under the Patriot Act, the FBI can obtain a FISA court order to seize "any tangible thing" pertaining to *anyone*, not just foreign powers or foreign agents.

Sanders explained, "Few who voted for the Patriot Act – I did not – knew that among its provisions was one that gave FBI agents the authority to engage in fishing expeditions to see what Americans read. . . . To remedy the excesses of the Patriot Act that threaten our right to read, I have introduced the Freedom to Read Protection Act. The bill, which has the support of Democrats and Republicans, progressives and conservatives, will establish once again that libraries and bookstores are no place for fishing expeditions."[66]

Rep. Ron Paul, a conservative Republican from Texas, is one of the co-sponsors of the Sanders bill. He voted against the Patriot Act because it violates the Fourth Amendment. "There are so many bad parts to the Patriot Act, I would repeal the whole thing," he told the booksellers publication *Bookselling This Week.* "The Freedom to Read Protection Act will be difficult to pass, but that's why it's important for people such as yourselves to rally your readership."[67]

Sanders, who was the keynote speaker at the ALA's annual conference in June 2003, has received strong support from librarians and booksellers. Indeed, he actually drafted his bill in response to an "open letter" signed by two-thirds of Vermont's independent booksellers and nearly 200 librarians from across the state. Last fall the Vermont Library Association Executive Board sent a letter to their representatives in Congress asking that they draft legislation to eliminate the provisions of the Patriot Act that "undermine Americans' constitutionally guaranteed right to read and access information without governmental intrusion or interference."[68] Local booksellers quickly followed with a similar letter.

Chris Finan, president of the ABFFE, said that concern among librarians and booksellers had mobilized support for the Sanders bill. "The rapid increase in the number of co-sponsors is very encouraging," he stated. "In addition, we are seeing a spike in the amount of press coverage that the issue is getting. Hopefully, this will enable us to maintain our momentum, but it is crucial that booksellers continue to contact their representatives in the House."[69]

On May 29, 2003, I spoke with Joel Barkin, press secretary for Rep. Sanders, who was enthusiastic about the Freedom to Read Protection Act's chances for passage:

Right now, our bill has 105 co-sponsors. As you probably know, 66 House members originally voted against the USA Patriot Act, so our co-sponsors are already twice the number that voted against the Patriot Act. That, in and of itself, is an interesting point. We have really tremendous support in the House, on both sides of the aisle, from progressives to moderate Democrats to conservative Republicans. If you look at those co-sponsors and where they come from, they make up huge chunks of geography from all over the country, and we think it will grow. I think there's a real chance that we could win this. The great thing about our bill is that it's very comprehensible. People understand it. It spells out very clearly the proper protection of their confidentiality in the use of libraries and bookstores, something they do every day. The Patriot Act, on the other hand, is a confusing piece of legislation. There's a lot in it that nobody understands.[70]

Barkin said he was pleasantly surprised at the political skills demonstrated by the library profession in their support for the Sanders bill. "I did not realize the lobbying infrastructure that they had," he admitted. "The library and bookselling communities have done a great job in rallying their members and their congressional representatives. People trust librarians, not just on this issue, but generally. I think the more they speak out on this issue, the more the public becomes engaged."[71]

Barkin was disturbed by the Justice Department's tendency to characterize critics of the Patriot Act as being soft on terrorism. "My boss will be the first to say that terrorism is a real threat and must be forcefully opposed, but we can't employ inappropriate tools like the Patriot Act, which goes far beyond what is needed to catch terrorists."

Barkin noted an interesting evolution in the Justice Department's response to general criticism of the Patriot Act and to the Sanders bill in particular. "The Department began by simply ignoring the criticism," said Barkin, "but when it grew in strength they began claiming, 'If you're not a bad guy, you have nothing to worry about.' But if you read the law, it's clear that the Patriot Act casts a much wider net than that. And now the Justice Department is claiming that the only people who are really worried about the Patriot Act are those in college towns and liberal states like Vermont. In reality, there have been local resolutions and ordinances passed against the Patriot Act in towns all over the country. And, of course, the members of Congress who have signed on to Rep. Sanders' bill represent every region of the country. So the Justice Department is using an entirely bogus argument. And now we're hearing about Patriot Act II and the CIA having jurisdiction in the states. People are worried about this sort of thing."[72]

As of November 2003, H.R. 1157 had attracted over 150 cosponsors in the House. When considering cosponsoring the Sanders bill, Rep. Don Young, a Republican from Arkansas, told reporters that "the Patriot Act was not really thought out. I'm very concerned that, in our desire for security and our enthusiasm for pursuing supposed terrorists, that sometimes we might be on the verge of giving up the freedoms which we're trying to protect. . . . I don't think it's anybody's business what I'm reading in the library."[73]

On May 23, 2003, Senator Barbara Boxer (D-CA) introduced the Library and Bookseller Protection Act (S. 1158), the Senate companion to Bernie Sanders' House bill. S. 1158 would

---

(1) exempt bookstores and libraries from FISA court orders (Section 215 of the Patriot Act) that require the production of "tangible things" for intelligence investigations and (2) exempt libraries from being considered "wire or electronic service providers" under Section 2709

of Title 18 of the U.S. Code, which provides for counterintelligence access to records. Section 2709 relates to NSLs, a kind of administrative subpoena that the FBI can issue internally without going to any judge. The FBI has told Congress that it is more likely to use NSLs to get at the electronic records (e.g., e-mail or Web usage) in libraries than Section 215 of the Patriot Act.

On July 30, Senator Feingold introduced the Library and Personal Records Privacy Act, which modifies portions of Section 215 of the Patriot Act. The bill would not repeal Section 215 altogether, but it would raise the standard for its use, requiring the government to show "specific and articulable facts" that warrant suspicion that an individual is "an agent of a foreign power." The bill would restore the pre-Patriot Act requirement that the FBI make a factual, individualized showing that the records sought pertain to a suspected terrorist. It would place similar limits on the use of NSLs, the FBI's "administrative subpoenas," which have been used increasingly since passage of the Patriot Act. Feingold said his bill "would restore the privacy of Americans while also allowing the FBI to follow up on legitimate leads," adding that it "recognizes that under certain circumstances the FBI should have access to library, bookseller, or other personal information and simply puts safeguards in place to protect the rights of law-abiding citizens."[74]

The Feingold bill is cosponsored by Jeff Bingaman (D-NM), Edward Kennedy (D-MA), Maria Cantwell (D-WA), Dick Durban (D-IL), Ron Wyden (D-OR), Daniel Akaka (D-HI), Jim Jeffords (I-VT), and Jon Corzine (D-NJ).

Timothy Edgar, an ACLU legislative counsel, stated, "We are encouraged that Members of Congress are taking steps to restore the privacy safeguards that were undermined by portions of the PATRIOT Act. The introduction of Senator Feingold's bill . . . signal[s] that Congress is taking seriously the broad, grassroots movement against the excesses of the PATRIOT Act."[75]

On July 31, 2003, Senators Lisa Murkowski (R-AK) and Wyden introduced the Protecting the Rights of Individuals Act, a bipartisan bill that would restore many of the civil liberties taken away by the Patriot Act. In particular, the Murkowski-Wyden bill would protect First Amendment rights of political protesters by changing the definition of "domestic terrorism" included in the Patriot Act; improve Section 215 of the Patriot Act by providing greater judicial oversight and restoring pre-Patriot Act limits of the FBI's ability to obtain records through FISA orders, requiring even higher probable cause standards before granting access to "business records" such as library, bookstore, and medical records; require the attorney general to issue annual public reports on searches conducted under the Patriot Act; ban federal agencies from engaging in data mining without explicit congressional authorization; and strengthen protections against government abuse by requiring that FISA warrants be issued only when foreign intelligence gathering is the "primary purpose" of the investigation, rather than simply "a purpose" as specified in the Patriot Act. It also addresses the use of NSLs and limits the kinds of communications that could be captured with pen register or trap-and-trace orders.

"Increasing numbers of Americans—liberals, conservatives, and independents alike—are beginning to recognize that the PATRIOT Act went too far," said Laura Murphy, director of the ACLU Washington Legislative Office. "By adopting this bipartisan bill, Congress can demonstrate that we can be both safe and free. The Murkowski-Wyden bill is a reasonable compromise that protects our civil liberties. We do not need to trample on privacy or civil rights to protect our national security."[76]

The ABFFE promptly endorsed both the Feingold and Murkowski bills but said it would continue to "strongly support" H.R. 1157 and S. 1158, the Sanders bill in the House and Boxer's companion bill in the Senate. "The Feingold and Murkowski bills will discourage the FBI from engaging in fishing expeditions in the private reading habits of American citizens," said ABFFE President Chris Finan.[77]

Senator Leahy's Domestic Surveillance Oversight Act of 2003 (S. 436) makes no direct changes to the Patriot Act, instead amending the FISA to improve the administration and oversight of foreign intelligence, including the Patriot Act. The bill, cosponsored by Republican Senators Charles Grassley (R-IA) and Arlen Specter (R-PA), authorizes FISA courts to establish rules and procedures regarding electronic surveillance and to transmit such rules and procedures to FISA judges, the chief justice of the United States, and to specified congressional committees. It requires the attorney general to issue an annual public report on the aggregate number of U.S. persons targeted for FISA orders and the number of times the attorney general has authorized that such information be used in a criminal proceeding. It also requires the FBI to report semi-annually on the number of requests for telephone and transactional records in public libraries, secondary school libraries, and institutions of higher education. Finally, it requires that the attorney general's semiannual report on requests for financial records and credit agency disclosures be sent to the congressional judiciary committees.

The House companion to the Leahy bill is the Surveillance Oversight and Disclosure Act (H.R. 2429), introduced on June 11, 2003, by Representatives Joseph Hoeffel (D-PA), Sam Farr (D-CA), and John Conyers (D-MI). The bill would require better reporting by the Justice Department on the Patriot Act, including special reports about how library records are obtained and used. The specific requirements of Hoeffel's bill are as follows:

1. An annual public report on the number of FISA surveillance orders issued for U.S. citizens and for noncitizens in each of four categories (electronic surveillance, physical searches, e-mail pen registers, and access to records), and on the number of times such information is used in criminal proceedings.

2. A semiannual report to congressional intelligence committees on all requests made for records from public or school libraries.

3. A report to Congress on the rules and procedures of the FISA court and any changes thereto [the proceedings of the FISA court are conducted in secret].

Hoeffel, who voted for the original Patriot Act, stated, "The Department of Justice, and Attorney General Ashcroft in particular, have been extremely reluctant and slow to provide information to Congress or to the public about the use of the new authority they have under the PATRIOT Act. There has been too much secrecy and too much 'trust me' rhetoric from the Attorney General. He and the Justice Department should have to report to Congress and the American people on their activities under this legislation. . . . It is important that Congress and the American People have a full understanding of how these powers have been utilized and how it has affected the country and the civil liberties on which it is built."[78]

The ALA promptly issued a press release saying that it "strongly supports" the Surveillance Oversight and Disclosure Act and "believes that this bill will result in increased public oversight and review, the protection of established liberties, and government accountability pertaining to some provisions of the USA PATRIOT Act."[79]

ALA President Maurice Freedman said, "We have been trying to get such legislation passed since the USA PATRIOT Act first became law. History has taught us that our government works best when it is subject to constant public scrutiny and review, and the public trust is eroded when government works in secret—behind closed doors where only the powerful and privileged reside." Incoming ALA President Dr. Carla Hayden concurred, "America's libraries will continue to support legislation like the Surveillance Oversight and Disclosure Act, which seeks to protect the many freedoms that we enjoy as Americans—including the constitutional rights of our patrons."

On March 12, 2003, Senators Leahy, Carl Levin (D-MI), Jeffords, Joseph Lieberman (D-CT), and Robert Byrd (D-WV) introduced the Restoration of Freedom of Information Act of 2003 (S. 609), which would (1) remove the broad FOIA exemption for "critical infrastructure information" created by the Homeland Security Act, (2) protect the actions of legitimate whistle-blowers, (3) allow the use of such information in civil court cases to hold companies accountable for wrongdoing or to protect the public, and (4) respect, rather than preempt, state and local FOIA laws.

In May 2002, Del. Eleanor Holmes Norton, congressional representative for the District of Columbia, introduced the Open Society with Security Act, a bill authorizing a presidential commission "to investigate how our country can meet the high standards necessary to effectively fight the dangerous menace of international terrorism while accommodating and affirming the central American values of privacy, openness, and public access."

Norton explained, "Like the Kerner Commission, the Open Society with Security Commission would help us to chart a safe course through deep waters without surrendering the very values that lead us to insist upon defending our country and our way of life. We can do better than blunt and often untested and ineffective instruments that crush our liberty. . . . Personal privacy and the right to be left alone, especially from interference by government, is an identifying characteristic of what it means to be an American."[80]

Norton, who has called the Patriot Act "legislation that is out of control,"said, "We have to focus people on the need for an open society. . . . [E]lected officials have allowed the militarization of security."[81] While acknowledging the threat of terrorism, Norton warned against the extreme measures embraced by the Justice Department:

> The example that the federal government is offering leaves much to be desired. Federal officials are quickly throwing up new approaches and systems—from shutdowns, barricades, and public exclusion, to camera surveillance, wholesale roundups and electronic surveillance, without regard to the Fourth Amendment or other constitutional protections, and without notice and public hearings, or even any public explanation.[82]

On October 22, 2003, another important bill to restrict the powers of the Patriot Act was introduced into the House of Representatives shortly after its introduction in the Senate. The Security and Freedom Ensured (SAFE) Act featured the sponsorship of two Republicans, Rep. Butch Otter of Idaho and Rep. Jeff Flake of Arizona. The Senate version of the bill had been introduced by Senators Larry Craig (R-ID) and Richard Durbin (D-IL).

The SAFE Act would permanently narrow the "sneak and peek" provision of the Patriot Act and would preclude investigative fishing expeditions under Section 215 by requiring evidence that the targets of a FISA warrant have some connection to a foreign government or organization. Finally, the SAFE Act would replace the Patriot Act's broad definition of "domestic terrorism" with a narrower definition linked to more serious federal crimes such as bombing, kidnaping, hijacking, etc.

The SAFE Act has bipartisan cosponsors in the House and Senate as well as broad support from organizations like the ACLU, the ALA, the Free Congress Foundation and the American Conservative Union.

The most ambitious of the recent bills to rein in the Patriot Act came on September 24, 2003, when presidential candidate Rep. Dennis Kucinich (D-OH) and Rep. Ron Paul (R-TX) introduced the Benjamin Franklin True Patriot Act (H.R. 3171). In addition to repealing 11 sections of the Patriot Act, the sweeping bill would also repeal two provisions of the Homeland Security Act and a variety of post-9/11 regulations.

The bill would repeal the following sections of the Patriot Act:

1. Section 213, relating to "sneak and peek" searches;

2. Section 214, relating to pen registers for foreign intelligence purposes;

3. Section 215, relating to government seizure of business records;

4. Section 216, relating to government use of pen registers in criminal cases;

5. Section 218, relating to the Foreign Intelligence Surveillance Act;

6. Section 411, relating to new grounds for deportation;

7. Section 412, relating to mandatory detention of certain aliens;

8. Section 505, relating to national security letters;

9. Section 507, relating to seizure of educational records;

10. Section 508, relating to collection and disclosure of personal information under the National Education Statistics Act of 1994;

11. Section 802, relating to the broad definition of domestic terrorism.

The True Patriot Act would also repeal two provisions of the Homeland Security Act:

1. Section 214, relating to an exemption from the Freedom of Information Act;

2. Section 871, relating to an exemption to the Federal Advisory Committee Act;

The Act would also repeal a provision of aviation security law that excludes permanent resident aliens from being hired as baggage checkers. And finally, the bill would revoke a number of immigration regulations, the attorney-client monitoring regulation, Attorney General Ashcroft's guidelines against compliance with the Freedom of Information Act, and any regulations altering the Thornburg guidelines on religious institution spying.

Rep. Pete Stark (D-CA), one of the 22 original cosponsors of the True Patriot Act, said, "Attorney General Ashcroft has used the Patriot Act to engage in an out-and-out assault on basic civil liberties. He has made a mockery of due process, violated basic privacy protections, and authorized federal agents to spy and snoop under a shroud of absolute secrecy. . . . Every American, regardless of their background, has the right to live free of unwarranted government intrusion. Repealing the worst provisions of the Patriot Act will reign in this gross abuse of power and restore to everyone our basic constitutional rights."[83]

As of the publication date of this book, none of the bills described above have become law, but several amendments to the Patriot Act, strategically attached to appropriations bills, have passed either the House or Senate and seem to offer the best chance for change to the Patriot Act since its passage. On July 22, 2003, the House of Representatives voted 309 to 118 to attach a provision to the Commerce, State and Justice appropriations bill that would block the Justice Department from funding secret sneak-and-peek searches under the Patriot Act.

Sometimes called "black-bag" jobs, these warrants allow agents to search homes, confiscate property, and bug computers without notifying the subject of the search. Providing notice of a search is essential to a citizen's Fourth Amendment rights, because it allows him to point out irregularities in a warrant, such as the fact that the police are at the wrong address or are exceeding the scope of the warrant. Without notice, government agents have unsupervised discretion over a search. In 2003 the Justice Department admitted to Congress that it had executed forty-seven sneak-and-peek searches and sought to delay notification of search warrants in 250 cases. Rep. Dennis Kucinich (D-OH) responded, "I would suggest to you that just one would constitute a threat to our Bill of Rights."[84]

It is important to note that 119 Republicans voted for the amendment, causing the amendment's sponsor, Rep. C.L. "Butch" Otter (R-ID), to declare, "Congress is coming to its senses. This is just the beginning of a crusade to which more and more of my colleagues are rallying."[85] Otter explained: "Not only does this provision allow the seizure of personal and business records without notification, but it also opens the door to nationwide search warrants and allowing the CIA and NSA to operate domestically." Laura Murphy, director of the ACLU's Washington Legislative Office, said, "Given its overwhelming passage this evening, the amendment is highly significant and a herald of more fix-Patriot measures to come."[86]

The success of the sneak-and-peek amendment came only after another amendment to the same appropriations bill had been denied on questionable procedural grounds. That amendment, proposed by Representatives Sanders, Otter, and Conyers, would have accomplished virtually everything in Sanders' pending Freedom to Read Protection Act, but it was blocked on the false claim that it imposed new budgetary obligations on the Justice Department, something the House does not allow on appropriations. Sanders and company quickly changed the language of the bill, keeping its provisions intact while avoiding any suggestion of new fiscal obligations, but this time the amendment was blocked by the Republican leadership in a highly unusual procedural maneuver that prohibited any amendments to amendments. The arrangement was reached without the knowledge of most House members, despite the fact that such agreements traditionally require advance notice to members.

Finally, on the advice of Rep. Stenny Hoyer (D-MD), Sanders offered the same amendment to the foreign operations appropriations bill, and that amendment did pass the House. The weakness of that amendment was not in its provisions—it would restrict State Department funding for FISA warrants on libraries and bookstores just as the previous amendment would have done to Justice Department funding—but there is relatively little relevant funding in the foreign operations budget. It was, nonetheless, a beginning.

Finally, let's mention a local ordinance that boldly presumes to oppose federal law. As described in Chapter 1, state library confidentiality laws have been passed in forty-eight of our fifty states (Hawaii and Kentucky rely upon attorney general guidelines to accomplish the same purpose), but those laws are trumped by the Patriot Act. Now we have an ordinance, passed in March 2003 in the northern California city of Arcata, which outlaws voluntary compliance with the Patriot Act by city officials. The ordinance, passed by a 4-to-1 vote of the city council, has the nearly unanimous approval of Arcata residents, but what power does it have against federal laws like the mighty Patriot Act?

"It's our citywide form of nonviolent disobedience," said David Meserve, the city councilman who drafted Arcata's ordinance. "The ordinance went through so easily that we were surprised. We started going up to people asking what they thought. They thought, 'Great.' "[87]

Nancy Talanian, codirector of the Bill of Rights Defense Committee in Florence, Massachusetts, believes that the Arcata ordinance has the authority for more than civil disobedience. "[I]n the case of the Patriot Act, the federal government can't really tell municipalities that you have to do the work that the INS or the FBI wants you to do. The citizen can say, 'No, I'm sorry. We hire our police to protect our citizens and we don't want our citizens pulled aside and thrown in jail without probable cause."[88]

State, Local, and Professional Resolutions Opposing the Patriot Act

As of August 13, 2003, more than 140 cities and counties, in addition to state legislatures in Alaska, Hawaii, and Vermont, have passed resolutions against the Patriot Act, some of them imposing restrictions on compliance. Supporters of these resolutions cover the entire political spectrum. For example, the key sponsors of the resolution in Anchorage, Alaska, are representatives of the National Association for the Advancement of Colored People (NAACP) and the National Rifle Association (NRA). Eventually, the resolution was passed in the state House by a vote of 32 to 1 and in the Senate by 19 to 0. Both chambers of the Alaska legislature are heavily dominated by Republicans, yet they passed the following resolution:

> It is the policy of the State of Alaska to oppose any portion of the USA PATRIOT Act that would violate the rights and liberties guaranteed equally under the state and federal constitutions; and, in accordance with Alaska state policy, an agency or instrumentality of the State of Alaska, in the absence of reasonable suspicion of criminal activity under Alaska State law, may not (1) initiate, participate in, or assist or cooperate with an inquiry, investigation, surveillance, or detention, (2) record, file, or share intelligence information concerning a person or organization, including library lending and research records, book and video store sales and rental records, and other personal data, even if authorized under the USA PATRIOT Act, (3) retain such intelligence information; (and that) an agency or instrumentality of the state may not,

(1) use state resources or institutions for the enforcement of federal immigration matters, which are the responsibility of the federal government; (2) collect or maintain information about the political, religious, or social views, associations, or activities of any individual, group, association, organization, corporation, business, or partnership, unless the information directly relates to an investigation of criminal activities and there are reasonable grounds to suspect the subject of the information is or may be involved in criminal conduct; (3) engage in racial profiling; law enforcement agencies may not use race, religion, ethnicity, or national origin as factors in selecting individuals to subject to investigatory activities except when seeking to apprehend a specific suspect whose race, religion, ethnicity, or national origin is part of the description of the suspect.[89]

The bill goes on to say the state legislature implores the U.S. Congress "to correct provisions in the USA PATRIOT Act and other measures that infringe on civil liberties, and opposes any pending and future federal legislation to the extent that it infringes on Americans' civil rights and liberties."

Just one month earlier, Hawaii had passed its resolution against the Patriot Act. In part it reads, "Whereas the residents of Hawaii during World War II experienced first hand the dangers of unbalanced pursuit of security without appropriate checks and balances for the protection of basic liberties. . . . " Hawaii resolves that "to the extent legally possible, no state resources—including law enforcement funds and educational administrative resources—may be used for unconstitutional activities, including but not limited to the following under the USA Patriot Act:

1. Monitoring political and religious gatherings exercising their First Amendment rights

2. Obtaining library records, bookstore records, and Web site activities without proper authorization and without notification

3. Issuing subpoenas through the United States Attorney's Office without a court's approval or knowledge

4. Requesting nonconsensual releases of students and faculty records from public schools and institutions of higher learning

5. Eavesdropping on confidential communication between lawyers and their clients."[90]

A similar resolution has been passed by the Vermont House, which characterizes the Patriot Act as "perhaps, the most severe legislative attack on civil liberties since the passage of the Alien and Sedition Acts in the 1790s." The resolution specifically attacks Sections 213, 215, 216, 218, 358, 411, 412, 508, 223, and 901 of the Patriot Act, but singles out library surveillance as its greatest concern:

Whereas, there has been an especially strong outcry in Vermont against the ability of federal authorities, under Section 215 of the Act, to obtain judicially-issued warrants for library or bookstore patron records based on minimal information, and the accompanying prohibition on librarians and bookstore personnel from revealing any information regarding the request, and

Whereas this provision runs directly counter to the intent of the Vermont General Assembly to protect the privacy of a library patron's records as codified in Title 3, Sect. 317(c)(19) of the Vermont Statutes Annotated, and the code of ethics of the American Library Association, and . . .

Whereas, both the Fletcher Free Library Commission and the Vermont Library Association have expressed their strongest possible concerns that the U.S.A. Patriot Act undermines constitutionally-guaranteed rights and the privacy of library patrons, and

Whereas, Congressman Bernard Sanders has announced his intention to sponsor legislation to exempt libraries and booksellers from the disclosure requirements of the U.S.A. Patriot Act, and . . .

Whereas, the law gravely threatens the civic values, personal freedoms, and rights that constitute the foundation of our national existence, now therefore . . .

Resolved: That the General Assembly strongly urges the United States Congress to revise the U.S.A. Patriot Act in order to restore and protect our nation's fundamental civil liberties, and, in particular, to enact Representative Sanders' proposal to exempt libraries and bookstores from the provision of the Act, and be it further . . .

Resolved: That the General Assembly requests that the office of the Vermont Attorney General offer legal support to any public library which is subject to a federal suit or administrative enforcement action for refusing to comply with the provisions of the Act related to library patrons' records."[91]

Oregon and New Mexico are currently considering statewide resolutions against the Patriot Act, but meanwhile, close to 200 cities and municipalities have passed local resolutions of the same kind. Most of these are symbolic affirmations of due process and free speech rights in the face of Patriot Act restraints, but some actually instruct local agencies to refuse to participate in Patriot Act investigations. For example, under a 2002 resolution passed in Detroit, Michigan, city police may decline to cooperate with "investigatory fishing trips" under the Patriot Act, such as compiling a list of mosque attendees.[92]

Predictably, professional organizations representing libraries and bookstores have been the most outspoken in their opposition to the Patriot Act. Library associations or boards of directors in forty-six states plus the District of Columbia have passed resolutions opposing the Patriot Act, and the remaining four states have resolutions in the works.

At its 2003 midwinter meeting, the ALA adopted its Resolution on the Patriot Act and Related Matters that Infringe on the Rights of Library Users. The resolution warned of the dangerous consequences for privacy and free expression not only from the Patriot Act but also from the revised FBI guidelines and "other recently enacted laws, regulations, and guidelines" that "increase the likelihood that the activities of library users . . . may be under government surveillance without their knowledge or consent."

After urging all librarians to educate their users, staff, and communities to the implications of the Patriot Act, the ALA resolution concluded,

"RESOLVED, that the American Library Association considers that sections of the USA PATRIOT Act are a present danger to the constitutional rights of library users and urges the United States Congress to:

1. provide active oversight of the implementation of the USA PATRIOT Act and other related measures, and the revised Attorney General Guidelines to the Federal Bureau of Investigation;

2. hold hearings to determine the extent of the surveillance on library users and their communities; and

3. amend or change the sections of these laws and the guidelines that threaten or abridge the rights of inquiry and free expression."[93]

Notes

1. *Congressional Record—Senate*, October 11, 2001, p. S10585.

2. Ibid., p. S10593.

3. Adam Clymer, "Justice Dept. Balks at Effort to Study Antiterror Powers," NYTimes.com, August 15, 2002, p. 2.

4. Ibid., p. 3.

5. Ibid.

6. Jerry Berman and James X. Dempsey, "CDT's Guide to the FBI Guidelines: Impact on Civil Liberties and Security—The Need for Congressional Oversight," Center for Democracy and Technology, June 26, 2002, p. 3.

7. Ibid.

8. Ibid.

9. December 23, 2002, letter from Daniel J. Bryant, Assistant Attorney General, to Patrick J. Leahy, Chairman, Committee on the Judiciary, U.S. Senate, in response to May 8, 2002, Judiciary Committee hearing.

10. Ibid.

11. December 23, 2002, letter from Daniel J. Bryant, Assistant Attorney General, to Patrick J. Leahy, Chairman, Subcommittee on the Constitution, Committee on the Judiciary, U.S. Senate, in response to July 25, 2002, Judiciary Committee hearing.

12. Ibid.

13. December 23, 2002, letter from Daniel J. Bryant, Assistant Attorney General, to Russell D. Feingold, Chairman, Subcommittee on the Constitution, Committee on the Judiciary, U.S. Senate.

14. Federal Bureau of Investigation, Memo to all Divisions from Office of the General Counsel, "New Legislation: Revisions to FCI/IT Legal Authorities Foreign Intelligence Surveillance Act," October 26, 2001, p. 6.

15. Ibid., p. 5.

16. Letter from F. James Sensenbrenner and John Conyers, Jr., to Attorney General John Ashcroft, June 13, 2002. www.house.gov/judiciary/ashcroft061302.html.

17. *The Marc Steiner Show*, WNPR National Public Radio, August 21, 2002.

18. Letter from Daniel J. Bryant, Assistant Attorney General, to F. James Sensenbrenner, Jr., Chairman, Committee on the Judiciary, U.S. House of Representatives, July 26, 2002, pp. 3–4.

19. Letter from Daniel J. Bryant, Assistant Attorney General, to F. James Sensenbrenner, Jr., Chairman, Committee on the Judiciary, U.S. House of Representatives, September 20, 2002, p. 3.

20. Federal Bureau of Investigation, "New Legislation: Revisions to FCI/IT Legal Authorities Foreign Intelligence Surveillance Act," p. 5.

21. Letter from F. James Sensenbrenner and John Conyers, Jr., to Attorney General John Ashcroft, April 1, 2003. www.aclu.org/SafeandFree/SafeandFree.cfm?ID=12302&c=207&Type.

22. Eric Lichtblau, "Justice Dept. Lists Use of New Power to Fight Terror," *New York Times*, May 21, 2003, p. A1.

23. "Report: Justice Dept. Sent Agents to 50 Libraries in 2003," American Library Association News, May 26, 2003, pp. 1–2. www.ala.org/Template.cfm?Section=News&template=/Content/Management/Content.

24. Maurice J. Freedman, "American Library Association Statement Responding to the Department of Justice May 20, 2003, Report and Testimony to the U.S. House Judiciary Committee," American Library Association, May 21, 2003, p. 1. www.ala.org/Template.cfm?Section=News&template=/Content/Management/Content.

25. Remarks of Rep. James Sensenbrenner, Chairman, House Judiciary Committee, Hearings on the USA Patriot Act, June 5, 2003. Televised hearings on CSPAN.

26. Ibid.

27. Ibid.

28. "The Patriot Act," *NewsHour with Jim Lehrer*, PBS Television Network, August 19, 2003.

29. Nat Hentoff, "The Soldier of the Constitution," *Village Voice*, August 23, 2002, p. 3. www.villagevoice.com/issues/0235/hentoff.php.

30. Telephone interview by author with retired Rep. Don Edwards, July 10, 2003.

31. "ACLU Asks Government to Account for Its Use of Vast New Surveillance Powers," October 24, 2002, www.aclu.org/Privacy/Privacy.cfm?ID=11048&c=130, p. 1.

32. Ibid., p. 2.

33. Ibid., p. 1.

34. "ABFFE Sues Justice Department for Data on Patriot Act Subpoenas," American Booksellers Foundation for Free Expression, October 24, 2002, p. 1. www.freeexpression.org/newswire/1024_2002.html.

35. "ACLU Presses for Full Disclosure on Government's New Snoop Powers," American Civil Liberties Union, News, January 17, 2003, p. 1. www.aclu.org/SafeandFree/SafeandFree.cfm?ID= 11638&c=206.

36. Ibid., p. 2.

37. Ibid.

38. Charles Levendosky, "Patriot Act Chills First Amendment Freedoms," *FACT: First Amendment Cyber-Tribune*, January 19, 2003, pp. 1-2. http://fact.trib.com/1st.lev.noinfoDOJ.html.

39. *American Civil Liberties Union et al., v. United States Department of Justice*, US District Court for the District of Columbia, Civil Action No. 1:02CV2077 (ESH), "Reply Memorandum in Support of Defendants' Motions for Summary Judgment, March 28, 2003, pp. 1–2.

40. Ibid., p. 5.

41. Ibid., p. 7.

42. Ibid., p. 9.

43. Ibid., p. 10.

44. Ibid., p. 16.

45. *American Civil Liberties Union et al., v. United States Department of Justice*, U.S. District Court for the District of Columbia, Memorandum from Ann Beeson , Jameel Jaffer, and Arthur B. Spitzer (ACLU) and David L. Sobel (EPIC), April 4, 2003, pp. 2–3.

46. Ibid., pp. 4–5.

47. Ibid., p. 10.

48. Jenner & Block, LLC, Memorandum from Theresa Chmara to Freedom to Read Foundation Board, January 21, 2003, p. 7.

49. Don Eggen, "Seizure of Business Records Is Challenged," *Washington Post*, July 31, 2003, P. A2.

50. Ibid.

51. Dan Eggen, "Patriot Act Faces New Challenge in Court," *Washington Post*, August 6, 2003, p. A8.

52. Danziger Cartoons, June 25, 2002. www.danzigercartoons.com/cmp/2002/danziger1363.html.

53. Chris Adams Wendt, "Reading Between the Lines," Rhinelander District Library, August 18, 2002, p. 1. http://wvls.lib.wi.us/RheinlanderDistrictLibrary/RBTL8-11-02.html.

54. Donna M. Hart, "New American Landscape under the Threat of Terrorism," *Arts4All Newsletter*, Issue 20, pp. 2–3. www.arts4all.com/newsletter/issue20/hart20.html.

55. Danziger Cartoons, June 25, 2002.

56. Hart, "New American Landscape," pp. 2–3.

57. Doug Moe, "Baraboo Shuts Down Cartoonist," *Capital Times*, October 31, 2001, p. 2. www.solidarity.com/hkcartoons/artshow/persche.html.

58. Ibid.

59. "USA Patriot Art," www.solidarity.com/hkcartoons/artshow/artshow.html.

60. Mike Konopacki, "A Call to Resist Illegitimate Authority," Resist, Inc., 2002. www.resistinc.org/newsletter/issues/2002/11/Konopacki2.html.

61. Ibid.

62. "USA Patriot Art," www.solidarity.com/hkcartoons/artshow/tomorrow.html.

63. Ian Bishop, "Booksellers Back Sanders' Measure," *Brattleboro Reformer*, May 16, 2003, p. 2. http://bernie.house.gov/documents/articles/20030516152555.asp

64. "Book Groups Call for Patriot Act Amendment," American Booksellers Foundation for Free Expression, May 15, 2003, p. 1. www.freeexpression.org/newswire/0515_2003.html.

65. Ibid.

66. Rep. Bernie Sanders, "Pulling FBI's Nose out of Your Books," *Los Angeles Times*, May 8, 2003, pp. 1–2. http://bernie.house.gov/documents/opeds/20030508100516.asp.

67. "Congressman Ron Paul Urges Booksellers to Rally in Support of H.R. 1157," *Bookselling This Week*, March 27, 2003, pp. 1–2. http://news.bookweb.org/freeexpression/1281.html.

68. Becca MacLaren, "Sanders Introduces 'Freedom to Read Protection Act,' " *The Advocate*, March 14, 2003, p. 1. http://bernie.house.gov/documents/articles/20030319102732.asp.

69. "Sanders Bill to Amend Patriot Act Attracts Seven More Co-Sponsors," April 4, 2003. http://news.bookweb.org/1314.html.

70. Author interview with Joel Barkin, press secretary for Rep. Bernie Sanders (I-VT), May 29, 2003.

71. Ibid.

72. Ibid.

73. Nancy Kranich, "The Impact of the USA PATRIOT Act: An Update," The Free Expression Policy Project, August 27, 2003, p. 3. www.fepproject.org/commentaries/patriotactupdate.html

74. "Bills Would Limit FBI's Patriot Act Access to Library Records," American Libraries Online, August 4, 2003. www.ala.org/alonline.

75. "ACLU Welcomes Measures to Restore Civil Liberties Lost Post 9/11," *American Civil Liberties Union News*, July 31, 2003. www.aclu.org/SafeandFree.cfm?ID=13260&c=206.

76. Ibid.

77. "Booksellers Endorse Senate Bill Amending Patriot Act," American Booksellers Foundation for Free Expression, July 31, 2003. www.abffe.com.

78. "Hoeffel to Introduce Bill That Would Require Greater Reporting by Justice Department on Patriot Act Activities," June 11, 2003.

79. "Reps. Conyers, Hoeffel and Farr Introduce Surveillance Oversight and Disclosure Act," *ALA Washington Office Newsline*, volume 12, number 54, Washington, D.C., June 13, 2003, pp. 1–2.

80. "District of Columbia Subcommittee Hearing on Privacy v. Security: Electronic Surveillance in the Nation's Capital," *DC Watch*, March 22, 2002, pp. 1–3. www.dcwatch.com/issues/privacy02.html.

81. Joan Steinau Lester, "Patriot Act Games," *San Francisco Chronicle*, May 18, 2003, pp. 1–2. www.sfgate.com/cgibin/article.cgi?file=/chronicle/article/2003/05/18/IN45628.DTL.

82. "District of Columbia Subcommittee Hearing on Privacy v. Security: Electronic Surveillance in the Nation's Capital," p. 3.

83. Rep. Pete Stark, "Stark Calls on Congress to Repeal Provisions of the Patriot Act that Violate the Constitution, Civil Liberties," www.house.gov/stark/news/news_2003-09-24_PatAct.html

84. Andrew Clark, "House Takes Aim at Patriot Act Secret Searches," *Reuters*, July 22, 2003. http://story.news.yahoo.com/news?tmpl=story&cid=564&ncid=564&e=44&u=/nm/2003072.

85. Nat Hentoff, "Getting It Right," *Editor & Publisher.com*, August 27, 2003, p. 1. www.mediainfo.com/editorandpublisher/features_columns/article_disply.jsp?vnuhttp://www.mediainfor.com/

86. Ibid.

87. Evelyn Nieves, "Local Officials Rise Up to Defy the Patriot Act," Washington Post.com, April 20, 2003, p. 3. www.washingtonpost.com/wp-dyn/articles/A64173-2003Apr20.html.

88. Ibid., p. 2.

89. David Lindorff, "Fighting the Patriot Act: Now It's Alaska," *Counterpunch*, May 14, 2003, pp. 2-3.

90. "Hawaii Renounces Patriot Act," www.capitol.hawaii.gov/sessioncurrent/bills/scr18_.html.

91. Resolution as Introduced, State of Vermont, House of Representatives, J.R.H. 9. www.leg.state.vt.us/docs/legdoc.cfm?URL=/docs/2004/resolutn/JRH009.HTML.

92. Elsa Wenzel, "Who's Afraid of the Patriot Act?" *PC World.com*, May 27, 2003, p. 3. www.pcworld.com/news/article/0,aid,110880,00.asp.

93. "Resolution on the Patriot Act and Related Matters That Infringe on the Rights of Library Users," *Newsletter on Intellectual Freedom,* May 2003, p. 93.

Conclusion

Ashcroft on the Offensive

As the year 2003 approached its close, the status of the battle over the Patriot Act seemed clear: Section 215 of the Act, which allows the seizure of business records, including library records, was the provision most feared by libraries and most frequently targeted in proposed legislation to scale back the Act. A hard-fought court victory had allowed the Justice Department to withhold all data on its use of the Patriot Act from the public, leaving libraries in the dark. Public opinion seemed to be turning against Attorney General Ashcroft and toward support for library confidentiality. Then came a bombshell.

In the course of his nationwide publicity tour designed to whip up support for the Patriot Act, Ashcroft made public a previously confidential memo to FBI Director Robert Mueller stating, "The number of times [Section 215] has been used to date is zero." Ashcroft said he had decided to declassify that previously secret data because of his "concern that the public not be misled about the manner in which the U.S. Department of Justice, and the FBI in particular, have been utilizing the authorities provided in the USA PATRIOT Act." Ashcroft explained, "To date we have not been able to counter the troubling amount of public distortion and misinformation in connection with Section 215. Consequently, I have determined that it is in the interest of law enforcement to declassify this information."[1]

Opponents and defenders of the Patriot Act were confounded and confused. Why had the Justice Department squandered so much of its financial and political resources in the legal battle to prevent the release of data on the use of the Patriot Act if the most controversial provision had never been used? Why had Ashcroft and his Assistant Attorney General Viet Dinh argued so emotionally before Congress that the removal of any of the tools provided by the Patriot Act, and Section 215 in particular, would immediately make the United States vulnerable to another terrorist attack? Why did Ashcroft bother opposing the Sanders bill, whose major provision was the revocation of Section 215, if he believed that the bill was essentially irrelevant and harmless? By alleging that the Justice Department had never used Section 215, Ashcroft raised more questions than he answered, and his comments during his nationwide tour certainly added to the confusion.

In a September 15, 2003 speech before the National Restaurant Association, Ashcroft ridiculed reports that FBI agents were monitoring libraries. "According to these breathless reports and baseless hysteria, some have convinced the American Library Association that under the bipartisanly enacted PATRIOT Act, the FBI is not fighting terrorism; instead, agents are checking how far you've gotten in the latest Tom Clancy novel," he said. "Do we at the Justice Department really care what you are reading? No. The law enforcement community has no interest in your reading habits. Tracking reading habits would betray our high regard for the First Amendment, and even if someone in government wanted to do so, it would represent an impossible workload and a waste of law enforcement resources. . . . [I]t's simply ridiculous to think that we would track what citizens are reading."[2]

DOJ spokesman Mark Corallo tried to soften Ashcroft's remarks by saying that the ALA "has been somewhat duped by those who are ideologically opposed to the Patriot Act."[3] Nonetheless, just one day after Ashcroft released his memo alleging "zero" uses of Section 215, he continued his attack on libraries and librarians in a speech to police and prosecutors in Memphis, Tennessee. "[T]he Department of Justice has neither the staffing, the time nor the inclination to monitor the reading habits of Americans," he said. "No offense to the American Library Association, but we just don't care. . . . The charges of the hysterics are revealed for what they are: castles in the air built on misrepresentation; supported by unfounded fear; held aloft by hysteria."[4]

In response to Ashcroft's attack, ALA President Carla Hayden said, "We are deeply concerned that the Attorney General should be so openly contemptuous of those who seek to defend our constitution. Rather than ask the nation's librarians and Americans nationwide to 'just trust him,' Ashcroft could allay concerns by releasing aggregate information about the number of libraries visited using the expanded powers created by the USA Patriot Act."[5]

But librarians suspected that full data on the use of the Patriot Act would never be forthcoming. All they had to work with were Ashcroft's leaked memo and his recent speeches in defense of the Patriot Act. Civil liberties advocates thus began examining Ashcroft's statements, parsing his words, seeking clarification. Was he telling the truth? Was it the full truth? Was it nothing but the truth?

The Truth, the Whole Truth, and Nothing but the Truth?

Setting aside Ashcroft's sarcastic rhetoric, we can cull two simple claims from his recent statements: 1) Section 215 of the Patriot Act has never been used; 2) No American citizen has had his library records reviewed under the authority of the Patriot Act.

On the first claim, as alleged in Ashcroft's leaked memo, there can be no direct evidence in refutation, because confirming the use of Section 215 is a felonious act in itself. But there is *indirect* evidence and testimony that questions the truth of Ashcroft's claim. First, in October 2002 the University of Illinois survey of 1,505 public library directors (see Chapter 3 and Appendix A) showed that 10.7% had received government requests for patron information since September 11, 2001, and 32.6% of those requests came from the FBI. Over three quarters of requests were for lists of books borrowed, web sites visited, etc., by a particular person, and 22.3% of the requests were accompanied by subpoenas, some of which contained gag orders. The most telling revelation in the survey was the disclosure that 10.3% of those library directors who received a court order said the order referenced Section 215 of the Patriot Act.

Were all of these library directors lying, or is Ashcroft's veracity in question? A more recent survey by the California Library Association (CLA), conducted for the *Sacramento Bee*, also casts doubt on the Ashcroft claim. The CLA study of California libraries (see Chapter 3 and Appendix B) was broader than the University of Illinois survey in its range of libraries (of the 344 libraries surveyed, 260 were public, 47 academic, and the other 27 were schools, special libraries, or library schools), but was less specific in addressing Patriot Act visits to libraries, asking only about "formal" and "informal" government visits since September 11, 2001. Informal visits were assumed to be those without a court order and formal visits were those accompanied by a court order. The CLA study found that 14 libraries had "formal" visits from the FBI and that 11 of the visited libraries complied with the requests. In addition, 16 libraries had "informal" contacts with FBI agents and six of them complied with requests for information.

Karen Schneider, who oversaw the survey as chair of CLA's Intellectual Freedom Committee, told me, "It was funny, the timing ended up being perfect. Just a few days after Ashcroft's publicity tour on behalf of the Patriot Act and his claim that there had been 'zero' use of Section 215 we did a survey that *suggested*, didn't prove, that even at the tip of the iceberg this wasn't true. There had been a fountain of informal and formal inquiries at libraries."

I asked whether the CLA study had cast further doubt on Ashcroft's "zero use" claim.

"I completely don't believe it," said Schneider. "I think that is such a fairy tale and was simply intended to silence criticism of the Patriot Act. It took them two years to respond to questions about the use of Section 215, and then they come up with zero? That's right up there with the weapons of mass destruction. Department of Justice statements before, during and after Ashcroft's publicity tour have been so contemptuous of our concern about the Patriot Act that I don't believe they are taking any of this seriously."[6]

Patrice McDermott of the ALA's Washington Office says of Ashcroft's "zero use" memo: "I find it hard to believe, and I have heard a lot of skepticism on the Hill as well. Ashcroft's statement didn't just say Section 215 hadn't been used in libraries, it said it hadn't been used at all."[7]

Some members of Congress have publicly expressed their doubts about the accuracy of the memo. "I have to question that document," said Rep. Butch Otter (R-ID), who said confirming Ashcroft's claim is impossible. "How would you know? Librarians are forbidden to tell anyone. It would be a violation of the law."[8] Otter speculated that "there may be [FBI] agents out there who have asked for this information that, quite frankly, the head of the Justice Department in Washington, D.C., is unaware of."[9]

In a November 2003 television appearance, Bob Barr, former Republican congressman from Georgia, expressed his doubt about the Ashcroft memo: "Even though the government says, 'Just trust us, we're not using that provision,' there are a number of different ways under the Patriot Act that the government can get the same information. . . . One has to presume that if the government has a certain power, it's going to use it. I know of no instance in which government has sought and has been given a particular power. . . . and never used it. . . . And I think we have to legitimately and realistically presume that they are using these powers. . . . The problem here is that the powers are exercised in secret, so you never know what the government is doing."[10]

On September 25, 2003, Joel Barkin, press secretary for Rep. Bernie Sanders, told me, "There is some question about whether Ashcroft was accurate in his statement that Section 215 had not been used, a claim that was questioned by Republican member Butch Otter at a press conference yesterday. You can't be sure because of the gag order."[11]

When I asked Charles Levendosky, columnist for the *Casper* [Wyoming] *Tribune* and prominent First Amendment advocate, if he believed Ashcroft's claim that Section 215 had never been used, he answered, "No, I don't believe it. The University of Illinois survey and the recent California Library Association survey contradict Ashcroft's claim."[12]

There is indirect evidence supporting the claim of "zero use" of Section 215. It came in a July 26, 2002 letter to the House Judiciary Committee from Assistant Attorney General Daniel J. Bryant. In answering a question about the use of Section 215 to acquire library records, Bryant said: "If the FBI were authorized to obtain the information the more appropriate tool for requesting electronic communication transactional records would be a National Security Letter (NSL)."[13]

The frequency with which the DOJ has used NSLs was revealed in documents acquired through an ACLU Freedom of Information Act request (see Chapter 2). The released DOJ documents included five pages of logs for NSL usage between October 2001 and January 2003. The size of the logs and the DOJ commentary indicated that NSLs are indeed a preferred surveillance tool to acquire information from places like libraries and bookstores. National Security Letters have always been a powerful tool for government surveillance because they do not require judicial review, but under the Patriot Act, NSLs are more readily available to the FBI than before, and they have a gag order attached, just like the Section 215 search warrants.

Because the FBI has reneged on its promise to the ALA's Washington Office to provide copies of NSL forms to assist librarians in recognizing and appropriately responding to them, it could be that librarians have mistaken FBI visits under the authority of NSLs as visits under Section 215. After all, both have gag orders attached, sowing confusion about the exact authority being presented. Perhaps, but given the very specific identification of Section 215 provided by a number of library directors in the University of Illinois survey, it seems unlikely that the library directors in each of those cases failed to note what government authority was being used.

Even if one takes Attorney General Ashcroft at his word, one would have to say he told the truth, but not the whole truth. If NSLs are being used routinely to acquire library records, with an accompanying gag order, it is misleading to hide that fact under the claim of "zero use" of Section 215. The only honest thing for Ashcroft to do would be to provide full aggregate data on the use of NSLs, Section 215, and any other tool that has intruded on library confidentiality.

And what are we to make of Ashcroft's second claim, that no American citizen has had his library records reviewed under the authority of the Patriot Act? First, we need to decode this statement. It's real meaning is: Only non-citizens have had their library records reviewed under the Patriot Act. Upon first hearing, this statement has a ring of truth. After all, the FBI has historically targeted foreigners in its surveillance programs, particularly its library surveillance. As we saw in Chapter 1, the FBI's Library Awareness Program was aimed primarily at those with "foreign-sounding names and foreign-sounding accents." And the Patriot Act itself clearly makes immigrants and foreigners, particularly Muslims, its preferred targets. But there have been enough publicized examples of surveillance of American citizens under the Patriot Act to suggest some ambiguity in Ashcroft's claim.

We must remind ourselves that the Patriot Act rewrote countless federal statutes, transforming them into powerful surveillance tools. As we have seen, the Patriot Act lowered the standards under which National Security Letters could be issued. It did the same to the "trap and trace" laws, and it facilitated the approval of warrants by the secret FISA court. The disturbing power of the Patriot Act lies not so much in its entirely new provisions as in its revision of previously existing law in ways that offend the Fourth Amendment. Unfortunately, the Justice Department seems to feel that when one of these revised statutes is used, it is not an application of the Patriot Act. Under such an interpretation, Ashcroft would have been able to ignore the use of, say, National Security Letters in acquiring the library records of Americans and claim that no such action had been taken "under the authority of the Patriot Act."

In conclusion, we know little more about the government's use of the Patriot Act in libraries than we did before Ashcroft's dramatic revelations. Only a full public disclosure of government surveillance of libraries will clear the air, and that is highly unlikely, given the Bush administration's predisposition toward secrecy. Nonetheless, we have enough survey data and anecdotal evidence to establish that library surveillance is alive and well in the United States of America and the Patriot Act is the prime enabler behind this continuing intrusion.

Attorney General Ashcroft has given us some truth, but certainly not the whole truth, and surely a good deal beyond the truth. His self-righteous denial of any FBI interest in library circulation records is a blatant contradiction to the Bureau's documented policy for the last 30 years. From the beginning of the Library Awareness Program in the 1970s to the Patriot Act surveillance in the new millennium, the Bureau has been tracking the reading habits of "foreigners" and those Americans they have called "unwitting agents." Only the steadfast opposition of the library profession stopped the Library Awareness Program, and even then the FBI responded with punitive investigations of librarians who publicly opposed the program. We can expect the same kind of struggle over the Patriot Act.

Notes

1. Dan Eggen, "Ashcroft: Patriot Act Provision Unused," *Washington Post*, September 18, 2003, p. A13.

2. "John Ashcroft Delivers Remarks at National Restaurant Association's Annual Public Affairs Conference," September 15, 2003, Political Transcripts by Federal Document Clearing House.

3. Eric Lichtblau, "Ashcroft Mocks Librarians and Others Who Oppose Parts of Counterrorism Law," *New York Times*, September 15, 2003, p. A23.

4. Dan Eggen, "Patriot Monitoring Claims Dismissed," *Washington Post*, September 19, 2003, p. A2.

5. "Ashcroft Says FBI Hasn't Used Patriot Act Library Provision, Mocks ALA for Hysteria," American Library Association News, September 22, 2003, p. 1. www.ala.org/Template.cfm?Section=News&template.

6. Author interview with Karen Schneider, California Library Association, October 20, 2003.

7. Author interview with Patrice McDermott, Washington Office, American Library Association, October 10, 2003.

8. Ian Bishop, "Sanders Battles USAPA," *Brattleboro Reformer*, September 25, 2003, p. 1.

9. "California Survey Reveals FBI Visited 16 Libraries," *American Library Association News*, September 29, 2003, p. 2. www.ala.org/Template.cfm?Section=News&template=ContentManagement/Content

10. *Now, with Bill Moyers*, PBS television series, November 16, 2003.

11. Author interview with Joel Barkin, press secretary for Rep. Bernie Sanders (I-VT), September 25, 2003.

12. Author interview with Charles Levendosky, *Casper* [Wyoming] *Tribune*, October 4, 2003.

13. Letter from Daniel J. Bryant, Assistant Attorney General to F. James Sensenbrenner, Jr., Chairman, Committee on the Judiciary, U.S. House of Representatives, July 26, 2002, p. 4.

Appendix A:
Public Libraries and Civil Liberties Questionnaire

Public Libraries' Response to the Events of 9/11/2001: One Year Later, Library Research Center, Graduate School of Library and Information Science, University of Illinois.

1. In response to events of September 11, 2001, to the best of your knowledge, has your library changed any of its policies regarding patron use of the Internet? (CIRCLE 1 FOR "YES" OR 2 FOR "NO.")

   Yes 9.7%
   No...90.3->(SKIP TO Q.3)
   100.0%

   (IF "YES" TO Q.1):

2. In response to the events of September 11, 2001, has your library . . .

	Yes	No
Restricted access to Web sites?	3.5%	96.5%
Opened access to previously blocked Web sites?	0.0%	100%
Started to require identification from patrons to use the Internet terminals?	40.5%	59.5%
Stopped requiring identification from patrons to use the Internet terminals?	14.6%	85.4%
Begun to monitor what patrons are doing, visually or by reviewing the cache/history?	33.5%	66.5%
Installed software that erases the cache/history after each use, or at regular intervals?	34.1%	65.9%
Started keeping a sign-up sheet of users of your computer terminals?	56.8%	43.2%
Stopped keeping a sign-up sheet of users of your computer terminals?	32.5%	67.5%

3. Since September 11, 2001, has your library voluntarily withdrawn any materials that might be used to assist terrorists, such as material on bomb making or bio-terrorism?

   Yes 1.3%
   No..98.7%
   100.0%

4. In response to the events of September 11, 2001, are any of your staff members...

	Yes	No
More likely to monitor the kinds of materials people are checking out?	8.7%	91.3%
Believing there are circumstances in which it would be necessary to compromise the privacy of patron records?	8.9%	81.1%
Made other changes in attitude or treatment of library patrons?	5.7%	94.3%

5. Has your library adopted or changed any policies in response to the passage of the USA Patriot Act?

Yes 7.2%
No...78.3%
No, but in process of developing policies 14.5%
                                                                                                                        100.0%

6. In the past year have you instructed staff or library board regarding...

	Yes	No
The provisions of the USA Patriot Act and/or on what to do should a search warrant or subpoena be served?	60.0%	40.0%
Library policies regarding patron privacy?	69.1%	30.9%
Library security?	55.7%	44.3%

7. Have you received any expressions of concern from patrons about their privacy rights under the USA Patriot Act?

Yes 7.1%
No...92.9%
                                                                                                                        100.0%

You should be aware that the Patriot Act contains a secrecy provision that, in certain circumstances, prohibits libraries from disclosing that the government has asked them for information. (The government may interpret the secrecy provision even more broadly.) NOTE THAT THE SECRECY PROVISION APPLIES ONLY TO REQUESTS THAT REFERENCE SECTION 215 OF THE PATRIOT ACT OR TITLE 50, SECTION 1862 OF THE UNITED STATES CODE. If you have received a request for information that references one of these statutory provisions, you may want to consult counsel about the applicability of the secrecy requirement before you disclose information in response to that particular request.

8. In the year preceding September 11, 2001, about how many requests about your patrons did you receive from authorities such as the FBI, INS, or police officers?

None..84.5%
Only 1 ....10.3%
2–5 ....3.4%
6–10 .... 0.1%
More than 10..0.0%
Don't know/Unsure..1.7%
                                                                                                                        100.0%

9. Have authorities (e.g., FBI, INS, police officers) requested information about any of your patrons since September 11, 2001?

   Yes 10.7%
   No ....89.3% -> (SKIP TO Q.18)
   100.0%

10. About how many separate requests about your patrons have you received since September 11, 2001?

    Only 1 ....81.3%
    2–5 ....18.1%
    6–10 ....0.6 %
    More than 10..0.0%
    100.0%

11. Who requested information? (CIRCLE ALL THAT APPLY.)

    FBI...32.6%
    INS...0.6%
    Police...68.2%
    Secret Service...0.6%
    Other 7.6%

12. What kinds of information were requested? (CIRCLE ALL THAT APPLY.)

    Information about specific library materials (e.g., asked you to
       provide a list of patrons who borrowed a certain book)...........................5.4%
    Information about a specific patron (e.g., asked you to provide list
       of books borrowed, or web sites visited, by a particular person)..........76.0%
    Other 22.3%

13a. What form(s) did the request take? (CIRCLE ALL THAT APPLY.)

    Verbal request for voluntary cooperation 83.1%
    Written request for voluntary cooperation 8.9%
    Subpoena...22.3%
    Court order...17.4%
    (IF "REQUEST FOR VOLUNTARY COOPERATION"):
    b. Did you cooperate?
       Yes 49.7%
       No...50.3%
       100.0%

14. If one or more requests (Q.13a) was a court order, did any of the orders prohibit you from telling patrons that the authorities had requested information about them?

    Yes 3.1%
    No...14.3%
    No court orders received...82.6% -> (SKIP TO Q.16)
    100.0%

15a. Did any of the court orders reference Section 215 of the Patriot Act or Title 50, Section 1862 of the United States Code?

Yes 10.3%
No ....89.7% -> (SKIP TO Q.16)
Don't know/Unsure.......................................0.0% -> (SKIP TO Q.16)

(IF "YES") :

b. How many such orders did you receive?

Only 1 ....33.3%
2–5 ....66.7%
6–10 ....0.0%
More than 10..0.0%
$\qquad$ 100.0%

16. Have you, ever sought legal advice regarding your library's obligation to respond to a request for information?

Yes 64.8%
No..35.2%
$\qquad$ 100.0%

17. Is there any part of Q.9 through Q.16 above that you did not answer, or did not answer completely, because you believe you are legally prohibited from doing so?

Yes 2.6%
No..97.4%
$\qquad$ 100.0%

18. Has anyone on your library staff ever voluntarily reported patron records and/or behaviors to outside authorities (e.g., FBI, police) in relation to terrorism or suspected terrorist activities?

Yes 4.1%
No..95.9%
$\qquad$ 100.0%

19a. Have any of your patrons ever reported concern about the behavior of another patron specifically in relation to terrorism or suspected terrorist-activities?

Yes 8.3%
No ....91.7% -> (SKIP TO Q.20)

b. To whom was this report made? (CIRCLE ALL THAT APPLY.)

To library staff 64.3%
To outside authorities...32.6%
To you, yourself...35.7%

20. As noted above, the Patriot Act contains provisions that prohibit those served with requests from disclosing the specifics of those requests, to anyone else. Do you feel this is an abridgment of First Amendment rights?

Yes 59.9%
No...37.2%
Depends, no clear answer 0.7%
Refused to answer question..0.1%
Don't Know 2.1%
100.0%

We would like also to ask a few general questions about your views as a citizen.

21. Do you think the U.S. government should remove information from its web sites that might potentially help terrorists, even if the American public has a right to know that information?

Yes 35.3%
No...48.5%
No Opinion 14.9%
Depends, no clear answer 1.1%
Refused to answer question..0.3%
100.0%

22. Do you think the U.S. government should not put information on its web sites that might potentially help terrorists, even if the American public has a right to know that information?

Yes 41.2%
No...41.4%
No opinion 15.8%
Depends, no clear answer 1.3%
Refused to answer question..0.3%
100.0%

23. Do you think private businesses such as airlines and utility companies should remove information from their web sites that might help terrorists, even if it limits the American public's information about these companies?

Yes 41.7%
No...40.3%
No opinion 16.7%
Depends, no clear answer 1.0%
Refused to answer question..0.3%
100.0%

24. Do you think private businesses such as airlines and utility companies should not put information on their web sites that might help terrorists, even if it limits the American public's information about these companies?

Yes 44.4%
No...36.0%
No opinion 18.2%
Depends, no clear answer 1.2%
Refused to answer question...0.2%
100.0%

25. Since 9/11/2001, have you heard or read about the government pulling information from its web sites, fearing terrorists might make use of that information?

Yes 34.1%
No...56.9%
No opinion 8.6%
Depends, no clear answer 0.2%
Refused to answer question...0.2%
100.0%

26. Since 9/11/2001, have YOU noticed that information that you expected to be on any government web sites you visit was missing?

Yes 4.3%
No...84.2%
No opinion 11.0%
Depends, no clear answer 0.2%
Refused to answer question...0.3%
100.0%

27. Some government agencies HAVE removed information from their web sites, saying that they are worried that the information could be useful to terrorists. Do you think that this action actually does hinder terrorists or do you think it does not make any difference?

Does hinder terrorists...22.0%
Does not make any difference...42.2%
No opinion/Unsure..35.2%
Depends, no clear answer 0.2%
Refused to answer question...0.4%
100.0%

Finally, we would like to ask you one hypothetical question.

28. If law enforcement officials asked you for information about one of your patrons and ordered you not to disclose that they had asked for information, would you challenge their order by disclosing the request to anyone (e.g., the patron, the press, and/or a public interest organization such as the ACLU) other than your library's attorney?

Definitely would 5.5%
Probably would 16.1%
Probably would not 53.7%
Definitely would not 21.4%
Depends, no clear answer 1.0%
Refused to answer question 1.0%
Don't know 1.3%
100.0%

Appendix B:
California Library Association
Patriot Act Survey

The results of the survey are displayed below. Individual responses are restricted. Zoomerang is not responsible for the answers submitted to any survey or for the results generated by survey responses. Zoomerang does not make any representations regarding the use of the results. Zoomerang makes no warranty that the survey, survey responses, survey results, and data or presentations of any or all surveys will meet with your requirements or that they are correct, reliable or accurate.

1. What type library are you affiliated with?

    Public 260 (76%)
    Academic 47 (14%)
    School 11 (3%)
    Special 10 (03%)
    Library school 6 (2%)
    Other 10 (03%)
                                      344 (100%)

2. What is your role in your organization?

    Director 98 (28%)
    Assistant Director 25 (7%)
    Branch Manager 47 (14%)
    Supervisor 45 (13%)
    Librarian 80 (23%)
    Library worker 15 (4%)
    Library student 10 (3%)
    Board member 8 (2%)
    Volunteer 1 (0%)
    Other 15 (4%)
                                      344 (100%)

3. Since September 11, 2001, has your library conducted an audit of policies and procedures related to privacy?

   Yes 200 (59%)
   No 141 (41%)

4. Has your library instituted any new policies as a result of the USA Patriot Act?

   Yes 140 (41%)
   No 201 (59%)

5. If you answered yes to the previous question, identify the type of policy/policies. Check all that apply:

   Patron confidentiality 72 (50%)
   Retention of library records.............................120 (83%)
   Other, please specify...32 (22%)

6. http://www.libraryprivacy.org/ is a Web site with information about the USA Patriot Act that is a joint project between the ACLU and CLA. Have you used this web site to . . . Check all that apply.

   Learn more about the Patriot Act 141 (91%)
   Read about the Freedom to Read Protection Act.....85 (55%)
   Download bookmarks or posters 17 (11%)
   Order bookmarks or posters for your library.........16 (10%)

7. Indicate the privacy-related procedures your library introduced for the first time since September 11, 2001. Check all that apply.

   Internet sign-in...35 (32%)
   Public Internet use 16 (15%)
   Library event and program sign-up sheets 11 (10%)
   Staff Internet use..9 (8%)
   Circulation records 23 (21%)
   Computer log files 32 (29%)
   Library book reserves 12 (11%)
   Interlibrary loan 9 (8%)
   Electronic mail..11 (10%)
   Other, please specify..31 (28%)

8. Indicate the pre-existing privacy-related procedures your library has updated, improved, or otherwise enhanced since September 11, 2001. Check all that apply.

Internet sign-in..142 (64%)
Public Internet use 97 (44%)
Library event and program sign-up sheets 24 (11%)
Staff Internet use..37 (17%)
Circulation records 109 (49%)
Computer log files 64 (29%)
Library book reserves...38 (17%)
Interlibrary loan..42 (19%)
Electronic mail...31 (14%)
Other, please specify..20 (9%)

9. What privacy-related procedures does your library perform on a routine basis? Check all that apply.

Shredding paper documents, such as
    computer sign-in sheets 223 (78%)
Deleting computer files, such as logs,
    proxy caches 208 (73%)
Other, please specify..29 (10%)

10. What steps has your library taken to educate library staff about the Patriot Act? Check all that apply.

Sent staff to videoconferences, talks,
    Webcasts, or training 110 (34%)
Held training programs......................................47 (14%)
Addressed related topics at staff meetings.......219 (67%)
Provided written guidance or procedures 153 (47%)
Encouraged staff to research the topic
    and share information with others 118 (36%)
Haven't taken any steps yet...............................56 (17%)
Other, please specify..23 (7%)

11. What steps has your library taken to educate users about the Patriot Act? Check all that apply.

Distributed bookmarks or flyers.......................40 (13%)
Encouraged public service staff to
    share knowledge 78 (25%)
Distributed related web sites through
    e-mail or through link on library web site 34 (11%)
Held a public informational program 21 (7%)

Shared information at a library board or
   town council meeting...93 (30%)
Posted signs warning patrons about the
   provisions of the act.......................................35 (11%)
Invited public members to videoconferences,
   Webcasts, or in-house training sessions 3   (1%)
Have not done user education..........................156 (50%)
Other, please specify..37 (12%)

12. Which of the following activities would be VERY effective with library users in YOUR specific library community? Check all that apply.

Distributing bookmarks or flyers....................153 (49%)
Encouraging public service staff to
   share knowledge 116 (37%)
Distributing related web sites through
   e-mail or link on library web site..................93 (30%)
Holding a public informational program...........94 (30%)
Sharing information at a library board
   or town council meeting 94 (30%)
Posting signs warning patrons about the
   provisions of the act.....................................123 (40%)
Inviting public members to videoconferences,
   Webcasts, or in-house training sessions 21   (7%)
None of the above, because 35 (11%)

13. Among your stakeholders, who has expressed concern about the potential impact of the Patriot Act on library confidentiality? Check all that apply.

Library administrators 190 (57%)
Library staff..239 (71%)
Library board members 116 (35%)
Library users..141 (42%)
Library volunteers 45 (13%)
Local government officials...............................70 (21%)
Local reporters...85 (25%)
No one 42 (13%)
Other, please specify..18   (5%)

14. Has your library had any informal contact from the FBI since September 11, 2001?

Yes..16   (5%)
No 304 (95%)

15. If your library had informal contact from the FBI after September 11, 2001, did your library comply with its requests?

    Yes..6 (3%)
    No 31 (13%)
    Not applicable 198 (84%)
    235 (100%)

16. Has your library had any formal contact from the FBI since September 11, 2001?

    Yes...14 (4%)
    No 298 (96%)

17. If your library had formal contact from the FBI since September 11, 2001, did you comply with their requests?

    Yes...11 (5%)
    No 15 (6%)
    Not applicable..217 (89%)
    243 (100%)

Appendices C–F:
Court Order Forms

The following court order forms (U.S. Attorney Preservation Demand Letter, U.S. District Court ECPA Order w/Schedule, U.S. District Court Search Warrant, and U.S. District Court Criminal Trial Subpoena) were probably the most frequently used legal orders to acquire library and bookstore records *prior to* the passage of the USA Patriot Act. Since that time, the two legal authorities that libraries and bookstores have come to fear most are Foreign Intelligence Surveillance Act (FISA) warrants and National Security Letters (NSLs), the latter having been identified by the Justice Department as the most likely authority under which the FBI would seek library records. Unfortunately, the Justice Department has been unwilling to make those forms available to librarians, who have frequently complained that they are unable to recognize the various legal authorities under which the FBI visits their libraries and are therefore unsure of their rights and obligations. To make matters worse, both FISA warrants and NSLs carry a gag order with them, preventing librarians and bookstore employees from revealing such visits.

The court orders contained in Appendices C–F are the most relevant orders available to us, and they were provided by the American Library Association's (ALA's) Office for Intellectual Freedom. The Electronic Communication Privacy Act (ECPA) Order in Appendix D (18 U.S. § 2703 (d)) is very similar to an NSL, and indeed, the ECPA is one of the three statutes under which NSLs can be issued. Among the options which 18 U.S. § 2703 (d) offers is "an administrative subpoena" requiring a provider of electronic communication or computing service to disclose to a government entity the name, address, local and long distance telephone connection records, length of service and types of service utilized, telephone or instrument number, and means and source of payment. The primary difference between the attached ECPA Order and an NSL is that the attached order is granted by a court, whereas an NSL is an administrative order issued by an FBI official without court oversight.

Appendix C:
U.S. Attorney Preservation Demand Letter

U.S. Department of Justice

United States Attorney
District of Columbia

United States Courthouse, Room 2800
Constitution Avenue and 3rd Street N.W.
Washington, D.C. 20001

Director
Gotham City Public Library
101 Main Street
Gotham City

    VIA FAX to (xxx) xxx-xxxx

Dear Director:

    I am writing to confirm our telephone conversation earlier today and to make a formal request for the preservation of records and other evidence pursuant to 18 U.S.C. §2703(f) pending further legal process.

    You are hereby requested to preserve, for a period of 90 days, the records described below currently in your possession, including records stored on backup media, in a form that includes the complete record. You also are requested not to disclose the existence of this request to the subscriber or any other person, other than as necessary to comply with this request. **If compliance with this request may result in a permanent or temporary termination of service to the accounts described below, or otherwise alert the subscriber or user of these accounts as to your actions to preserve the referenced files and records, please contact me before taking such actions.**

    This request applies only retrospectively and does not in any way obligate you to capture and preserve new information that arises after the date of this request. This preservation request applies to the following records and evidence:

A. All stored communications and other files reflecting communications to or from [Email Account / User name / IP Address or Domain Name (between DATE1 at TIME1 and DATE2 at TIME2)];

B. All files that have been accessed by [Email Account / User name / IP Address or Domain Name (between DATE1 at TIME1 and DATE2 at TIME2)] or are controlled by user accounts associated with [Email Account / User name / IP Address or Domain Name (between DATE1 at TIME1 and DATE2 at TIME2)];

C. All connection logs and records of user activity for [Email Account / User name / IP Address or Domain Name (between DATE1 at TIME1 and DATE2 at TIME2)], including:

    1. Connection date and time;
    2. Disconnect date and time;
    3. Method of connection (e.g., telnet, ftp, http);
    4. Type of connection (e.g., modem, cable / DSL, T1/LAN);
    5. Data transfer volume;
    6. User name associated with the connection and other connection information, including the Internet Protocol address of the source of the connection;
    7. Telephone caller identification records;
    8. Records of files or system attributes accessed, modified, or added by the user;
    9. Connection information for other computers to which the user of the [Email Account / User name / IP Address or Domain Name (between DATE1 at TIME1 and DATE2 at TIME2)] connected, by any means, during the connection period, including the destination IP address, connection time and date, disconnect time and date, method of connection to the destination computer, the identities (account and screen names) and subscriber information, if known, for any person or entity to which such connection information relates, and all other information related to the connection from ISP or its subsidiaries.

D. All records and other evidence relating to the subscriber(s), customer(s), account holder(s), or other entity(ies) associated with [Email Account / User name / IP Address or Domain Name (between DATE1 at TIME1 and DATE2 at TIME2)], including, without limitation, subscriber names, user names, screen names or other identities, mailing addresses, residential addresses, business addresses, e-mail addresses and other contact information, telephone numbers or other subscriber number or identifier number, billing records, information about the length of service and the types of services the subscriber or customer utilized, and any other identifying information, whether such records or other evidence are in electronic or other form;

E. Any other records and other evidence relating to [Email
Account / User name / IP Address or Domain Name (between DATE1
at TIME1 and DATE2 at TIME2)]. Such records and other evidence
include, without limitation, correspondence and other records of
contact by any person or entity about the above-referenced
account, the content and connection logs associated with or
relating to postings, communications and any other activities to
or through [Email Account / User name / IP Address or Domain
Name (between DATE1 at TIME1 and DATE2 at TIME2)], whether such
records or other evidence are in electronic or other form.

                             Very truly yours,

                             _____

                             Assistant United States Attorney

Appendix D:
U.S. District Court ECPA Order w/Schedule

UNITED STATES DISTRICT COURT
FOR THE EASTERN DISTRICT OF VIRGINIA

IN RE: APPLICATION OF THE)
UNITED STATES OF AMERICA   )   MISC. NO.
FOR AN ORDER PURSUANT TO   )
18 U.S.C. § 2703(d)   )

Filed Under Seal

ORDER

This matter having come before the court pursuant to an application under Title 16, United States Code, Section 2703,(b) and (c), which application requests the issuance of an order under Title 18, United States Code, Section 2703(d) directing Gotham City Public Library, an electronic communications service provider and a remote computing service, located in the Eastern District of Virginia, to disclose certain records and other information, as set forth in Attachment A to the Application, the court finds that the applicant has offered specific and articulable facts, showing that there are reasonable grounds to believe that the records or other information and the contents of a wire or electronic communication sought are relevant and material to an ongoing criminal investigation.

AND IT APPEARING that the information sought is relevant and material to an ongoing criminal investigation, and that prior notice of this order to any person of this investigation or this application and order entered in connection therewith would seriously jeopardize the investigation;

IT IS ORDERED pursuant to Title 18, United States Code, Section 2703(d) that Gotham City Public Library will, within three days of the date of this order, turn over to agents of the Federal Bureau of Investigation the records and other information as set forth in Attachment A to this Order;

AND IT IS FURTHER ORDERED that the Clerk of the Court shall provide the United States Attorney's Office with three (3) certified copies of this Application and Order;

AND IT IS FURTHER ORDERED that the application and this Order are sealed until otherwise ordered by the Court, and that Gotham City Public Library shall not disclose the existence of the Application or this Order of the Court, or the existence of the investigation, to the listed subscriber or to any other person, unless and until authorized to do so by the Court.

AND IT IS FURTHER ORDERED that the notification by the government otherwise required under 18 U.S.C. 2703(b)(1)(B) be delayed for a period of (ninety days).

Appendix E:
U.S. District Court Subpoena in a Criminal Case

AO 89 (Rev 7/95) Subpoena in a Criminal Case

United States District Court

DISTRICT OF UNITED STATES OF AMERICA
                V.

SUBPOENA IN A
CRIMINAL CASE

CASE NUMBER:

TO:

YOU ARE COMMANDED to appear in the United States District Court at the place, date and time specified below, or any subsequent place, date and time set by the court, to testify in the above referenced case. This subpoena shall remain in effect until you are granted leave to depart by the court or by an officer acting on behalf of the court.

PLACE
COURTROOM

US District Court, District of
XXX Avenue
XXX City, XXX

DATE AND TIME

YOU ARE ALSO COMMANDED to bring with you the following document(s) or object(s):

U.S. MAGISTRATE JUDGE OR CLERK OF COURT

_____ (BY) DEPUTY CLERK

_____ ATTORNEY'S NAME AND PHONE NUMBER

AO 89 (Rev. 7/95) Subpoena in a Criminal Case

PROOF OF SERVICE

RECEIVED BY SERVER DATE

Date   Place

SERVED

_____ SERVED ON (PRINT NAME)

FEES AND MILEAGE TENDERED TO WITNESS

YES   NO   AMOUNT $

SERVED BY (PRINT NAME)

DECLARATION OF SERVER

I declare under penalty of perjury under the laws of the United States of America that the foregoing information contained in the Proof of Service is true and correct.

Executed on _____ _____ Date

              Signature of Server

_____ Address of Server

ADDITIONAL INFORMATION

Appendix F:
U.S. District Court Search Warrant

Search Warrant
AO 93 [Rev. 5/85] Search Warrant

United States District Court

_____ DISTRICT OF

In the Matter of the Search of
[Name, address or brief description of person or property to be searched]

SEARCH WARRANT
CASE NUMBER:

TO: _____ and any Authorized Officer of the United States

Affidavit(s) having been made before me by_____

Who has reason to believe that   Affiant

on the person of or

on the premises known as (name, description, and/or location)

in the _____ District of _____ there is now
concealed a certain person or property, namely (describe the person or property)

I am satisfied that the attidavit(s) and any recorded testimony establish probable cauise to
believe that the person or property so described is now concealed on the person or premises
above-described and establish grounds for thr issuance of this warrant.
YOU ARE HEREBY COMMANDED to search on or before
Date
(not to exceed 10 days)the person or place named above for the person or property specified,
serving this warrant and making the search (in the daytime—6:00 A.M. to 10:00 P.M.) (at any
time in the day or night as I find reasonable cause has been established) and if the person or
property be found there to seize same, leaving a copy of this warrant and receipt for the person
or property taken, and prepare a written inventory of the person or property seized and promptly
return this warrant to _____ as required by law.
U.S. Judge or Magistrate

_____ at _____ Date and time issued

City and State

_____   _____

Name and Title of Judicial Officer   Signature of Judicial Officer

Search Warrant

AD 93 (Rev. 5/85) Search Warrant

DATE WARRANT RECEIVED   DATE AND TIME WARRANT EXECUTED   COPY OF WARRANT AND RECEIPT FOR ITEMS
LEFT WITH

INVENTORY MADE IN THE PRESENCE OF

INVENTORY OF PERSON OR PROPERTY TAKEN PURSUANT TO THE WARRANT

CERTIFICATION

I swear that this is a true and detailed account of the person or property taken by me on the warrant.

_____

Subscribed, sworn to, and returned before me this date.

_____

U.S. Judge or Magistrate   Date

Selected Bibliography

Brown, Cynthia, ed. *Lost Liberties: Ashcroft and the Assault on Personal Freedom*. New York: The New Press, 2003.

Chang, Nancy, et al. *Silencing Political Dissent: How Post-September 11 Anti-Terrorism Measures Threaten Our Civil Liberties*. New York: Seven Stories Press, 2002.

Cole, David. *Enemy Aliens*. New York: The New Press, 2003.

———. *Terrorism and the Constitution*. New York: The New Press, 2002.

Congress, House Committee on the Judiciary, *FBI Counterintelligence Visits to Libraries*, 100th Cong., 2d Sess., June 20 and July 13, 1988 (Washington, D.C.: U.S. GPO, 1989), p. 125.

Ewing, Alphonse B. *The USA PATRIOT Act*. Hauppauge, NY: Nova Science Publishers, 2002.

Foerstel, Herbert N. *Surveillance in the Stacks: The FBI's Library Awareness Program*. Westport, CT: Greenwood Press, 1991.

Halperin, Morton, et al. *Freedom vs. National Security: Secrecy and Surveillance*. Broomall, PA: Chelsea House Publishers, 1980.

Intellectual Freedom Manual, 6th edition. Office for Intellectual Freedom. Chicago: American Library Association, 2001.

Leone, Richard C. and Anrig, Gregory, Jr., eds. *The War on Our Freedom: Civil Liberties in an Age of Terrorism*. New York: Public Affairs, 2003.

Phillips, Peter, ed. *Censored 2004: The Top 25 Censored Stories*. New York: Seven Stories Press, 2003.

Reams, Bernard D., Jr. and Anglem, Christopher. *USA PATRIOT Act: A Legislative History of the Uniting and Strengthening America by Providing Appropriate Tools Required to Interdict and Obstruct Terrorism Act*. New York: Fred B. Rothman & Co., 2002.

Rehnquist, William H. *All the Laws but One: Civil Liberties in Wartime*. New York: Knopf, 1998.

Schulhofer, Stephen J. *The Enemy Within: Intelligence Gathering, Law Enforcement, and Civil Liberties in the Wake of September 11*. New York: The Century Foundation Press, 2002.

The USA PATRIOT Act in Practice: Shedding Light on the FISA Process. Hearing before the Committee on the Judiciary, U. S. Senate, 107th Congress, 2nd Session, September 10, 2002. Washington, D.C.: U.S. Government Printing Office, 2002.

Theoharis, Athan, ed. *From the Secret Files of J. Edgar Hoover*. Chicago: Ivan R. Dee, 1991.

Turner, William W. *Hoover's FBI*. New York: Thunder's Mouth Press, 1993.

Welch, Neil J. and Marston, David W. *Inside Hoover's FBI: The Top Field Chief Reports*. New York: Doubleday, 1984.

Index

About the Author

HERBERT N. FOERSTEL is the former Head of Branch libraries at the University of Maryland, College Park, and currently serves on the advisory boards of the Freedom to Read Foundation and the National Security Archive. He has authored nine books on First Amendment topics and numerous articles and reviews, the most recent of which was the review of the four-volume set, *Censorship: A World Encyclopedia* for the *Journal of Information Ethnics*. Among his previous publications are: *Freedom of Information and the Right to Know: The Origins and Applications of the Freedom of Information Act* (1999); *From Watergate to Monicagate: Ten Controversies in Modern Journalism and Media* (2001); and *Banned in the Media: A Reference Guide to Book Censorship in Schools and Public Libraries, revised and expanded edition* (2002).